teach yourself...
PowerPoint for Windows

Tom Badgett

MIS:
PRESS

A Subsidiary of
Henry Holt and Co., Inc.

First Edition—1994

ISBN 1-55828-367-6

Printed in the United States of America.

10 9 8 7 6 5 4 3 2 1

MIS:Press books are available at special discounts for bulk purchases for sales promotions, premiums, fund-raising, or educational use. Special editions or book excerpts can also be created to specification.

For details contact: Special Sales Director
MIS:Press
a subsidiary of Henry Holt and Company, Inc.
115 West 18th Street
New York, New York 10011

DEDICATION

To the creative part of each of us that is freed only with the permission of those whose lives we share.

ACKNOWLEDGEMENTS

My name is on the front of this book, but I couldn't have written this book alone.

I'd like to thank my patient and flexible editor, Debra Williams Cauley, who managed short deadlines and beta software with apparent ease.

As you can see from the color section in this book, the creative folks at Genigraphics—especially Joey Schroth and Rosemary Abowd—went out of their way to show some creative images. Their quick work and expert advice added significant material to this book.

The Microsoft technical support team helped make sense of last minute design changes under tight deadlines.

I also commend the following manufacturers and their products, used to prepare this book:

Gateway 2000 4DX2-66V computer. Gateway 2000, 610 Gateway Drive, N. Sioux City, SD 57049, 800-846-2000.

TurboModem Plus, 14.4Kbps modem. The Complete PC, 1983 Concourse Drive, San Jose, CA 95131, 408-434-9600.

Sound Blaster Pro, multimedia interface card, Creative Labs, 1901 McCarthy Boulevard, Milpitas, CA 95035, 408-428-6622.

Mustek MFS-6000CS color, 1200 dpi flatbed scanner. Mustek, Inc., 15225 Alton Parkway, Irvine, CA 92718.

Finally, thank you, the readers of this book, for buying it. Your comments and suggestions are welcome at:

MCI Mail: Tbadgett
CompuServe: 74365, 1003
Internet: tBadgett@usit.net

Contents

CHAPTER 8: POWERPOINT AND THE MICROSOFT OFFICE SUITE 287

Introduction

Microsoft PowerPoint 4.0 is either a powerful stand-alone presentation application, or one of many powerful tools contained in the *Microsoft Office* suite of products. However you view PowerPoint, if your software needs include the ability to construct graphics and text slides for screen presentation or projection, PowerPoint 4.0 is a good choice for getting the job done.

What is PowerPoint?

PowerPoint helps you create a variety of presentation tools, from relatively simple on-screen (using the computer) *slide shows*, to a full portfolio of materials including overhead projection slides, audience *handouts*, speaker outlines or notes, 35mm slides, and more. You could also use PowerPoint to construct accent sheets for a printed company report—title pages, graphs, text charts and lists, scanned images, and photographs—but the program's forte is presentation materials.

Version 4 will offer special appeal to users of Microsoft Word 6 because it has been designed to look, feel, and act like this newest Microsoft word processor. From the menu to the toolbar to the pop-up *Tip of the Day*, PowerPoint 4.0 is very Word-like in appearance and function.

There are some obvious differences between these two products, as well. One difference is the way PowerPoint handles graphics files. Because PowerPoint is designed from the start as a presentation package, there is strong support for *clip art* (a significant resource supplied with the program), graphics files, text charting, and more. But as a Word 6 user you will find a lot of familiar ground to travel with this program. If you're not a Word user, you still will find PowerPoint 4.0 easy to learn and use. I'll show you more in this chapter and in the next one that should convince you of that idea, so read on.

The Highlights of PowerPoint Version 4.0

PowerPoint 4.0 has a number of new features that enhance functionality and that also make the program easier to learn and to use. Some of these features are very obvious—such as the Tip of the Day, part of the online help system that displays every time you start PowerPoint—and some are more subtle. While a number of smaller enhancements, changes, and improvements are included in this version, we will discuss them later in the book. However, the features that I've listed below are highlights of PowerPoint 4.0.

Click here...

PowerPoint 4.0 includes a number of pre-configured templates and slide designs. When you select them from a graphics window, PowerPoint presents a dummy design on the screen. With most of these dummy slides the sections reserved for text have a simple prompt that reads, "Click here to add text." When you position the *mouse pointer* over this prompt and press the left mouse button once, the prompt text is removed. Now the insertion point is positioned inside the text field so that you can type your own text for this section of the slide. PowerPoint will automatically adjust the font and text attributes according to the design of the screen.

Other text prompts ask for specific information: "Click to add title," for example. And, when the slide includes a place for clip art, you're prompted to "Double click here to add clip art." A small clip art image accompanies this prompt to make sure you understand. This simple concept can help you create a whole series of slides very quickly, especially if you have done a little design work on your presentation before you start creating the illustrations with PowerPoint.

Clip Art Selector and Viewer

This version of PowerPoint is supplied with about 1,000 clip art images. That's twice as many as were in the previous version of the product. In the past, to choose a clip art image you had to scan an onscreen list of file names and pick the one you wanted from the list. That works, but even when the names are fairly descriptive, with 1,000 choices it can be difficult to locate what you want.

In PowerPoint 4.0 you select clip art images from a *ClipArt Gallery* display. Images are organized into categories, such as Academic, Backgrounds, Cartoons, and so on. When you choose the category, postage stamp-sized images from that group are displayed on the screen. You can scroll through this visual list to find the clip art that you want to use. Figure I.1 shows what this screen looks like.

Figure I.1 ClipArt Gallery Main Screen

Customizable Toolbars

Graphics *toolbars* help you conduct many PowerPoint operations. The program is configured with three toolbars that contain common tasks, but you can use the Customize Toolbars dialog to add, move, or delete the *toolbar buttons*. Again, if you are familiar with Word 6, the toolbars supplied with PowerPoint will be easy to learn. Many of the buttons you use in Word are also used in PowerPoint. The Customize dialog groups buttons by task (File, Edit, View, and so on) and displays buttons for each of the menu choices under these main headings. You can use the mouse to drag and drop buttons where you want them.

Direct Mail

Computing today has come full circle. When I first started working with computers in the mid 1970s, each user connected to a central machine through a serial terminal. We shared disk space, printers, programs, memory, and mail. Then along came the PC. Users sought the power, speed, and privacy of their own personal machine. Now, we're getting back together. Products such as *Windows for Workgroups*, a *Microsoft Windows* environment that networks machines, let individual users share disk and printer resources, and exchange mail.

PowerPoint 4.0 includes a link to network mail so you can stick an electronic *routing slip* onto a PowerPoint presentation and send it across the network to one or more addresses. This lets you show other people what you're working on, send interesting mail with clip art or text charts, or ship works in progress around the company for help from different people.

Graph Generator

In PowerPoint 3 you had to use Excel to generate spreadsheet graphs. In version 4 you can use a separate graphing application to enter data and draw graphs. This application also is available in Word 6. While this utility won't replace a full-featured spreadsheet, it works well for simple graph data for visual comparisons, and removes the requirement that you have Excel installed to use graphs with PowerPoint.

OLE 2.0 Support

Object Linking and Embedding (OLE) is an important feature in the Windows environment. It lets different applications share information through real-time, *"live"* links. With OLE 2.0, the latest OLE standard, it is easier to share information among applications, and you can use the current application (PowerPoint, in this case) as the user interface into the remote program. With the previous version of OLE you had to launch the application that contained the linked data before you could edit it. With OLE 2.0 you can edit remote data in place.

PowerPoint also uses this feature to provide another interesting capability: linking. With a PowerPoint link you can insert special icons on your slides that are linked to another presentation or presentation segment. If you click on a HyperLink icon, the linked presentation is launched. When it is completed, you are returned to the calling application. This is like a subroutine call (for you programmers) that can make it easier to create presentation modules for use across a wide range of presentations. For example, you could create a short sequence of slides that illustrates the current sales activity for a specific product. Then you can call this from within a sales promotion presentation, an annual report, a sales strategy session, or wherever this data is applicable.

Pop-up Cue Cards

With PowerPoint 4.0 the job of constructing attractive slides is much easier. With minimal practice, just about anybody can make a computer presentation. What most of us don't know is what makes a good slide: what size type should you use, what type of graphic or illustration is appropriate, what colors work well together and carry the proper message. A new feature, the *Cue Card*, provides running hints about what makes a good slide. You receive suggestions about the size of type, how many lines to use on a single screen, how to provide variety in your presentation, and so on. In addition to design help, the Cue Cards offer suggestions on adding sound or video to slides, editing clip art, and more. A sample Cue Card is shown in Figure I.2.

Figure I.2 Sample Cue Card

Though Cue Cards are not a substitute for studying presentation design, or learning your way around PowerPoint, they can help to keep you pointed in the right direction.

Report It Word 6 Link

As mentioned earlier, PowerPoint 4.0 is well-integrated with Word 6 and other Office applications. Right on the PowerPoint tool bar is a Report It icon that launches Word 6 automatically and inserts the outline from the current presentation as a Word document. This is done by converting the outline to an RTF (Rich Text Format) document before it is loaded into Word. You can use the full features of Word to edit and format the outline, then return it to PowerPoint.

Tip of the Day

An addition to the PowerPoint help system, the Tip of the Day dialog pops up when you first launch the program. The random tips offer suggestions on how to do various PowerPoint tasks. You can disable the automatic Tip of the Day, or you can use the Help menu to display the Tip dialog at any time. Once the dialog is on the screen, you can step through a series of tip screens if you wish.

ToolTips

Icon-based toolbars are nice, but the newer applications are so complex it can be difficult to remember what the little pictures mean. And, if you are using a high resolution screen (say, 1,024 x 768 resolution) and you're already myopic from years of sitting in front of glowing screens, you can't always see the pictures anyway.

That's where ToolTips comes in. In PowerPoint, when you place the mouse pointer over one of the toolbar icons a pop-up yellow note bar tells you what the tool does. If you already know the tool you're about to use, the ToolTips display won't bother you because there is a slight delay between the time you point to the icon and when the ToolTips text pops up. That way, you can step through tools without any interference from the pop-up text if you wish. On the other hand, if you need a little help remembering what a specific tool does, simply place the pointer over the icon and wait about a second.

Wizards

A *Wizard* is Microsoft's newest buzzword for built-in, interactive macros that help you conduct software operations. This version of PowerPoint has two Wizards: the AutoContent Wizard and the Pick a Look Wizard. Figure I.3 shows a typical Wizard screen. As you can see, the Wizards pre-set a lot of PowerPoint features by asking you questions.

Figure I.3 Typical Wizard Interactive Screen

The AutoContent Wizard suggests a sequence of slides that fit together to make a complete presentation. Many beginning presentation program users don't have experience in organizing a presentation. They may neglect some elements that should be included. The AutoContent Wizard automatically inserts a Title and Subject slide as well as other slides in the proper sequence to help you build a successful presentation.

The Pick a Look Wizard helps you select an output style based on the type of output you want for the presentation slides. It automatically picks a template from the ones supplied with PowerPoint, then customizes it based on the responses you give to questions from the Wizard. You can launch the Pick a Look Wizard at any time during presentation design and production, not just when you open a new presentation.

Why Use PowerPoint?

The question Why use PowerPoint? involves two issues. The first is, What is the application for PowerPoint, how will it help you in your business or personal life, what jobs can it make easier or more professional? The second is, Why use

PowerPoint instead of Lotus Freelance, Harvard Graphics, or other graphics and presentation applications?

Let's look at the second question first. There are many similarities among the top presentation programs on the market today. I don't want to get into a blow-by-blow dissection of each package or a strength vs. limitations argument here. Depending on your perspective, each of the current offerings can be the best for different applications. There are some obvious reasons to choose PowerPoint over another application, however.

The main argument in favor of PowerPoint is that if you already are using Microsoft Word or another of the Office applications, you are familiar with Microsoft's approach to software design and user interface. You can move into PowerPoint from Word 6 very easily. The screens look quite similar and, in fact, some of the utilities and features from Word are also a part of PowerPoint.

Also, by sticking with the products of a single vendor you can be reasonably assured that they will work well together. In today's Windows environment it is increasingly important to be able to share information among different programs. Besides, if you bought Microsoft's Office suite of software so you could use Word 6 and Excel 5, for example, you already have PowerPoint as part of the package. It is like getting another application free. Why buy another package when you have this one?

Now let's look at the What can PowerPoint do for me? question. If you've read the first part of this introduction you can see some of the applications already. This is a presentation package that is designed to support you in preparing stand-up presentations or moderated slide shows as an aid in conveying information to an audience. I suppose you could use it for a user-conducted, interactive presentation with the HyperLink feature, but this is not what PowerPoint is designed to do. It doesn't include enough checks and *branching* features to make it a strong player in this application area.

Notice that you shouldn't look at PowerPoint as only a formal presentation builder. Anytime you are presenting information to someone else, whether it is to a large group or one-on-one to your boss or co-worker, this software can help you organize your own thoughts and present ideas in a professional manner. It is much easier to generate simple comparison graphs with PowerPoint than with Excel or 1-2-3, for example. So if you want to sit down to discuss sales figures or cost projections with someone, you can key the figures into the PowerPoint graph generator quickly and easily to produce a professional graph of this information.

The pre-designed screens and Wizards help you step through a presentation design so you can make sure you have thought of all the components you need, and then PowerPoint helps you build a presentation with professional-looking slides or illustrations. PowerPoint isn't for everybody, but an awful lot of us have it as part of the Microsoft Office suite. Don't automatically write it off because you never give stand-up presentations in the board room. It is equally useful for less formal, short presentations from office planning discussions to homework assignments.

About This Book

This is just one of a whole series of books in the *Teach Yourself...* line from MIS:Press. The intent is for this book to do just what the title implies. It will help you teach yourself how to use PowerPoint. You can approach this task from a number of perspectives. One that will get you up and running with PowerPoint very fast is to take the Weekend Tour that begins in Chapter 2, either as the first thing you do after reading this introduction, or after you at least browse the Getting Started chapter. There is enough information in these two chapters alone to help you achieve a fairly high degree of expertise with PowerPoint in a relatively short period of time.

In addition, there is a section to help you design presentations that should help you get the most out of PowerPoint, and there is plenty of information on using the program and its features. For a quick look at what else is in this book, look at the section What's in This Book later in the introduction.

Conventions We Use

Before we get started, let's agree on some terms and ways of doing things. I'll try to keep the format of this book as simple and as straightforward as possible while, at the same time, making clear the various commands, files, and structures we need to discuss.

First of all, in addition to plain text, you'll find throughout this book icons (small pictures) designed to draw your attention to certain sections. When you see the Note icon, you know we have some special information that applies to the main text in that area, and that we feel is important enough to point out.

Beyond that, we have other ways of presenting data in this book that can guide you toward understanding:

- New terms are italicized. These are words we are introducing for the first time and likely will use later in the book. You probably also will find them described in the glossary.

- Keystrokes, file names, commands, and specific options are presented in boldface. Information you enter from the keyboard is shown in boldface, but you won't enter everything you see in boldface. We'll tell you specifically when to type something on the keyboard.

- The individual PowerPoint presentation elements are called slides in this book, even if you may use these elements in ways other than for a slide show. This is a good, general term that describes the screens you design with the software.

In addition, I assume you are reasonably familiar with Microsoft Windows. I may offer some hints to show you better or easier ways to do some Windows-specific tasks, but in general I assume you are familiar with the Windows user interface so that, for example, if I say click on something you know what that means. You should also know the difference between click and double-click, and you should know how to pull down Windows menus and how to manipulate dialog boxes. (However, I will give you a short Windows refresher in Chapter 1, mainly so we can agree on terms and procedures.)

What's In This Book

I've already hinted at some of the things I'll cover in this book. Here is some more detail on what you will find.

In Chapter 1, I'll help you get started with PowerPoint by showing you the major features of the PowerPoint screen and the user interface.

Chapter 2 gives you a Weekend Tour of PowerPoint. This is a way to read about and try most of the major features of PowerPoint in a relatively short period of time (you don't have to work on PowerPoint over the weekend if you don't want to!). If you study this chapter and try the exercises I suggest, you'll come away with a fairly firm grasp on what PowerPoint can do and how to do it. After that, you can use the other areas of the book for reference and to refine the skills you learned in this chapter.

As I mentioned earlier in this introduction, using PowerPoint to create presentation support slides is relatively easy. The harder part may be learning how to design presentations in the first place. The object of this book is to teach you PowerPoint, but in Chapter 3 I'll also give you some hints on designing presentations for PowerPoint.

PowerPoint is full of pre-formed templates and slides, Wizards and other sub-applications to help you build presentations. In Chapter 4 you will learn how to use PowerPoint templates, clip art, and Wizards. You will use some of these features whenever you use PowerPoint, even as part of the exercises in the Weekend Tour and in the Getting Started section, but this chapter gives you some additional detail.

One useful and fairly easy application for PowerPoint is to design a speech or other presentation around slides you can show from your computer. You can use the standard computer screen if the group is small, or you can project the images for a large group presentation. Chapter 5 shows you how to use PowerPoint to create computer slide shows.

Chapter 6, Printing From PowerPoint, offers some hints on producing printed output from PowerPoint. Your printer can produce outlines, speaker notes, audience handouts, or presentation samples. You'll learn how to configure your printer and how to print these portions of a PowerPoint presentation in this chapter.

In addition to straight printing, you may want to create other types of presentation material with PowerPoint. In Chapter 7 I'll show you about creating presentation output with PowerPoint. This might include 35mm slides, overhead projector foils, or video.

Among the strong features of PowerPoint is its high level of integration with other Microsoft products. In Chapter 8 I'll show you how PowerPoint fits in with other products in the Microsoft Office suite of applications.

It may seem strange, but "help on help" can be quite useful. The PowerPoint help facility is powerful and includes many features that you can use but which may need a little introduction. In Chapter 9 I'll describe the features of PowerPoint help and show you how to use them.

Finally, there are two appendices and a glossary as part of this book. Appendix A discusses some of the hardware issues around using PowerPoint, and Appendix B serves as a useful command reference to PowerPoint.

To Sum Up

One way to look at PowerPoint is as a focused word processor. Much, if not most, of the functionality of PowerPoint is already included in many word processors such as Word 6. You can insert text fields, partition screens, include clip art video or sound, produce graphs, and more. The difference between PowerPoint and Word, however, is that PowerPoint screens are pre-formatted, making design a lot easier. In addition, the clip art supplied with PowerPoint offers more variety than is included with the Word package, and the clip art viewer makes it a lot easier to use.

As part of Microsoft's newest Office suite, PowerPoint helps demonstrate the next phase of software that includes common user interfaces, common features, tight integration, and single-vendor packages. You may not find that PowerPoint answers all of your presentation needs, but it will go a long way in helping you produce professional, understandable presentations. I hope the hints and guidance in this book help you get the most out of this package.

— Tom Badgett
   Knoxville, TN

Getting Started

15

Everything has to start somewhere. Your beginning with PowerPoint may have come as you installed the Microsoft Office suite of products, or when you decided you needed a presentation product and chose this one, or you may be beginning with PowerPoint with this book.

Whatever your status with PowerPoint, this chapter is a good starting point or a good place to refresh your memory if you already have a little experience with this software.

What is PowerPoint?

PowerPoint is a Microsoft Windows-based presentation package. You will use it to design and build slides to support a variety of presentations. It is a good tool for preparing a series of overhead projector foils, producing 35mm slides, printing title or accent pages for a company report, preparing computer-based slide shows, and more.

If you've never used presentation software, you'll be pleased at how easy PowerPoint is to learn. If you have some experience with presentation software, you'll find a lot to like here. PowerPoint's built-in slide designs and interactive Wizards can make the job go faster, help make sure your designs are complete, and help keep your presentations consistent time after time.

PowerPoint and Windows

PowerPoint is based on Microsoft Windows and carries many features of other Microsoft products, especially Word 6. As a Windows product, PowerPoint is easy to learn and has a user interface that is consistent with other Windows applications. In addition, when you use software that is fully Windows-compliant, you gain the benefit of interoperability through OLE (Object Linking and Embedding). PowerPoint, like most of Microsoft's latest Windows applications, supports OLE version 2.0, an advanced object linking protocol that makes it fairly easy to share data among different applications.

PowerPoint and Other Microsoft Software

OLE 2.0 is only one of the features of PowerPoint made possible by the Windows environment. Because Microsoft is interested in making the learning curve for PowerPoint as short as possible, they have designed it to look and act like their other products, and to work well with them.

From a screen appearance standpoint, PowerPoint is closer to Microsoft Word 6 than to anything else. See Figures 1.1 and 1.2 for a comparison of the two opening screens. As you can see, PowerPoint and Word 6 look a lot alike.

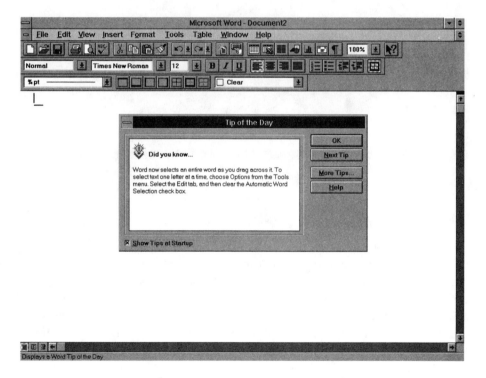

Figure 1.1 Microsoft Word 6 Opening Screen

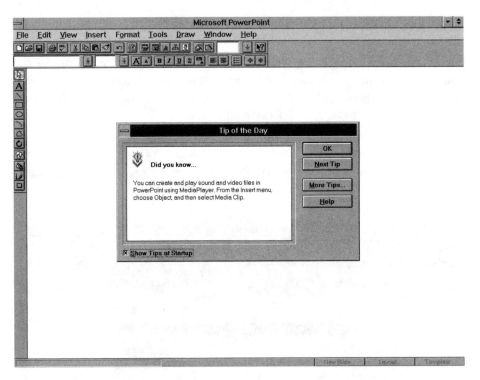

Figure 1.2 PowerPoint 4.0 Opening Screen

(Your versions of these screens may look a little different from these, depending on optional settings and your Windows display configuration.) Obviously this kind of interface consistency makes the transition from one product to another extremely easy. Many of the same tool buttons you find in Word are also available in PowerPoint. And, even when the actual menu selections aren't the same, the main menu titles are similar. Both products have File, Edit, View, Insert, Format, and Tools menu choices, and the format bars of the two products are very similar.

These two applications are also linked in ways other than through OLE 2.0. For example, when you want to edit a PowerPoint presentation outline, you can click on a Report It icon on the toolbar to launch Word and load the outline. When you are finished, you can exit Word and return to PowerPoint.

Installing PowerPoint

Installing PowerPoint is a simple process that resembles the installation of any other Windows-compliant program. The basic process is listed below:

1. Insert Disk 1 from the PowerPoint distribution diskette set into one of the floppy drives.

2. From the Windows Program Manager, use **File Run** to display the Run dialog.

3. In the **Command Line:** field of this dialog, type **A:\SETUP** (or **B:\SETUP** if you placed the diskette in the B: drive) and press **Enter** or click on **OK**. The initial setup screen shown in Figure 1.3 is displayed.

Figure 1.3 Initial PowerPoint Setup Screen

4. Accept Setup's defaults of directory and components to be installed, or customize the installation as required. Select the type of installation from the Installation Type dialog shown in Figure 1.4.

Figure 1.4 PowerPoint Setup Installation Type Dialog

PowerPoint Setup is similar to all Windows installation programs, so this part of the setup process should be straightforward. If you choose the Typical installation, there isn't much for you to do except insert new diskettes when Setup calls for them. If you select Complete/Custom installation, then you can choose which components of the software you want to install. Choose this option if you want to save disk space or make other custom choices in your installation of PowerPoint. Setup gives you the following options:

Microsoft PowerPoint Program Files	9767 K
Online Help, Tutorial and Cue Cards	640 K
Applets	8316 K
Converters, Filters and Translators	2298 K
Spelling Checker	264 K
Templates	6688 K
Clip Art Files	8402 K
Media Player	481 K
TrueType Fonts	1433 K
Tools	936 K
Genigraphics Driver & GraphicsLink	377 K

For the most complete installation, choose all of these options. That way you won't have to use Setup again to add or remove components, and you won't be surprised or frustrated when you try to do something that you think PowerPoint supports but which you didn't install. Of course if you don't have enough disk space to install everything, specify what you have room for; you can always add and remove components with Setup later if necessary.

PowerPoint Files and File Management

When you install PowerPoint you have the option of accepting Setup's default directory of **C:\Powerpnt**, or you can specify another directory of your choice. Once you have specified the main directory for PowerPoint files, Setup creates additional directories under this main directory for Setup and Template files. You don't make this choice.

In addition, Setup creates additional directories under the *MSAPPS* directory under your Windows directory. If you are using other Microsoft applications, the MSAPPS directory already exists. If not, PowerPoint Setup will create it for you.

Under this directory are a number of subdirectories that hold other Microsoft applications (or *applets*) that support main Microsoft applications. The *WordArt* utility, for example, is installed when you install Word 6. If you installed Word 6 before PowerPoint, this directory and its associated files are already in place. If you install PowerPoint first, then PowerPoint Setup creates this subdirectory and installs the program files in it (if you specify that you want to install PowerPoint applets).

The *Equation Editor*, OrgChart, clip art, and other PowerPoint utilities and support files also are installed in separate subdirectories under MSAPPS.

In the following section is a brief discussion of the various file groups that you can select as part of the PowerPoint installation.

Microsoft PowerPoint Program Files

You can't run PowerPoint without these files. On the other hand, you can make a very basic installation by installing just these program files. There would be a lot you couldn't do if this was all you installed, but you could run the program. You might want to use this choice if you have limited disk space and only need the bare bones basics.

Online Help, Tutorial, and Cue Cards

Chances are you'll want the online help, tutorial, and cue card files in addition to the program files. These files give you access to online help and electronic manual, the pop-up Cue Cards that offer hints on designing presentations, and a hands-on tutorial. I don't recommend that you try to install PowerPoint without these files.

Applets

These files contain PowerPoint utilities or small applications. You can do without them, but you would limit the power of PowerPoint. The applets include the Equation Editor, WordArt, OrgChart, and ClipArt Gallery.

Converters, Filters, and Translators

Most programs like PowerPoint include built-in conversion utilities to import data from and export data to other applications. If you don't install these files you may not be able to import data from external applications. If you do install these files, you should be able to share text and graphics files easily with most major applications.

Spelling Checker

This application does what the name says. It checks the spelling of the text portions of your PowerPoint presentations. If you don't install it you save 264K of storage, but you also lose the ability to spell check your documents.

Templates

PowerPoint templates are professional presentation designs that you can use as a starting point for your own presentations. If you don't install templates, you can still fully use PowerPoint, but the designs you use will be solely your own.

Clip Art Files

These files contain the 1,000 or so drawings supplied as part of PowerPoint to help you create colorful and graphic presentation slides. Without them, your slides will have a lot less oomph, but you'll save nearly eight and a half megabytes of storage. You make the choice.

Media Player

The Media Player is a utility for playing multimedia files and controlling some hardware. If you don't plan to use multimedia components in your presentations, then you don't need these files.

TrueType Fonts

TrueType fonts are a collection of Windows-compliant font sets that enhance the appearance of your applications and also help the screen display match what comes out on the printer.

Tools

These files provide an additional set of utilities, including an interface to Setup so you can re-configure PowerPoint if necessary. Also included is a system reporting utility that displays information about your system hardware and software.

Genigraphics Driver & GraphicsLink

This set of utilities lets you prepare presentations for transmission to Genigraphics company to make 35mm slides or color overhead foils. This type of capability is increasingly common with presentation software. Genigraphics is only one of several companies that offer this type of slide preparation service.

A Quick Windows and PowerPoint Primer

Before you can use PowerPoint effectively you should be thoroughly familiar with the Microsoft Windows environment. I can't teach you all there is to know about Windows within a short section of a book about PowerPoint, but it might be a good idea for you to scan this section, even if you are an experienced Windows user. That way we can agree on terms and processes. That'll make it easier for you to understand instructions about using Windows-based PowerPoint features.

The Windows Screen

Microsoft Windows provides a graphical user interface for your computer data and applications. The main Windows interface is the Program Manager screen, which consists of several application windows (the exact number depends on how many applications you have installed). Inside each application window is a group of icons that represent programs or utilities within that application group.

Figure 1.5 shows a Program Manager screen with basic Windows components, including the Main and Accessories application windows.

Figure 1.5 Program Manager with Main and Accessories Windows

When you install a new application such as PowerPoint, the Setup or Install program usually creates a new application window to hold the main program and any utilities and support programs that go with it. Figure 1.6 shows the PowerPoint application window created by Setup.

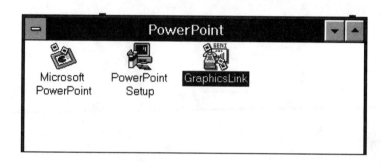

Figure 1.6 PowerPoint Application Window in Program Manager

If your system has several Windows-based applications and you use Windows regularly, then Windows probably launches automatically when you start your computer. If not, simply type **Win** at the DOS prompt to start the Windows operating environment.

Once you are in the Program Manager, you can start PowerPoint by first opening the PowerPoint application window (which may be titled Microsoft Office if you installed PowerPoint as part of Office or if you have previously installed Microsoft Word or another Office application). Then locate the Microsoft PowerPoint icon, and either double-click on it or select it and press **Enter**.

When PowerPoint starts, the main PowerPoint screen, complete with the Tip of the Day, is displayed (See Figure 1.7).

The Program Manager screen and the main PowerPoint screen show graphically the power of the Windows environment. These screens are full of little pictures (icons) that represent programs or program features. You select them with the mouse by clicking or double-clicking on the appropriate icon.

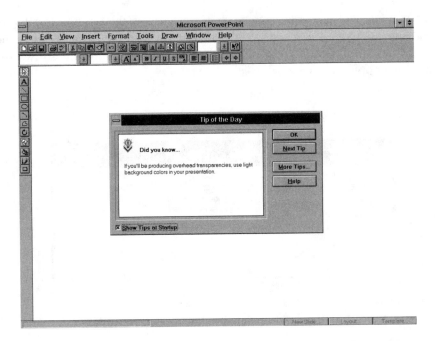

Figure 1.7 Main PowerPoint Screen with Tip of the Day

Using the Mouse

The mouse is a great improvement to computer interaction, and it seems so easy and natural when you watch someone with some experience use it. When you first sit down with a mouse, however, it is a pretty awkward experience. I can't teach you to feel comfortable with the mouse. That comes only with some experience. I can offer a couple of hints that make using the mouse easier, and I can share a couple of terms that you'll see throughout this book.

First of all, as you move the mouse pointer around the screen, notice that the shape of the pointer changes depending on the type of onscreen object under the pointer. When the pointer is over an object that can be selected, the pointer is an arrow point. When the pointer moves over a part of the screen that can hold text, on the other hand, the pointer changes to an I beam. This is the insertion point and it shows that you are pointing to a text portion of the screen.

If you click on the screen with the I beam showing, a text insertion point is fixed and the next text you type will appear at that location.

If you run out of desk before you have moved the mouse pointer where you want it, simply pick up the mouse and move it over to give you room to move.

NOTE

You can resize a PowerPoint object by moving the mouse pointer to the edge of the object until the pointer changes to a double-ended arrow. Press and hold the left mouse button and drag the edge of the object to the new position.

NOTE

As you move the mouse, keep your wrist on the desk and move the mouse with your hand. If you try to move the mouse by moving your whole arm, you will have less control and will get fatigued easily.

NOTE

Your mouse probably has two buttons, usually termed left and right. The left mouse button is the main one. When I instruct you to click or double-click or to hold down the mouse button in this book, I mean the left button. Some applications don't use the right button at all, but in PowerPoint you can use the right button to display additional menu choices. For example, if you press the right mouse button when the mouse pointer is inside a slide in the PowerPoint editing window, you will see a pop-up menu with eight frequently used selections on it (See Figure 1.8).

Figure 1.8 Right Button Command Menu

If you place the pointer within one of the displayed toolbars and press the right mouse button, you'll see another menu for customizing the toolbar displays (See Figure 1.9).

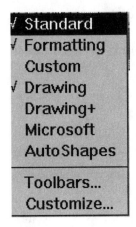

Figure 1.9 Right Button Toolbar Menu

When I tell you to click on a PowerPoint object, I mean to move the mouse pointer over the object and press the left mouse button momentarily. A double-click means to place the mouse pointer over an object and press the left mouse button twice in quick succession. A double-click operation can be a little complicated for some users. For one thing, there is sometimes a tendency to move the mouse pointer between clicks. This moves the pointer off of the object you are trying to select, so the double click doesn't take effect. In addition, you need to double-click with a close-spaced rhythm. If you leave too much space between the clicks, you won't make the selection you want.

Sometimes you want to select a menu item without actually executing it. When a double-click is required to start a specific menu item, you can use a single click to highlight or select the item. You can also drag a highlight cursor or selector by holding down the left mouse button while you move the cursor. A menu or dialog box selection that requires a single click will be executed when you move the highlight bar over the choice and release the mouse button.

When you are working with text, you can generally select a portion of text by placing the mouse pointer at the beginning of the block of text you want to select, holding down the left mouse button, and moving the highlight across as much text as you want to select. Once selected, the text can be manipulated as a unit or block.

You may want to point to an item without selecting it, as when you want to view the ToolTips for a toolbar button. To point to a screen object, simply move the mouse pointer over the object and pause without pressing any mouse button.

Understanding Menus

Any program that runs under Microsoft Windows has a menu scheme that is similar to the Program Manager menu system and to most other Windows products. Figures 1.10–1.12 show three Windows menus. Figure 1.10 is the basic Program Manager menu bar. It is relatively short, but uses the same structure as all Windows-compliant applications. Figure 1.11 shows the Microsoft Word 6 menu bar and Figure 1.12 shows the PowerPoint 4.0 menu bar.

Figure 1.10 Program Manager Menu

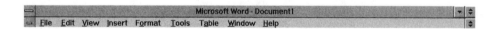

Figure 1.11 Microsoft Word 6 Menu

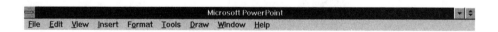

Figure 1.12 PowerPoint Menu

Notice the similarity among these menus. They are all arranged in a horizontal fashion (similar to the style first used by spreadsheets like Lotus 1-2-3). When an application is active, you are working in the main part of the screen. You may be entering information into a spreadsheet, typing in a word processor, or, in the case of PowerPoint, inserting text or graphics into a presentation slide. When you want to use a menu selection, you can access it in two ways:

- Use the mouse to point to the menu item and pull down the list.
- Press and release the **Alt** key to activate the menu, use the cursor movement keys to highlight the item you want, then press **Enter**. You can also press the underlined character in the menu name to activate the menu. In the PowerPoint menu in Figure 1.12, for example, you can access the View menu by pressing the **V** key after you press the **Alt** key to activate the menu bar.

Figure 1.13 shows a PowerPoint screen with a submenu pulled down from the main menu bar.

Figure 1.13 PowerPoint Format Pull-Down Menu

Note that some menu choices give you additional feedback about the way they work. A selection followed by three dots, for example, means that a dialog box will be displayed if you select that menu item. Once the dialog box is displayed, you can provide additional information or answer questions to get the desired results. (See the discussion of dialog boxes later in this chapter for more information.)

A menu item followed by a right-facing triangle (▶) means that a submenu will be displayed if you select that item. Figure 1.14 shows one such submenu displayed along with a pull-down menu from the main menu bar.

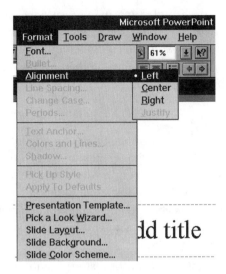

Figure 1.14 Second Menu Beside Main Menu

You can start some menu choices with a keyboard hotkey combination. These alternatives are shown beside the menu entries. See Figure 1.15 for an example of hotkey prompts on a pull-down menu from PowerPoint.

Figure 1.15 PowerPoint Edit Pull-Down Menu

Notice that the choices on a pull-down menu also have one character in each selection underlined. After you pull down the menu, you can either use the mouse to highlight and choose a selection, or you can simply press the keyboard character that is underlined in the selection you want. You don't have to press the **Alt** key in combination with the keyboard key in these submenus.

Understanding Toolbars

With a full-featured application such as PowerPoint, the menu structure can become extremely complex. Remembering where each choice is and how to use it can be difficult. That's why PowerPoint uses additional ways to get into its features. One of these is the toolbar. The PowerPoint toolbar is located directly under the menu bar. It consists of 20 standard buttons with pictures to help you understand what each button does.

To access a PowerPoint command or feature from the toolbar you just have to click on the right button. The button is a visual representation of a menu choice, a macro, or internal command. If you frequently use commands other than the ones supplied on the standard toolbar, you can easily customize the display to include the features you want (I'll show you how to do that in the next chapter).

Understanding Dialog Boxes

A dialog box is an interactive pop-up display that asks for more information before conducting the operation selected from a menu. Figure 1.16 shows a typical PowerPoint dialog box.

Notice that there are several features of this dialog that are common to most dialogs. The dialog box is definitely a separate entity from the rest of the display, for one thing. It is well defined and it carries a title.

Along the right side of the dialog are several buttons. Which buttons appear depends on the function of the dialog, but you are almost certainly sure to find a Help button, a Cancel button, and an OK button. If there isn't an OK button, there will be a button that says Go on or Execute. For example, if you display the Slide Show dialog (View **Slide Show...**), the selection to close the dialog and continue is **Show**. This is obvious, given the title of the dialog box and the menu choice you made to display it in the first place.

Figure 1.16 Typical PowerPoint Dialog Box

In addition to these buttons, most dialogs include one or more areas for user input. You may be asked to specify a disk drive, a directory, or a file name, or to make selections by clicking on buttons. A button is a (usually) round object that is selected or de-selected by clicking with the mouse. When a button is selected it is colored dark, or, in the case of three-dimensional buttons, appears to be depressed. These are toggles. The first time you click on it, the button is selected. On the second click it is de-selected.

Understanding Scroll Bars

Most of the time you work with a Windows application, all you are seeing on the screen at any one time is a portion of the total display. In a word processor, for example, you can only see a portion of one page of the document. In PowerPoint you usually are looking at only one slide at a time.

To see other parts of the document or presentation you can use scroll bars, the gray horizontal and vertical devices at the bottom and side of the screen. Notice the vertical scroll bar in Figure 1.17. Click on the upward facing arrow to move one slide up in the presentation; click on the downward facing arrow to move one slide down in the presentation.

In addition, there is a small box between the arrows on the scroll bar. This shows how far from the top or bottom of the file you are. You can grab this box with the mouse and drag it up or down on the bar to move rapidly across several slides.

Scroll bars frequently appear in dialog boxes as well, to let you select an item in a window that contains too many items to appear in the dialog at one time.

Figure 1.17 PowerPoint Screen with Scroll Bars

Arranging Windows

As a Microsoft Windows product, PowerPoint supports some multitasking. That means you can work on more than one presentation at a time, copy or move information from one presentation window to another, and view multiple presentations simultaneously to compare them.

As you work with multiple PowerPoint windows you may need to rearrange the open windows to make them easier to view, to move one out of the way, or to access a different presentation. There are several ways to display multiple PowerPoint windows. Each time you open a new presentation, PowerPoint overlays the latest presentation window over previous ones. After you have three or four of these open, it will be impossible to see previous displays. Use the Window **Arrange All** menu sequence to have PowerPoint shrink these windows and place them on the screen where you can see them all at once. Figure 1.18 shows a screen with three presentations open.

Even with just three presentation windows open at once, however, it is nearly impossible to see any detail in any of the screens. Another way to display these windows so you can tell what is open is to use the Window **Cascade** command. This stacks up the open windows like a deck of cards fanned out so that you can see the presentation titles, but you can only see the contents of the topmost presentation. Figure 1.19 shows a PowerPoint Cascade display.

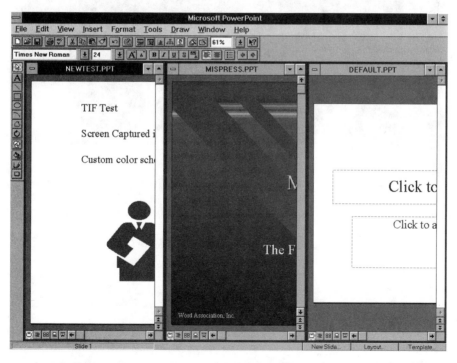

Figure 1.18 PowerPoint Screen with Three Open Presentations

You can activate any of these cascaded windows by simply clicking on the title bar of the one you want. Then you can enlarge the display by clicking on the **Restore** button (the upward facing arrow) at the far top right of the window. When you want to go back to another of the windows, first shrink the current presentation by clicking on the doubled-ended arrow on the right of the menu bar. Then you can click on the title bar of another presentation window and enlarge it as before to work with it.

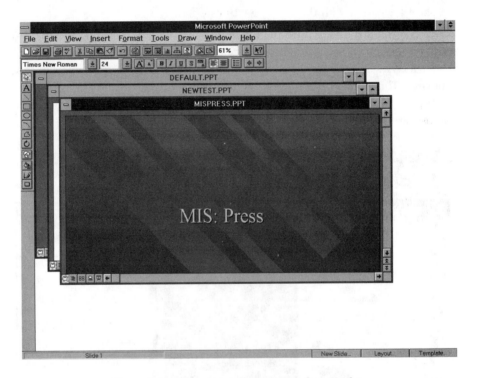

Figure 1.19 PowerPoint Cascade Window Display

To Sum Up

Whether you are new to Windows or have a lot of experience with other Windows programs, you shouldn't have much trouble getting up to speed with PowerPoint. After a little practice manipulating the PowerPoint menus, toolbars, and presentation screens, it should feel very natural. Just remember that the Windows user interface provides a standard of data presentation and manipulation that is similar to what you'll find in other major programs.

In the next chapter you'll walk through a tour of PowerPoint that will show all of this program's major screens and features. If you practice with your software as you read through this tour, you'll be creating your own basic presentations with PowerPoint quickly.

A Weekend Tour
of PowerPoint

PowerPoint is a powerful application. You can use it to produce professional presentations, create complex slides and slide shows, and more. Like most complex applications, there is a lot to learn to become proficient in using it. However, because PowerPoint is a Windows application and because it is part of the larger Microsoft Office suite, there is much you can accomplish with only a cursory introduction to presentation design theory and to PowerPoint itself.

In this chapter you'll learn the important concepts behind PowerPoint. You'll become familiar with its major screen components, and you'll use it to actually produce a useful presentation. If you step through this chapter and try the examples I show you, you'll end up with a strong working knowledge of PowerPoint.

The PowerPoint Screen

You've seen pieces of the PowerPoint screen in earlier chapters. In this section I want to provide additional detail about what's on the PowerPoint screen, how you access these components, and what you do with them.

Starting PowerPoint

First, let's talk about how to start PowerPoint from inside Windows. The PowerPoint *program icon* may be located in a PowerPoint application window or inside the Microsoft Office application window, depending on what other Microsoft software you have running. If you installed PowerPoint as part of the Microsoft Office suite, then the application window that holds the PowerPoint program icon is probably in the Office application window.

Figure 2.1 shows a Microsoft Office application window that has been shrunk to an icon. All application windows have the same icon in the Microsoft Windows environment. It is by the title that you tell what an individual window does. If you installed PowerPoint as a stand-alone application, the title of your application window icon may be PowerPoint.

Figure 2.1 Microsoft Office Application Window Closed

If you double-click on this icon, the application window opens, as shown in Figure 2.2. Inside the application window are several icons that relate to PowerPoint and other components of the Microsoft Office suite.

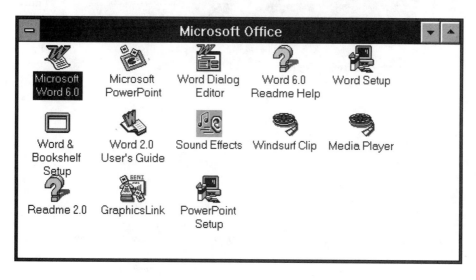

Figure 2.2 Microsoft Office Application Window Open

To launch PowerPoint, simply double-click on the program icon, shown in Figure 2.3.

Microsoft
PowerPoint

Figure 2.3 PowerPoint Program Icon

When you double-click on the PowerPoint program icon, the program starts and the main PowerPoint screen is displayed. Figure 2.4 shows the main PowerPoint screen with the major components labeled. Refer to this illustration as we discuss each of the labeled components in detail.

Figure 2.4 Main PowerPoint Screen with Components Labeled

The Menu Bar

The PowerPoint *menu bar,* like the menu bars of all Windows-compliant pro-grams, is a horizontal strip just below the title bar (see Figure 2.4 for the location of these screen elements). I described how to use menus in Chapter 1. In Figure 2.5 you can see a close-up of the PowerPoint menu bar.

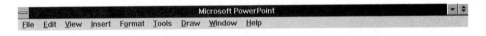

Figure 2.5 PowerPoint Menu Bar

Each of these nine menu choices holds additional selections that you can display by clicking on the menu bar or by using the **Alt+Key** combination, as discussed in Chapter 1. If you pull down a submenu list and some of its choices are light gray instead of black, that means you can't use them.

Why would a menu item appear that PowerPoint wouldn't let you use? There are a number of reasons, depending on the menu choice. However, the general reason is that PowerPoint (and all Windows-based programs) shows which commands aren't available. This works much better than letting you make the choice and getting an error message such as "Sorry. That command not available."

One example of commands that are on the menu but that can't be accessed are the **Cut** and **Copy** commands on the Edit menu. If there is nothing marked on the active screen, then you can't copy it or cut it. Therefore these options are grayed out. Also, if the *clipboard* is empty there is nothing to paste into the current document or presentation, so the **Paste** choice on the Edit menu will be grayed out.

There are many other situations in which a given menu item may not be available for use until some prerequisite condition is met. If you encounter an inaccessible menu item that you really want to use, find out what the prerequisite is, satisfy it, then try the command again.

In the following pages you'll find a PowerPoint command and menu reference. Use these figures as a quick reference to the commands available under each main menu choice. You can also see from these screens what the shortcut keys for some commands are. For more detailed information about each PowerPoint command, refer to Appendix B, Menu and Command Reference.

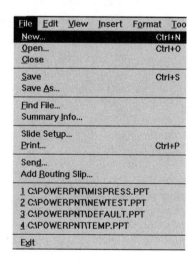

Figure 2.6 PowerPoint File Menu

Figure 2.7 PowerPoint Edit Menu

Figure 2.8 PowerPoint View Menu

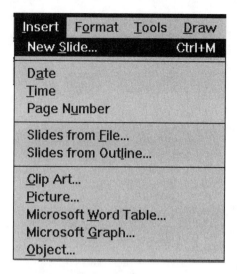

Figure 2.9 PowerPoint Insert Menu

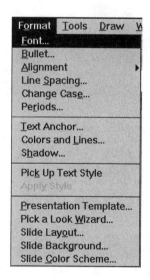

Figure 2.10 PowerPoint Format Menu

Figure 2.11 PowerPoint Tools Menu

Figure 2.12 PowerPoint Draw Menu

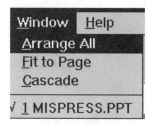

Figure 2.13 PowerPoint Window Menu

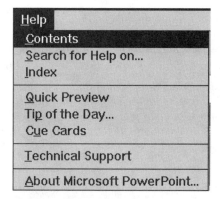

Figure 2.14 PowerPoint Help Menu

Remember the conventions of menu displays. A menu item followed by three dots means that a dialog box is displayed as a result of this menu choice. A right-facing triangle means that there's a submenu under this menu item. A control key combination shown after a menu entry means that you can bypass the menu bar and start this command by pressing the control key combination. If there is nothing displayed after a menu entry, you can launch that individual command by highlighting it and pressing **Enter**, or by clicking on the entry.

The Toolbar

The concept of a pictorial toolbar evolved as designers and users realized that certain menu commands are used heavily and are sometimes cumbersome to use or difficult to remember. In general, it is easier to scan a toolbar and pick out a picture to conduct a certain task than it is to remember which menu and which submenu to access to execute a specific command.

PowerPoint installs with three default toolbars but is configured with seven toolbars. In addition to this you can customize the toolbars by adding or removing commands through the Customize dialog. (Figure 2.4 shows the standard toolbars and their placement.)

To access a command represented by a toolbar button, simply point to the button and click once. If you can't remember what a particular toolbar button does, point to the button and wait about one second. PowerPoint's automatic ToolTips displays a one or two word description of that button's function.

Below is a toolbar reference that shows a close-up of each toolbar with labels that indicate what each button does. The toolbars that appear on the PowerPoint screen by default are shown first, then the ones that you can install through the Toolbars pop-up menu are shown.

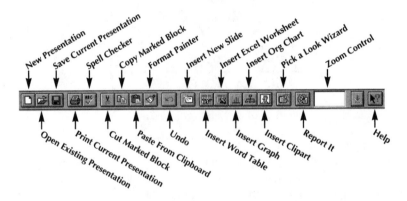

Figure 2.15 Standard PowerPoint Toolbar with Labels

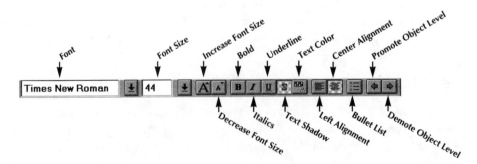

Figure 2.16 Format PowerPoint Toolbar with Labels

Figure 2.17 Drawing PowerPoint Toolbar with Labels

Figure 2.18 Drawing+ PowerPoint Toolbar with Labels

Rectangle Tool ➡ ◄— Parallelogram Tool
Trapezoid Tool ➡ ◄— Diamond Tool
Rounded Rectangle Tool ➡ ◄— Octagon Tool
Cross Tool ➡ ◄— Cube Tool
Ellipse Tool ➡ ◄— Balloon Tool
Pentagon Tool ➡ ◄— Hexagon Tool
Isosceles Triangle Tool ➡ ◄— Right Triangle Tool
Star Tool ➡ ◄— Seal Tool
Thin Right Arrow Tool ➡ ◄— Thin Left Arrow Tool
Thin Up Arrow Tool ➡ ◄— Thin Left Arrow Tool
Thick Right Arrow Tool ➡ ◄— Thick Left Arrow Tool
Thick Up Arrow Tool ➡ ◄— Thick Down Arrow Tool

Figure 2.19 AutoShapes PowerPoint Toolbar with Labels

You can add and remove PowerPoint toolbars easily. Point to any toolbar and press the right mouse button to display the Toolbars menu shown in Figure 2.20.

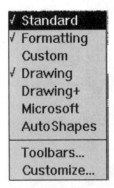

Figure 2.20 PowerPoint Pop-up Toolbars Menu

Notice that the default toolbars (Standard, Format, and Drawing) have a check mark beside them in this menu. That means they are being shown on the screen. These choices are toggles. If you click on any toolbar name that has a check beside it, PowerPoint removes the check and also removes that toolbar from the screen. If you click on a toolbar name that does not have a check beside it, PowerPoint adds a check and also adds that toolbar to the screen display.

If you click on the Custom toolbar name, PowerPoint displays the custom toolbar. Until you have created a custom toolbar, however, there are no tool buttons on it. A blank toolbar is shown in Figure 2.21.

Figure 2.21 Blank Custom Toolbar

To add your own choice of buttons to this blank custom toolbar, first display it. Then point to it and click the right mouse button to display the Toolbars menu again. Choose **Customize...** from this menu to display the Customize Toolbars dialog shown in Figure 2.22.

Figure 2.22 Customize Toolbars Dialog Box

In this dialog, highlight the name of the menu from which you want to select a command. PowerPoint displays the available toolbar buttons for that menu selection. To install one of these buttons on the custom toolbar, grab the one you want, drag it to the toolbar, and drop it. PowerPoint automatically resizes the toolbar to accept the new button. You can repeat this process as often as necessary to install additional buttons on the toolbar. If you change your mind about a tool button you already have placed on the custom toolbar, just grab it and drag it off of the bar. When you drop it, the button will disappear and will be removed from the toolbar.

In addition, with the Customize Toolbars dialog displayed, you can insert or remove tool buttons from any toolbar displayed on the screen. You can even move tool buttons from one toolbar to another. To install the same tool button on more than one toolbar, simply repeat the drag and drop process from the Customize Toolbar dialog as often as necessary to place the button on as many toolbars as you like.

As you add and remove buttons, PowerPoint automatically resizes the toolbar so it is just big enough to hold the buttons on the bar. You can remove the Custom and AutoShape toolbars without changing the buttons they contain by clicking on the **Control Menu** button on the upper left hand corner of these toolbars. (This is the same functionality offered by most Windows dialog boxes.)

One more thing. You can change the shape of the AutoShape and Custom toolbars by placing the mouse pointer at one edge until the pointer changes to a double arrow. Hold down the left mouse button and drag the shape of the box to a horizontal, vertical, or square orientation.

Note that some PowerPoint commands generate their own toolbars. If you insert a graph, for example, a toolbar to support the graphing operation replaces the default toolbars until you close the graphing utility and return to the regular PowerPoint screen.

The Format Bar

As you saw in the previous section, PowerPoint considers the Format Bar one of the available toolbars. However, because of the somewhat special nature of its operation, I wanted to give a little attention to this toolbar.

The Format Bar is used to format the text on a slide or within other presentation materials such as audience handouts or speaker notes. This is very similar to the Format Bar included with Microsoft Word, but it has some features specific to presentation applications.

The PowerPoint Format Bar includes the usual text formatting features, including boldface, underline, italics, text alignment, and bulleted list. The typeface and font size selections are there too, in the form of pull-down lists like the one in Figure 2.23.

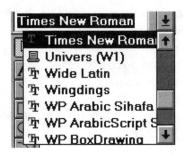

Figure 2.23 Format Bar Pull-Down Typeface List

There are some additional text formatting tools on this bar as well. For example, you can decrease the size of the current font by clicking on the **Decrease Font Size** button. Increase font size with the **Increase Font Size** button. You can see the results of each click right on the screen.

You can specify text color with the Text Color dialog and create shadowed text easily by selecting text and then clicking on the Text Shadow button.

PowerPoint is smart enough to know you want to change text formatting for the whole word where the insertion point rests; you don't have to select a word to format it. To change the format of more text than a single word, select it first.

Finally, left- and right-facing arrows on the Format Bar let you promote or demote outline levels on a PowerPoint slide screen.

Creating a Presentation

PowerPoint presentations can be simple or very complex. It depends on the message you're trying to impart with your presentation. A simple message requires a simple presentation design; a more complex message calls for a more complex presentation design.

Each PowerPoint presentation is contained in a single file. This one file, which you name when you save the presentation for the first time, stores the slides, speaker's notes, handouts, outline, and the formatting information that gives your presentation its particular appearance.

In the next chapter you will learn a few tips on planning and designing a presentation. In this section I'll show you how to begin with a basic concept and turn it into a series of slides in PowerPoint. If you step through this exercise, creating the sample presentation discussed here, then it should be fairly easy for you to substitute your own topics and design ideas for what is shown.

Sample Presentation Overview

For this exercise I'll show you how to construct a simple presentation about a topic you already know. Then you can use this same procedure to build another presentation about a topic of your own.

Let's assume that you want to build a brief presentation to tell someone about this book. You will provide a little background on the publisher (only what you can gather from the book itself), then you will show how the *Teach Yourself...* series fits into the other computer offerings from the publisher (I'll show you that). You will describe the general features of the series, present some specifics about this book in the series, and show the audience where to get more information.

Think for a moment about how to present this information within the framework of what you already know about PowerPoint. Remember that this presentation material is designed to support an oral presentation and not to stand alone, so the slides we create will carry minimal information.

One way to help design a new presentation is to list the general topics you want to cover, as I did above. Next, create a simple storyboard by drawing some squares on a piece of paper and labeling them. These squares represent the individual slides in your presentation. For a simple presentation, this may be all the planning you need. PowerPoint includes a number of tools to help you build a presentation, so you can let the individual slides evolve as you work with the software.

The drawing in Figure 2.24 shows my first attempt at a storyboard for this presentation. I didn't try to design each slide fully. I only wanted to get a general idea about the order of the information, to determine how many slides would be needed, and to identify the key slides in the presentation.

As you can see, this presentation will contain only eight slides, which is not very many but is enough for a short presentation and enough to help the audience retain the information you present. With this much background and planning, let's get on with building this presentation in PowerPoint.

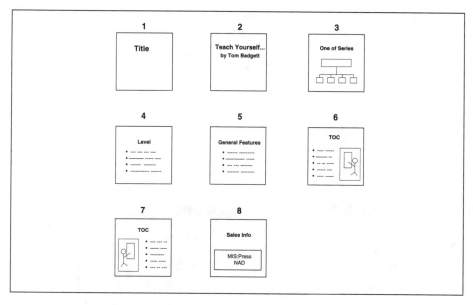

Figure 2.24 Sample Presentation Initial Storyboard

Starting a New Presentation

Starting a new presentation in PowerPoint is similar to creating a new document file in Word or another word processor. Use the File **New (Ctrl+N)** menu sequence to display the New Presentation dialog shown in Figure 2.25.

Figure 2.25 New Presentation Dialog

As you can see, there are many choices for starting a new presentation. For this sample we will use the Pick a Look Wizard. This interactive macro will help you set up the basic show by stepping through several screens which ask for your input. When the Wizard ends, the basic presentation configuration will be complete.

Using the Wizard

Here's how to select and use the Wizard:

Click on the **Pick a Look Wizard** button to select it, and then click on **OK** to display the first of nine interactive dialogs, shown in Figure 2.26.

Figure 2.26 Pick a Look Wizard — "Step 1 of 9" Dialog

Click on the **Next** button to present the second dialog, shown in Figure 2.27.

Figure 2.27 Pick a Look Wizard — "Step 2 of 9" Dialog

Accept the default selection, On-Screen Presentation, by clicking on the **Next** button to present the next dialog, shown in Figure 2.28.

Figure 2.28 Pick a Look Wizard— "Step 3 of 9" Dialog

Click on the **Blue Diagonal** button to specify the template design you want for this presentation, then click on the **Next** button to go on to the next dialog, shown in Figure 2.29.

PowerPoint includes more than 100 templates, so you're not limited to the ones listed on this dialog. Click on the **More** button to display a list of available templates if you'd like to try another selection.

N O T E

Figure 2.29 Pick a Look Wizard— "Step 4 of 9" Dialog

Accept the default selection on this dialog. PowerPoint can print several views of your presentation. For this sample let's assume you want them all. The next dialog is shown in Figure 2.30.

Figure 2.30 Pick a Look Wizard — Slide Options Dialog

Select the name **Microsoft** in the **Name, company, or other text** field on this dialog. Type in the name of your company or other text you want to appear on each slide. Accept the defaults on the rest of this dialog by clicking on the **Next** button to display the next dialog, shown in Figure 2.31.

Figure 2.31 Pick a Look Wizard — Notes Options Dialog

Assume you want to include all of this information on the Presentation notes, and click on the **Next** button to move on to the next dialog, shown in Figure 2.32.

Figure 2.32 Pick a Look Wizard — Handout Options Dialog

Again, assume you want to print full information on the handouts, and click on the **Next** button to move on to the dialog shown in Figure 2.33.

Figure 2.33 Pick a Look Wizard — Outline Options Dialog

To make all of the printed material contain the same information, click again on the **Next** button to accept the PowerPoint defaults and move on to the dialog shown in Figure 2.34.

Figure 2.34 Pick a Look Wizard — "Step 9 of 9" Dialog

Click on **Finish** to close out the Wizard and move on to entering information on the first slide. Figure 2.35 shows the default opening slide chosen by this Wizard.

Figure 2.35 Opening MIS:PRESS Presentation Slide

Creating the Slides

Click where the slide prompts "Click to add title" and type the title of the first slide:

MIS:Press

Click in the field that prompts "Click to add sub-title" and type

Teach Yourself... Series

Press **Enter** twice to add some spacing after this subtitle. Notice that PowerPoint automatically maintains formatting. Now type the last line of the subtitle text:

The Fast and Easy Way

This information comes right out of the book. Notice that at the bottom left of the slide is the company name you entered on the Slide Options dialog (Figure 2.30) earlier. In the middle of the slide you should see // and on the right **##**. These are place holders for the current date and slide number, which will be inserted when you print the slides or set them up for a computer slide show. The finished slide should look like the one in Figure 2.36.

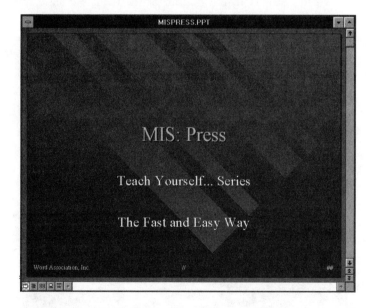

Figure 2.36 Completed Slide #1 in Sample Presentation

Click on the **New Slide...** button at the lower right of the PowerPoint screen to display the New Slide dialog shown in Figure 2.37.

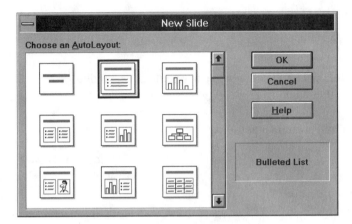

Figure 2.37 New Slide Dialog

Use the scroll bars (at the right of the Choose an AutoLayout window on this dialog) to move the display to the bottom of the available slide types. Choose the next-to-last AutoLayout slide, which has a single dark line at the top and has the rest of the slide blank (this is one slide to the left of the blank slide). To choose this slide, double-click on it, or select it by clicking once and then clicking on **OK**. The display should look like the one in Figure 2.38.

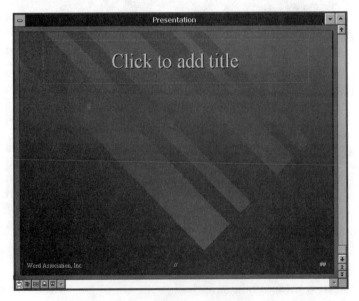

Figure 2.38 Blank Slide (Slide #2 in Presentation)

Click where the slide prompts "Click to add title" and type the following title:

Teach Yourself... PowerPoint

Using Text

Select the text tool from the Drawing toolbar at the left of the screen by clicking on it. (The text tool looks like a capital A.) Notice that the mouse pointer changes from the arrow point to a plus sign (sometimes called a cross hair). Move the cross hair below the slide title under the Y in Yourself. Click the left mouse button to set the text insertion point. Type the second line of the slide:

By Tom Badgett

Now use the text tool four more times to complete the slide. The text tool is canceled and the default pointer is selected when you finish entering information into a text field.

 You can drag a text box to preset the size before you start typing, or you can simply click once to position the insertion point and let the box grow as you type.

You can enter more than one line of text into a text field by pressing **Enter** at the end of each line, but as soon as you click outside the current text field, the text tool is canceled. When you finish, the slide should look like the one in Figure 2.39.

 You could have selected another type of slide that would do more of the text formatting for you, but I wanted to show you how to create your own text fields simply with the text tool from the Drawing toolbar.

Click on the **New Slide...** button at the bottom of the PowerPoint screen and once again choose the next-to-last AutoLayout slide (the same one you selected for the last slide). Click where the slide prompts "Click to add title" and type the title of this slide:

Teach Yourself: One of a Series

Next choose **Clip Art...** from the Insert menu to display the Microsoft ClipArt Gallery dialog shown in Figure 2.40.

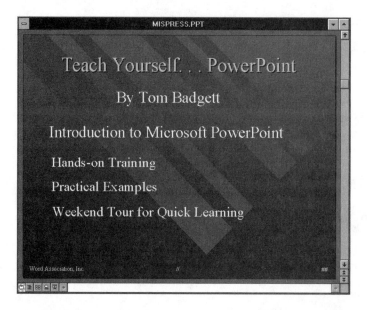

Figure 2.39 Completed Slide #2 in Sample Presentation

Figure 2.40 Microsoft ClipArt Gallery Dialog

Double-click on the blue book in position eight of the display (second row, last slide on the right). The book clip art will be inserted into the slide. Notice that PowerPoint automatically positions and sizes the clip art image in the lower part of this slide.

Now save the presentation. Use **File Save As...** (or use **Save** button on Toolbar) to display the Save As dialog. Enter the name **MISPRESS** in the **File Name** field of this dialog and click on **OK** to save the presentation to the default presentation directory. At this point **Summary Info** dialog box appears. Add any data you wish to the fields in this box and click on **OK**.

Use Insert **Object...** to display the Insert Object dialog shown in Figure 2.41.

Figure 2.41 Insert Object Dialog

Use the scroll bars at the right of the Object Type window of this dialog to locate the Microsoft Organization Chart 1.0 entry. Double-click on this line to launch the Organizational Chart utility (see Figure 2.42).

Notice that a sample organization chart is already on the screen. You will use this basic chart with one change. Click on the first **Co-worker** button (with the right-facing line). The mouse pointer changes to a Co-worker icon. Move the pointer to the first box on the left of the second line of the organization chart and click. The Organizational Chart utility adds another box to the left, creating a display with one box on the first row and four on the second.

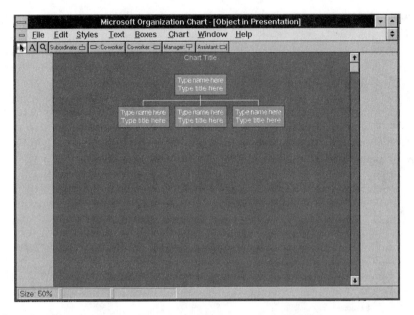

Figure 2.42 Microsoft Organizational Chart Application Screen

Click on the top box in the chart to select it. Now you can enter data from the place holder info. This doesn't work like the "Click here to add title" prompt on the main PowerPoint screen, so you'll have to select the line with the mouse. Move the pointer to the left of the line, press and hold the left mouse button, and move the mouse to select the line. Now what you type next will replace the prompt line.

Type the name:

MIS: Press

You can also select the prompt line by pressing **Enter** or **Tab** after double-clicking on the box. This will select the entire title line. Now press backtab (**Shift+Tab**) to select the Name line and start typing. To delete a prompt, press **Enter** or **Tab** to select the line and then press **Del**.

In the same way, enter the title in this first box:

Computer Books

Now start with the left box on the second row of the chart and enter a name in each box. The box names, left to right, should be:

Welcome to...

Teach Yourself...

Power of...

Power Shortcuts...

Click in the second box on the bottom row (Teach Yourself...) and use Text **Color** to display the text color bar. Click on a red bar to change the text color to red. This will produce red text against the default orange background.

Use Boxes **Box Color** to display another color bar. Click on the white box at the top of the color bar. The background color of the Teach Yourself... box changes to white. (Actually, you will see a black box unless you click on the box again or click outside the box to deselect it.) Now you have red text on a white background, which highlights the Teach Yourself... box and makes it stand out from the others.

Your finished organization chart should look similar to the one in Figure 2.43.

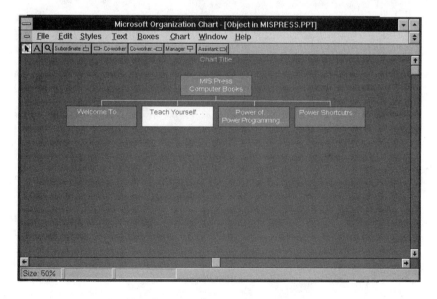

Figure 2.43 Completed Teach Yourself... Organizational Chart

Use File Update **MISPRESS.PPT** from the Organization Chart main menu to place the completed chart on the presentation slide. Use **Exit** and **Return to MISPRESS.PPT** to close the OrgChart application and return to your slide. The organizational chart you just constructed will be overlaid on the book clip art you inserted previously.

Click anywhere inside the organizational chart to select it. Notice the *handles* that appear on each edge of the chart. Grab a handle on the bottom horizontal edge of the chart and drag the edge until it is nearly at the bottom of the slide.

Grab the top horizontal handle and drag the edge until the top of the chart is near the top of the book. Now you have an organizational chart that is big enough to read, but it is distorted. Drag the left and right edges to change the aspect ratio of the chart so it looks more legible. The resulting slide should look like the one in Figure 2.44.

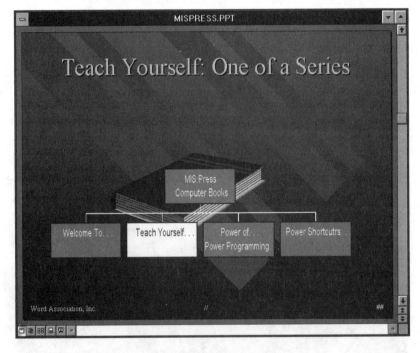

Figure 2.44 Completed Teach Yourself Series Slide

Click on the **New Slide...** button to display the New Slide dialog. Choose the next-to-last slide from the last, as before. This is the slide with space for a title and the rest blank. Click on the "Click to add title" line on this slide and type **Levels**. Use the mouse to select the text that you just entered, then click three times on the **Increase Font Size** button on the Format Bar. This will enlarge the title.

Click on the text tool icon on the Drawing toolbar and move the mouse cross hair about half way between the Levels title and the bottom of the slide. Click once to set the text insertion point. Type the following, pressing **Enter** at the end of each line:

> **Beginner/Intermediate**
> **IBM/PC**
> **and Compatibles**

Now click on the **New Slide...** button to display the New Slide dialog. Choose the second AutoLayout slide (double-click on it). This slide is the one with a title line at the top and a bulleted list at the bottom of the slide. Click on the "Click to add title" prompt and type the title for this slide:

> **General Series Features**

Click on the "Click to add text" prompt to enter the first line in the bulleted list:

> **Basic and instructional**

Press **Enter** to move to the next line in the list. Repeat this process until you have entered all six items in the list, as shown in Figure 2.45.

Click on the **New Slide...** button and choose the third AutoLayout slide down from the top in the left column. This is the slide with a title at the top, a bulleted list on the left, and a clip art image on the right. Add a title at the top of the slide. Press **Enter** after the first line of the title to type the second line:

> **Teach Yourself...PowerPoint**
> **Table of Contents**

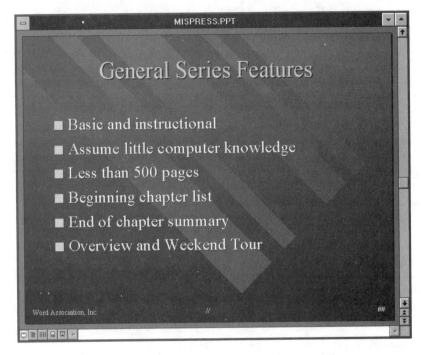

Figure 2.45 Completed General Series Features Slide

Next, click the mouse inside the top of the "Click to add text" box. Enter the five lines of the bulleted list for this slide:

Introduction

Getting Started

Weekend Tour

Designing Presentations

Using Templates, Clip Art and Wizards

Double-click on the clip art image at the right of this slide to display the ClipArt Gallery dialog. Choose the last clip art image on the top row. This is the drawing that shows a presenter standing before a large group with a pointer in the right hand. The finished slide should look like the one in Figure 2.46.

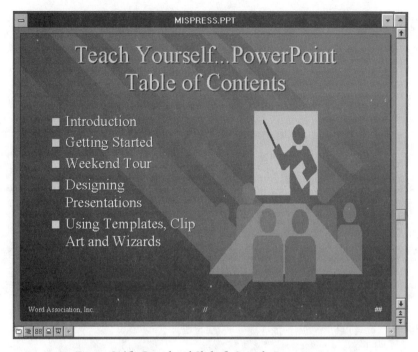

Figure 2.46 Completed Slide 6, Sample Presentation

Click on the **New Slide...** button and choose the fourth slide from the top in the left column. This is the slide with a bulleted list on the right and a clip art image on the left. Enter a title for this slide:

> **Teach Yourself...PowerPoint**
>
> **Table of Contents (2)**

Enter the rest of this book's table of contents as a bulleted list at the right side of the slide:

> **Computer Slide Shows**
>
> **Printing**
>
> **Presentation Output**
>
> **With Microsoft Office**
>
> **Using Help**
>
> **Hardware & Software**
>
> **Menu/Command Ref.**

Double-click on the clip art icon on the left of this slide to open the ClipArt Gallery. Choose the second image from the top in the left column. This is the image that shows a presenter in front of a small group with a pointer in the left hand. The finished slide should look like the one in Figure 2.47.

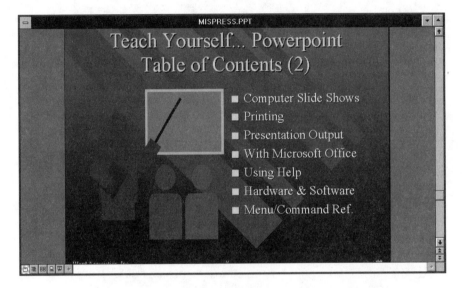

Figure 2.47 Completed Slide #7, Sample Presentation

Click on the **New Slide...** button to display the New Slide dialog one last time. Choose the next-to-last slide in the list, which is the one with a title at the top and the rest of the slide blank. Enter a title:

Sales/Purchase Information

Select the text tool from the Drawing toolbar and click near the middle of the slide to open a text box. Type the name and address of MIS: Press as found inside the front of this book. Press **Enter** at the end of each line to start a new line:

Special Sales Director

MIS:Press

a subsidiary of Henry Holt and Company, Inc.

115 West 18th Street

New York, NY 10011

Select the rectangle object tool from the Drawing toolbar and drag a rectangle around the name and address information on this slide. The default fill color is applied and the box is displayed in the foreground, covering up the text.

Use Draw **Send Backward** (on the Drawing+ toolbar, see Figure 2.18) to send the new box to the background and make the text visible. The box should still be selected. You can tell this by the presence of handles around the edges of the box. If the box is not selected, click on one edge of the box to re-select it. The handles should appear.

Point to the Drawing toolbar and press the right mouse button. Choose Drawing+ to add the second drawing toolbar at the left of the PowerPoint screen. Click on the first icon at the top of this new toolbar and choose red from the color samples displayed. The background of the selected box around the name and address should change to red.

Finally, format the text. Use the mouse to select the text inside the red box. Click on the **B** button on the Format Bar to bold the text. Click on the Text Color button on the Format Bar to pull down the text color bars. Choose White. The text inside the red box should change to bold white.

Use File **Save** to store the latest version of your presentation. The final slide should look like the one in Figure 2.48.

Congratulations! You have taken a basic presentation idea, designed a series of slides around it, and produced these slides in Microsoft PowerPoint. In doing so you have used many of the features you'll need from now on to make PowerPoint work for you in building successful presentations.

Your next step probably should be to come up with a design of your own. Think about something you already know about, or, like this book, something you can learn about easily, and design a series of slides to support a discussion of that topic. You could use an idea from your job that you already have had to present to others or something that you will soon present to someone else.

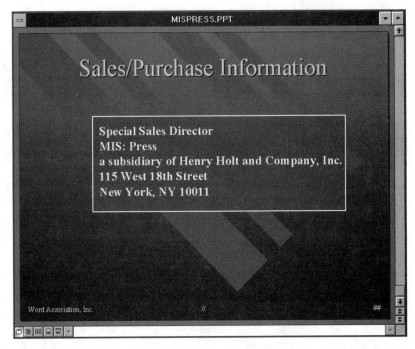

Figure 2.48 Finished Slide #8, Sample Presentation

You could choose a topic that you want to discuss at home with your children or spouse, or you could let your children help you select an idea from their current school work. (You'd be surprised at how quickly children take to the presentation idea!) Remember, for additional hints on designing presentations, refer to Chapter 3.

Printing and Presenting the Data

Now that you have a finished presentation, what do you do with it? That depends a little on how you will use the presentation—this one or the ones you create for yourself—but in this section you'll learn about the major options you have in PowerPoint. Later in this book you'll get a look at some additional information on outputting presentation slides.

At the very least you'll probably want to review the presentation you just created to see how things fit together and to decide whether you need to reorganize any of the information. There are a couple of ways to do that quickly in PowerPoint.

Especially for a short presentation like this one, the Slide Sorter view is an excellent way to get an overview of the slides you have and to see how they fit together into an overall presentation. Choose **Slide Sorter** from the View menu to see your presentation all together on one screen, like the view in Figure 2.49.

Figure 2.49 Slide Sorter View of Sample Presentation

 There is an icon at the bottom of a full-screen slide that lets you choose Slide Sorter view quickly. Locate and click on the icon that looks like four rectangles on a slide (the third icon from the left at the bottom of your slide). Return to full slide view by double-clicking on any slide in the Slide Sorter.

If everything looks alright in the Slide Sorter, click on the first slide in the presentation to select it, and then use View **Slide Show...** to display the Slide Show dialog. Accept the default of showing all slides with Manual Advance by clicking on the **Show** button. PowerPoint will display the first slide in your presentation as a full-screen image and will wait for you to press the left mouse button or any keyboard key to advance to the next slide. Press the right mouse button to back up a slide (you can also use the right and left cursor keys to move forward and backward in the presentation).

Notice that the full information you asked PowerPoint to include is now printed at the bottom of each slide: the company name you specified, the current date, and the slide number. You can return to the Slide Sorter view at any time by pressing **ESC** on the keyboard. When you advance past the last slide in the presentation, PowerPoint automatically returns to the Slide Sorter view (or whatever view was current when you started the slide show).

Remember that as you created the slides, PowerPoint was also creating some additional material for you, based on the answers you gave the Pick a Look Wizard when you started creating the presentation.

Outline View

For one thing, there's an outline of the presentation that you haven't seen yet. To get a look at the automatic PowerPoint outline, use View **Outline**. You should see the slide titles and text in an outline format like the one in Figure 2.50. (You can also click on the second icon at the bottom of the slide display—the one that looks like lines on a page—to display the outline view of your presentation.)

You can easily print the outline with the File Print dialog and selecting **Outline** in the Print What field. If you'd like to add more to the outline, simply type the additional data where you'd like it to appear. Just keep the notes or outline information within the boundaries of the correct slide. Then, even if you change the position of a slide in the Slide Sorter view, PowerPoint keeps your additional notes with the proper slide on the outline. Remember, however, the outline is a view of the slide; adding text to outline means it will show—and print—on the slide itself.

Note, too, that you can change the position of slides from within the outline. Those of us who have years of experience working with text documents and outlines probably find this view very comfortable. For example, to move a slide down in the presentation, simply place the insertion point on the first line of that slide in the outline, and then click on the down arrow on the outline tool-bar to the left of the outline display. Notice how the order of slides changes.

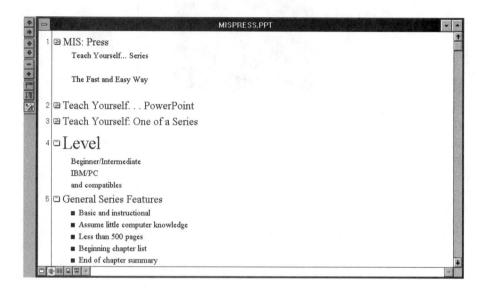

Figure 2.50 Sample Presentation Outline View

Speaker's Notes View

Another view is the Speaker's Notes view. You can display this view with the View **Notes Pages** command sequence, or by clicking on the Notes Pages View icon at the bottom of the screen (fourth icon from the left). Figure 2.51 shows a Notes View for the first screen of the sample presentation.

As you can see, this is a split page view that places each slide at the top of a page and leaves room at the bottom for information about the slide. This is a convenient tool to use for speaking notes.

Riding along with the notes pages is a Notes Master sheet that helps you do some additional formatting to the notes pages you print. Use View **Master** to display the Master menu. Then choose **Notes Master** to view the Notes Master page as shown in Figure 2.52.

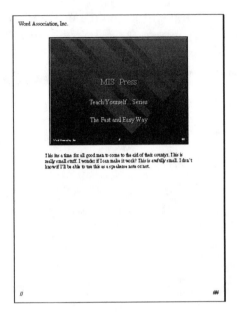

Figure 2.51 Notes Pages View for Sample Presentation After Notes Added

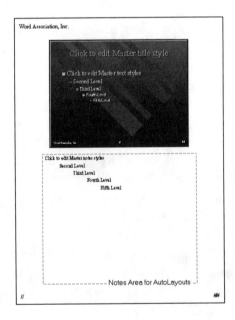

Figure 2.52 Notes Master Page Screen

By formatting the master page you establish the format for all notes pages associated with the current presentation. You can grab the slide image and move it around the page, add more graphics elements, and create master text.

Handouts

There is another way of looking at your presentation, one that is designed to serve as a handout for the audience. You can create handouts that contain two, three, or six slides per page. To create handouts, first use the View **Master** command sequence to display the Master menu. Choose **Handout Master** from this menu to display the Handout Master screen shown in Figure 2.53.

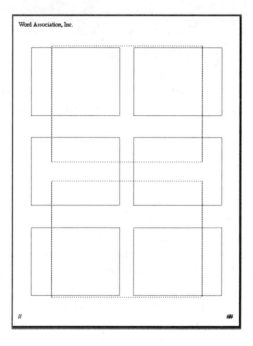

Figure 2.53 Handout Master Screen

You can use the master screen to add formatting, text, or graphics to the handout sheet. To generate handouts use the File **Print** command to display the Print dialog. Click on the down arrow at the right of the **Print What** field to produce a display like the one in Figure 2.54. Select the type of handout you want to create and click on **OK**.

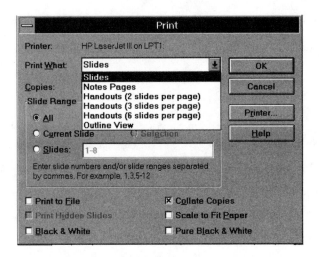

Figure 2.54 File Print Dialog with Print What List

The handout sheets can be helpful in providing an audience follow-along pages or sheets to carry away with them to help improve information retention.

To Sum Up

You've covered a lot of ground in this chapter. Later in this book we will step together through some of these same areas, but in more detail. In addition, you should try redoing this sample application with information of your own. We covered a lot of information about designing and producing your own presentations with PowerPoint. With the basic information in this chapter—screen components, menus, toolbars, views, clip art, and more—you have all the experience you need to produce your own presentations.

So why wait? Pick a topic from work, home, or school and start working with PowerPoint right now. At the same time, spend some more time with this book refining your skills and going beyond what we have covered in this introduction.

In the next chapter you'll learn how to make the presentation design process easier.

Designing Presentations
for PowerPoint

P owerPoint helps make the job of designing and producing professional and meaningful presentations a lot easier than in the old days of colored pens and flip charts. The computer tools coupled with the drawings, text tools, and forms packaged with the software help just about anybody look like a professional presentation designer.

However, the presentation business has reached the same stage that desktop publishing achieved several years ago. The tools are more powerful, they are easy to use, and they are widely available. However, those of us who have little or no experience in producing presentations can't always use these tools effectively.

A detailed treatise on professional presentation design is beyond the scope of this book—and beyond the expertise of your author. However, there are some design considerations that are easily learned and that, when considered during the design of your presentations as a whole and of the individual slides, can make your work more effective.

That's the topic of this chapter. I'll share some experience that can help you do a better job with the tools PowerPoint offers. As you study the hints offered here, keep in mind that PowerPoint is not designed as a stand-alone presentation tool. The slides and screens you design with it are intended to be accompanied by a human presenter. Even if you have used music and narration as part of a high-end presentation design with PowerPoint, you may well stand up to control the presentation, to answer questions, or to add personal comments during the show.

With that in mind, part of your planning and design of a PowerPoint presentation should focus on how the human presenter and the material you design can work together to achieve the ultimate goal. I'll talk about some general considerations about using PowerPoint presentation material, I'll show you some ways to help plan a presentation, and I'll talk about some of the issues involved with designing individual slides.

General Design Considerations

Let's look at some general ideas first. Presentations enhanced with PowerPoint carry a lot more weight than the old fashioned kind because of the way people gather information. Here's what research shows:

- 10 percent of what we learn comes from the words we hear.
- 40 percent of what we learn comes from the way the words are said.
- 50 percent of what we learn comes from what we see.

So, up to 50 percent of the information you provide your audience comes from what you present on your PowerPoint slides. That doesn't mean you can back off from preparing for the presentation, or that you should downplay the importance of text and facts. After all, the other 50 percent of what your audience learns comes from what you say and how you say it.

The key to successful presentations is twofold. As you design any presentation, be aware of the power of the visual part of it, but don't forget that the audience also expects to hear something. What the audience sees should be designed to supplement what is being said. The two methods of presenting information work together. You've probably noticed yourself that it can be distracting or even irritating to try to read a lot of material while someone is talking. You tune out the words to concentrate on the visual, or you skim the visual to listen to what is being said.

Therefore, the visual component of a presentation should be brief. You can shorten on-screen presentations by breaking some of the long-standing rules of language you were taught in school. A *bulleted list*, for example, doesn't always require a subject and verb, and you can use creative symbols in place of standard bullets to enhance the visual. That way the bullets themselves become part of the message. (See Figure 3.1.)

The goal is to help the audience grasp the information as quickly as possible and to help them retain it. Whatever you can do to make the experience a visual one will enhance the process.

Some of the same design rules and guidelines you would use for desktop publishing or photographic composition also apply to presentations. After all, the individual components of a presentation are slides or pages, individual units that are linked together to form the whole. The difference between PowerPoint slides and a printed page or a photograph, of course, is that you can use sound and even motion in addition to layout, color, shape, and shading to get your message across. The key to successful presentations is to use the tools at your disposal in a creative way that is appropriate to the audience you hope to reach and to the message you hope to convey.

Figure 3.1 Bulleted List without Standard English and with Custom Bullets

In designing a presentation, keep the ultimate goal in mind. Do you want the audience to remember specifics, for example, or is a general idea the more important consideration? In a sales presentation, for example, is it more important for the audience to remember technical specifications and statistics, or do you want to convey a concept or an overview of what the product can do for them or for their business?

There is no set answer. The correct response to that question depends on the type of selling you are doing and what you want the viewer to do, think, or feel at the end of the presentation. But we can make some observations on how to accomplish either of those goals.

To leave the viewer with a concept, feeling, or idea:

- Use motion video and photographs.
- Reduce the amount of text on screen.
- Show people doing something with the product.
- Show people who appear pleased or satisfied.
- Emphasize *what* is being done over *how* it is being done.

Remember, we retain visual information such as pictures better than text. So whenever you can, impart ideas visually. You'll have a better chance of keeping the audience interested, and the audience will have a better chance of retaining the information.

To emphasize factual details over concept:

- Use text and charts.
- Use no more than six lines per slide.
- State and restate ideas, using different methods and terms.
- Simplify screens.
- Use photographs or art to help the viewer link raw data to the real world.

Whatever the ultimate goal of the presentation is, you can see from the two lists that there are similarities in design concept. The common guideline is to keep things simple yet heavy on the visual to improve information retention.

The sample slide in Figure 3.2 is relatively simple and should be easy for the viewer to understand, interpret, and remember.

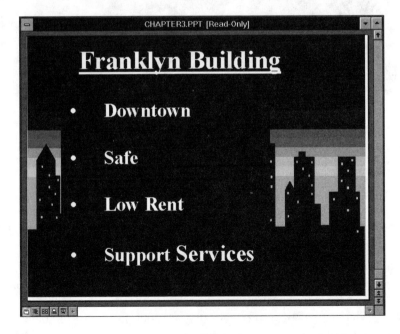

Figure 3.2 Simple Slide Easy to Interpret

The sample slide in Figure 3.3, on the other hand, is too complex. It has too much information on the screen, and would not be easy for most viewers to understand. Remember that presentation slides are designed to augment what a speaker says, not to carry all of the information.

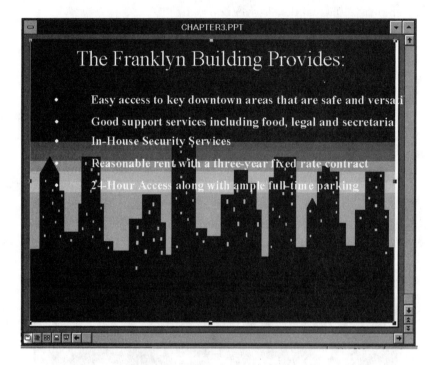

Figure 3.3 Complex Slide Difficult to Interpret

Another important concept is to design presentations for random control whenever possible. In other words, it strengthens your presentation if you can jump over certain slides or backtrack to previous ones. During a presentation, you should be aware of the level of audience understanding. If it becomes obvious that the audience is confused or (worse) bored, you should be able to back the show up or branch to an entirely different segment.

You can do this with interactive buttons on some or all presentation screens, and by having presentation screens that don't appear automatically. A presentation that is under the control of the presenter, who can select slides by clicking on objects that aren't obviously interactive, is much more flexible than one that proceeds automatically. In fact, PowerPoint is set up fairly well for this with its

Hypertext feature. While you can't make just any object a hyperlink, you can install specific icons that will serve that purpose. By designing icons that appear to be part of a background design or that fit into another part of the overall screen, you can make a link to another slide that is not obvious but that is readily available during the presentation.

Another technique you can use to help you during a presentation is to install some object on every screen—either an obvious or a secret symbol—that jumps to a screen with a full list of screens and interactive buttons. This display is used as an interim step to any slide in the presentation. That way you need to insert only a single link on each slide. The link is always to the interim slide list. The slide list contains as many links as there are slides in the presentation. Such a screen does a couple of useful things for the presenter. It lets you step back and review any screen as the result of an audience question or if you forget something. It also lets you skip slides if you realize you are running out of time or if you sense that the audience is not following some part of the presentation. The sample screen in Figure 3.4 illustrates this concept.

Figure 3.4 Concept Diagram of Presentation with Master List

With a relatively simple presentation, this type of preplanning may not be necessary. But for a lengthy or complex presentation, if you haven't designed a way to back up or jump to a specific location within the presentation, it may be difficult to respond to forced *branching* easily.

Another way to use this branching technique is to maintain two presentations, one behind the other. One presentation is a summary and can be used for audiences that need only cursory information. The other offers more detail and can be used for different audiences or to expand on an idea if the audience wants it.

In other words, by including links on the summary slide to another slide with more detail, you have the ability to compress or expand the information you present depending on audience needs. You might have a series of summary screens, and include on each one a button that could branch to a more detailed description of the topic if you felt it necessary during the presentation.

Another way to break up the information is to have a series of slides that uses common terms for the concepts you are trying to convey. These slides would be enough for non-technical or inexperienced audiences. When you have to make the presentation to a more savvy audience, on the other hand, you could expand it with more technical information and details.

The basic advice is to be creative. Look at the message you want to get across, consider the audience, and be aware of the broad range of presentation tools available in PowerPoint. Also, while there are some general rules that apply to all types of presentation design, some rules are meant to be broken. The dynamic nature of PowerPoint promotes experimentation. If you think of something that might work, try it. Then don't hesitate to listen to feedback from users and viewers of your finished product and make changes as necessary.

In the next section I'll talk a little about how to start with a basic idea and work toward a presentation design. This is an individual process and one that you're going to have to develop on your own. However, experience born of practice can help point you in the right direction.

The Design Process

Garrison Keillor, National Public Radio show host, always said he just started talking until he thought of something to say. Unfortunately, too many speeches and presentations are designed just this way. It is better to plan carefully all aspects of the show:

- What to say
- What you want the audience to learn or do as a result of what you say
- What type of room you will do the presentation in
- How you will dress

Making a presentation is a little like flying an airplane: while you are doing it there is so much going on that if any one thing goes wrong it could endanger the whole show. If, like flying, you have planned well from the beginning, then one or two mishaps along the way won't throw you off course or cause you to crash and burn.

Your approach may be different, or you may use some of these steps in a different order, but the general approach to designing a presentation should include some or all of these elements:

- Brainstorming
- Outlining
- Storyboarding
- Scripting
- Building the presentation
- Testing and debugging

We will discuss each of these processes in the next part of this chapter.

Brainstorming

Brainstorming can be a complex or a fairly simple process, depending on what you are trying to accomplish. We've all used the term at one point or another, but we usually mean something fairly simple. "Let's brainstorm and see if we can come up with a name for the dog," we might say. Then everyone sits around and throws out ideas until somebody hits on one everyone will accept. If you take brainstorming to another, more serious level, however, you can accomplish surprising things with it.

The first step to using brainstorming to help you design a presentation is to ask yourself some basic questions:

- WHO?
- WHAT?
- WHEN?
- WHERE?
- WHY?
- HOW?

These general questions can take more specific forms:

1. Who is the audience?
2. What does the audience know or believe about the subject of the presentation?
3. What does the audience expect to learn or achieve as a result of the presentation?
4. What do I want to accomplish: educating, motivating, informing? What should the audience feel, know, or do differently after the presentation?
5. When and how often will the presentation be delivered?
6. Where will the presentation be delivered, and under what conditions (what kind of room, what atmosphere, what time of day, etc.)?
7. Why am I giving this presentation?
8. How can I most effectively achieve my goals with the resources available?

Some of the answers you need will be immediately obvious. Your supervisor may tell you to prepare a show on a specific topic, perhaps, and will tell you in general what to say and what should be accomplished. Or you may be considering a presentation as the result of a request from a field office or sales force. You may decide to do it yourself as a result of a perceived need to train or inform some of your staff. In these examples, the goals are rather clear and the process fairly obvious.

Other questions may not be so obvious, such as what the audience already thinks or knows about the subject, how you will be most effective in achieving your goals, and what resources you have at your disposal. One tried and true technique to answering these questions, and others you probably haven't thought of, is brainstorming.

Brainstorming is most often associated with a group effort, and it can be effective in that context. But group brainstorming should be preceded by considerable individual effort. The brainstorming process works like this:

1. Use a notepad or word processor and write a topic word or phrase at the top of the first page. This should be the general topic if you are designing a presentation.
2. Spend the next 10 to 20 minutes thinking about the topic.

3. Write down every word or phrase that comes to mind during that time. Don't edit, judge, or qualify what you write down. Put on the paper or on the screen everything that comes to mind during the session, even if you can't see how it relates to the topic at hand.

4. When you have to force the ideas or when 20 minutes have passed, stop the session.

5. Don't try to consciously think about the topic for several hours—8 to 24 hours is a good break time.

6. Start another session by reading your previous work quickly.

7. Repeat steps 1 through 6 several times to build a long list of words and phrases. You are through with this first phase of brainstorming when it becomes difficult to come up with new topics.

This part of the brainstorming process can take from a couple of days to a few weeks, depending on the project and how much information you are trying to uncover.

You should be prepared to write down or record new ideas at any time. This is part of the brainstorming process. Relax and be creative. Don't worry about order at this point, but leave room under each item for some subtopics. Figure 3.5 shows the result of one brainstorming session about a presentation on the Internet.

Internet

Global
Growing at 1 Million/Month
Business
Difficult to use
Need software
Access difficult
What does it cost?
Training?
Hardware?
Why use it?
Who is using it?
Cost?
Is Sam on it?
Who is the bicycle guy?

Figure 3.5 Internet Brainstorming List

When you reach this stage of thinking, you should have a fairly lengthy list of words, phrases, and ideas. They may seem unrelated at this point. You may scan the list and wonder how you came up with such a wildly scattered set of topics. That's okay. You're now ready to try the next part of the process.

It is still too early to throw away anything from the list. All you want to do now is group the items, or expand the list for further brainstorming. First, use a separate screen or piece of paper for each of the words or topics you created before. If you ended up with 75 words and phrases, then you should have 75 pieces of paper with one word or phrase at the top of each one. Now go through the previous process (steps 1-7) with each piece of paper. You will end up with 75 sheets (or whatever the original number of topics was), with a collection of words and phrases on each sheet.

At this point you should begin editing the lists, making decisions about which ideas and concepts fit within the general limits of the current project and which ones are obviously beyond the scope of it.

NOTE Don't throw anything away. A particular page of ideas may help you later or may support a totally different project sometime in the future.

You are ready to begin sorting your topics and ideas. Start by reading the major headings at the top of each brainstorming sheet. If you find entire topics that seem not to fit the current project, lay them aside.

Now arrange the major topics in order of importance. Just stack the individual sheets in descending order. Highlight the important ideas under each major topic (use a highlight pen on paper or boldface type on your word processor). Finally, extract the important subtopics under each main topic into a list organized by order of importance.

The resulting material could take several forms, depending on your personality, the level at which you started, and the type of project you are working on. Whatever the form, you should have a list of topics for the current presentation. Now, consider each of these topics or groups of topics in the light of our WHO WHAT WHEN WHERE WHY HOW guidelines presented earlier in this chapter:

- Which of these is most important?
- How can you present the ideas most effectively?
- In what order should they appear?
- What resources do you have to help you present them?

At this point you may want to bring other people into the process. Make an informal presentation that shows what you have accomplished, including your goals for the presentation, and ask for creative input. Whether you are primarily responsible for the project and are just asking for help, or whether you are part of a team charged with designing the presentation, be sure to give the others involved a definite deadline for their feedback. This should be no more than a few days from when you make your initial presentation to them. In addition, make the following clear:

1. The form of feedback you wish: written report, telephone call, another meeting, sample screens.
2. The date, time, and place to submit input.
3. Project goals and the nature of their involvement.
4. Project schedule and whether you will want additional help in the future.

You should now be ready to start an outline. Don't try to outline a presentation until you have finished brainstorming, which is the creative part of the design process. An outline is only an organizational tool. It will help you put in the proper order the creative data you collected during brainstorming.

Creating an Outline

I have worked with a lot of writers and presentation designers, each a creative individual with their own approach to getting the job done. With few exceptions, the general attitude among these people about outlining is fairly negative. Far too many people view an outline as unnecessary baggage in the creative process. That's far from the truth. And the longer or more complex the project, the more important outlining becomes. Whatever preconceived notions about outlining you bring to the presentation table, try to set them aside. Outlining is a useful tool that augments the creative process.

The purposes of an outline are:

- To help organize
- To highlight important areas
- To identify minor ideas or concepts
- To discover irrelevant ideas or concepts

In addition, a well-designed outline can help others see your vision for the presentation. I find that having one or more people review an outline can help you identify weaknesses and omissions in your work before you have progressed too far to make changes easily.

While there are some classic outline forms from which to choose, you can safely design your own. Remember that the outline is an organizational tool, so the more organized the outline is, the better it can do its job. The formality of your outline style should vary directly with the number of people you expect to read it. If your outline is simply for your own reference—a way to guide you toward a storyboard design—then adhering to strict outline format is less important. If, on the other hand, you expect to distribute the outline to several other people, a more formal approach is desirable.

NOTE

PowerPoint has a useful outline view of each presentation. This outline is simply another view of the slide show. You can use the outline view to help you visualize the organization of your presentation. But the outline process I am talking about here is more formal and is designed to help you understand the overall presentation—slides and narration. This outline should be created in Word 6 or another quality word processor.

Here are some outlining guidelines you may find helpful:

1. Use a consistent numbering system that ranges from high to low level. The classic form is Roman numerals at the highest level, followed by capital alphabetic characters, then numbers followed by periods, and so on. You word processor can provide a workable numbering system.

2. Provide at least two entries at each level (no *A.* without a corresponding *B.*, no *1.* without an accompanying *2.*).

3. Use consistent style: single words and phrases (topical outline) or sentences (sentence outline) at each level.

4. Use parallel headings and subheadings so that the same type of material is placed in similar levels.

5. Use consistent wording among entries at the same level.

6. Use main headings that represent slide topics to make storyboard development easier.

7. Use headings that convey sufficient information for other readers to understand.

A fragment of an outline for the sample presentation about this book (described in Chapter 2) is shown in Figure 3.6. Obviously this is not the only format, but it is a basic design that should serve your personal needs and the needs of others in your organization who may have occasion to review it with you.

Teach Yourself...PowerPoint Outline

I.   **Introduction**
      A.   **Who is MIS: Press?**
      B.   **Teach Yourself... Concept**

II.   **Title and Features**
      A.   **What is PowerPoint?**
      B.   **Author**
      C.   **Features**

III.   **Series Concept**
      A.   **Other MIS: Press Computer Books**
      B.   **Where Teach Yourself... Fits**

IV.   **Target Level**
      A.   **Audience**
      B.   **Coverage**

V.   **General Features**
      A.   **Teach Yourself vs other books**
      B.   **Series Goals**

Figure 3.6 Sample Show Outline—Teach Yourself...

If you conduct the brainstorming and outlining steps properly, then when it comes to building the storyboard, the hard work is done. All you will really need to do is use the main outline headings as slide titles and fill in the description from the subheadings on each slide.

If you are designing an *interactive presentation,* or one that includes some direct branching (discussed earlier in this chapter), then you may want to build a *flow chart* between the outline and the storyboard. A flow chart shows graphically any branches or decision points that occur in the show. In an interactive application, the user/viewer can change the direction of the presentation at certain points as the result of prompts or other stimuli. A simple flow chart is shown in Figure 3.7.

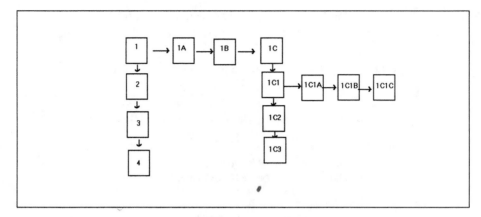

Figure 3.7 Sample Presentation Flow Chart

When the outline is finished you are ready to draw a simple storyboard. We will show you one way to do that in the next section.

Using a Storyboard

Think of a *storyboard* as a graphical representation of the outline. A storyboard can be a simple hand drawing on a yellow pad, or a complex, well-drawn creation. Whether you draw a storyboard by hand or use a computer-based drawing tool, the storyboard is an important part of the creative process. Particularly as presentations get more complex, you'll ultimately save time by drawing a storyboard before you start actually constructing the presentation in PowerPoint.

I'll submit to one exception to this storyboard rule. In PowerPoint, the Slide Sorter view can help you visualize your presentation. You can use it to build a storyboard while you construct the presentation. In this case you are using PowerPoint to construct a storyboard that is really part of the presentation itself.

For all but the simplest shows, however, the best approach is to rough out the story line on paper. The idea is to use the outline as a basis for drawing a simple representation of each slide you will have in the program.

Think of a PowerPoint presentation as a series of slides, modules, or events—some of them placed sequentially (end to end), and some of them lying parallel. One of these lines contains the images (slides) you will use during the presentation. Associated with each slide is another unit that represents music, sound, or narration. In addition, you can specify a special effect (fade, wipe, dissolve, etc.) as the *transition* between slides.

The sample storyboard fragment in Figure 3.8 shows this concept. Any art such as drawings or photographs is shown, plus placement of text, windows, and other special effects. You can note on the drawing what sound, if any, will be associated with each slide.

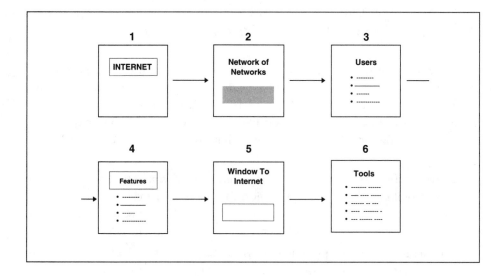

Figure 3.8 Presentation Storyboard Fragment

The first storyboard after the outline can serve as a doodling session—part of the initial planning. This is a chance for you to put in a primitive visual form the outline you have developed during brainstorming. As with other steps in the design process, you may have to go through this procedure several times to refine the design, locate problems, add new ideas, and get input from other members of the design team or other experts in your organization.

If all of this seems overly complicated, don't let it be. You won't spend very long on any of these steps for a simple presentation, and for a longer presentation, focusing on an organized procedure can make the whole process relatively easy. Besides, storyboarding in particular, can be fun. It is not difficult or complicated, and it can make designing the final presentation a lot easier.

Working with a storyboard can accomplish a number of important things:

- Establish the order of the slides
- Determine the number of slides

- Create the general design of each slide
- Identify special effects (sound, video, wipes, etc.)
- Determine what resources are needed to produce the slides
- Give other team members a vehicle for reviewing the presentation and making changes
- Provide an archival copy of the information

As you work with sound, artwork, and other resources, you may want to brainstorm again. Try writing artwork and sound ideas next to each topic or on the storyboard. Don't worry if your ideas seem strange when you think of them—write them down! Later, what seemed like a bad idea may be the unique angle you were looking for, or it may make you think of an even better way of doing something.

As you refine the storyboard, add additional information. This makes the process of building the actual application in PowerPoint even easier. You may wish to include notes on the file names for any graphics or scanned images, or to jot down a list of resources and their locations beside each slide drawing.

For a relatively simple presentation, your storyboard will likely include every slide. The storyboard for a complicated presentation, however, may show only the first slide or two in a multi-slide series so that you can track modules of information.

What you learn while working with the storyboard can feed back to the outline, causing you to change the basic design of the presentation. The visual process is a good polishing step that helps you to see how a show shapes up.

Remember that you are trying to tell a story, make a point, sell an idea, or change an opinion. How you do this depends on the audience, the material being presented, and your own personality. There are, however, a few recognized ways of telling a story. For example, you can begin at the beginning with little detail, then build until you have provided the audience with a lot of information:

> **The computer may seem like a new idea, but the conceptual design for machines we use today is over 100 years old...**

On the other hand, you can start with some piece of important information well into the story, then bring the audience up to date a little at a time:

Today's desktop PC can process information at more than 112 million instructions per second, speed and power that...

Consider these ways of organizing information for a story:

Deductive Organization: Moves from the general to the specific.

Inductive Organization: Moves from the specific to the general.

Chronological Organization: Begins at the beginning and describes a sequence of events in the order in which they occurred.

Process Organization: Presents the steps involved in a process or procedure where each step must occur in a given order.

Agenda Organization: Presents information in a random order, frequently without logic. However, a successful agenda organization must tell the audience what the order is.

You can design other ways to organize a presentation that are combinations of these methods. In fact, it is rare to see a clean organization that strictly follows one of these presentation designs. It is more important to know the audience, to understand what end result is desired, and to select a combination of tools and organization to achieve this goal.

You should accept the fact that your carefully planned design will change when you begin production. While the outline and storyboard are excellent organizational tools, they shouldn't become overpowering or cause limitations in your thinking as you work on the script and prepare the slides for the presentation.

Writing the Script

Like a movie script, the presentation *script* provides a textual representation of all of the elements of the final show. Whereas the storyboard is a visual representation of all or part of the show elements, everything that will be part of the presentation should appear on a script, including:

- Slide descriptions
- Text and how it will be presented
- Slide number
- Duration of each module

- Narration (if any)
- Sound effects
- Music
- Graphics elements
- Video
- A portion of a PowerPoint presentation script is shown in Figure 3.9.

Introduction to Internet
Working/Design Script – Preliminary
Version 1.2

AUDIO	VIDEO
FADE UP: MUSIC File: Intro.WAV	**SLOW FADE UP FROM BLACK** Slide #1: Introduction
NARRATOR: The global Internet is one of the newest business and personal fads to hit the country. Whether or not you know what Internet is, it is only a matter of time before it directly affects your life.	
MUSIC OUT	Slide #2: Network of Networks
NARRATOR: One problem with understanding the Internet is the physical design. Internet is more than a network of computers – it is a network of networks . . .	

—

Figure 3.9 PowerPoint Script Fragment

Like storyboarding, scripting is a personal activity. You can design your own script format and style, but you should keep these ideas in mind:

- Who will use the script?
- Are several people working on the production?
- How complex is the production?
- How will the presentation be produced?

The answers to questions such as these will help you determine how serious you need to be about designing a complete and consistent script style. Here are some guidelines or suggestions to help you develop your own style:

1. Split the page, placing audio information on the left side of the page and visual information on the right.
2. Number the scenes or slides in each module.
3. Include file names or other information where possible.
4. Write instructions in all upper case, and narration in upper and lower case.

Remember that, while you want to include a lot of detail in a working script, you also want to strive for clarity and an uncluttered appearance. This helps those who may be unfamiliar with the show to help you during production or during the proofing and testing process. Just as you want to achieve an open, uncluttered feel to each of the slides you design, the script used to produce the presentation should also feel open and accessible.

When the script and storyboard are completed and you are satisfied with the order of the slides, the content, and the mood of the presentation, you are ready to begin building the show.

Designing the Screens

Once you have completed a detailed outline, a storyboard, and a script, you already have accomplished much of the work in building a presentation. From this point, here are the general steps to completing the presentation design:

1. Construct individual slides or screens by creating titles and adding text or graphic elements.
2. Set the duration or control (how will the slide change).
3. Add sound, music, or narration as required.

After the elements of the presentation are in place, test it to make sure that everything functions as you intend and that the program produces the desired effect.

In some ways, a slide or a computer screen is like a printed page. Taken together, all of the elements in either medium create a *layout*. A layout is the arrangement of the elements that make up the page or screen. Some of the possible elements of a PowerPoint screen are:

- Text
- Graphics
- Photographs
- Boxes and other static objects
- Motion Video
- Color Space

No single element of a layout is intended to stand on its own. Every slide element should relate in some way to every other element and, in some cases, with one or more elements on previous or following slides.

If you change the *typeface* or *typestyle* used for a heading, for example, it may change how much information will fit on the page and it may require a change in the type used for the rest of the screen (see the section on fonts later in this chapter for more information on using typefaces). If you open up a screen with more colored space, you may not be able to fit all of the elements you had on the screen before. And, if you change the font or background on one slide, you should consider making the same changes to other slides in the presentation for consistency.

Here are general guidelines to remember as you work on slide design:

- Each slide should address a single concept or idea.
- Slides should follow a logical progression, each building on the other.
- In general, a simple design is best.
- The viewer must be able to digest each slide quickly and easily.
- Use no more than six lines of text on any one slide.
- Use upper and lower case text, NOT all caps.
- Choose a color appropriate to the mood you want to convey.
- Avoid using too many colors (five colors per slide maximum).
- Use photographs and video wherever possible.

In addition, be aware of how most of us view a page, a screen, or a photograph. The scanning pattern usually is a reverse "S" that starts at the upper left corner, moves to the middle toward the right side, zooms to the left about three-fourths of the way down, and exits on the lower right. Obviously, items you want to emphasize should be placed at points on the "S" that reinforce the natural scanning pattern.

Also, consider using motion to focus the viewer's eye on the desired area of the slide. In PowerPoint you can insert short video clips, for example. You could also insert a brief sound element to encourage the audience to focus on a particular slide. I'll show you later in this book how to use such features of PowerPoint to enhance a presentation.

As you design each screen, remember this general rule. Visual material augments a presentation. It adds information to what the speaker is saying or helps the audience to retain or interpret what the speaker is saying. Don't use motion video, animation, or any other technique simply because you can; use it because it is the proper thing to do in a given situation.

One way to think about this is to ask what questions a visual may answer. If it provides information about *where* something is, *how* something works, *how much* is involved (cost, quantity, etc.), *who* is involved or affected, *when* you do something or use something, or *why* this information is important, then that visual is doing its job.

A number of attention-getting concepts can help you enhance a PowerPoint presentation. I've summarized some of them in Table 3.1.

Table 3.1 Relative Impact of Presentation Screen Elements

High Interest	Low Interest
Photos	Words
Color	Black & White
White (Blank) space	Solid copy
Bold type	Italic type
ALL CAPS	Lower case
Large type	Small type
Wide lines	Thin lines
Large area	Small area
3D	2D

Use the guidelines in Table 3.1 along with the other guidelines you learn in this chapter. For example, the table shows that ALL CAPS get more attention than upper and lower case (initial caps) text. However, you don't want a chart with all text in upper case because it is too difficult to read. We are used to reading text in upper and lower case. Use all caps for headings, titles, and other text you want to emphasize, then revert to normal initial caps for the rest of the text.

In the following sections, I'll give you additional suggestions for using specific slide elements as part of your presentation design.

Using Text Charts

I've spent a fair amount of time in this chapter talking about the many color and graphics tools you can use to enhance PowerPoint presentations. However, you shouldn't ignore the importance of text. At least half of business-oriented presentation material is still text-based. With PowerPoint you can use motion and music to augment what is on the screen, but it is still true that you will likely be using a lot of *text charts* as part of your PowerPoint shows.

A text chart is used for tables of organization, flow charts, timetables, sales presentations, and summaries. The name notwithstanding, text charts may incorporate a variety of graphic elements—scanned images, graphs, and clip art—as well as grids, boxes, lines, and shading, along with basic text.

At its simplest level, a text chart may be nothing more than a bulleted list. After all, one of the reasons for designing a PowerPoint presentation in the first place is to convey some type of information. The advantage of PowerPoint is that you can organize and present this text information in creative ways to catch and keep the viewer's attention and to improve retention of the data. Language, properly applied, is still a good way to present information.

Here are some of the ways a text chart helps you to convey information in a PowerPoint Presentation:

* Presents information that includes too many data types or too much information to present logically in a graph.
* Shows exact values instead of graphic approximations.
* Shows information that covers a very broad range between the highest and lowest numbers.
* Shows data when the exact amount is critical.

The guidelines for designing a text chart slide are generally the same as for any other slide:

- Choose typefaces and type sizes carefully.
- Place relatively small amounts of data on each slide.
- Keep information on each slide closely related.
- Highlight the benefits or results of your ideas.
- Be as specific as possible; avoid generalities.
- Keep each sentence or phrase as short as possible.
- Keep slides in a series consistent by using the same combination of fonts, and by using similar size and layout ratios from slide to slide.
- Use both upper and lower case characters, not all upper case (Except for titles or other emphasis).
- Drop extra or unnecessary words, even if incomplete sentences result.
- Generally, you should avoid the use of hyphens; they can break up the flow of data.

Designing with Text (Fonts)

I've talked about general concepts of using text in your presentations. Now let's look at text elements in more detail. The characters you put on the screen are an important part of your message. Not only does the typeface you select help convey information, it also imparts a mood or style that is an integral part of the message.

What is a typeface? It is a distinctive shape and design of type that makes a collection of letters recognizable. Typefaces are generally identified by name, such as Times Roman, Helvetica, Palatino, and Century Schoolbook. In addition to the design of characters, you can also control the size of text in PowerPoint.

The size of the type you use is measured in *points*. One point is equal to 1/72nd of an inch, so 72-point type is about one inch tall. In most typefaces, 12-point type is standard for printed pages and is also a readable on-screen size. A 30- or 50-point size is appropriate for titles and headings or for a bulleted list when the viewer will be a longer-than-normal distance from the screen.

Most typefaces can be presented in different styles and stroke weights. Examples are bold, italic, bold italic, or shadow. A font is a collection of all of the characters available for a particular typeface and style. Times Roman Italic, for example, is a font, as is Palatino Bold or Helvetica Bold Italic.

As you choose type for a presentation slide, also be aware of *serif* and *sans serif* designs. Serif type includes finishing strokes at the end of main strokes. Most typefaces use serifs, and serif type is usually easier to read than typefaces without serifs (sans serif type). Times is a serif type: **Times**

Helvetica is a popular sans serif type: **Helvetica**

Notice the difference between a font and a typeface. A typeface is a named shape or design of character, whereas a font is a collection of all of the available characters in a particular typeface in a specific style.

PowerPoint supports a wide range of text styles, sizes, and colors. However, you should work with a limited number of fonts and styles within any given presentation. It is best to stick with the same type style for the same positions across all slides. For example, if you have a series of slides that includes a title or header line on each slide, all of the title text should use the same font and (usually) the same font size. Likewise, captions for the images on these slides should all use the same size and font; running text or bulleted lists should be the same, and so on.

Two or three fonts on the same slide should be the maximum. You might use one basic type style for body copy—the text used in the middle of the screen for description or for lists—and one or two accent faces for captions or emphasis. Accent faces can be an italic, bold, extended, or condensed version of the basic body type, or they can be a related new font. Related type means type of the same general style. You don't want body copy of clean, modern Helvetica, for example, mixed with large titles drawn in florid Old English.

As a general rule, sans serif fonts are a better choice for presentations than serif fonts. Serifs tend to disappear or blur, particularly if you are projecting the image.

Size of type is important in any page, screen, or slide design. Presentation professionals have some guidelines about type size, but the most general rule is, Can the audience read it? You can find this out by testing the presentation with co-workers or friends in an environment similar to where the presentation will be given.

A good rule of thumb is that the maximum viewing distance from a presentation screen is six times the screen diameter. So, if you are projecting images onto a 30- x 40-inch screen, you should plan the presentation so that no one in the audience must sit further than 20 feet away (40 in. x 6 = 240 in./12 = 20 feet). If you are making the presentation on a standard 14-inch PC screen, on the other hand, no one in the audience should sit further than about 7 feet away (14 in. x 6 = 84 in./12 = 7 feet).

Test these guidelines by simply pushing your chair away from your PC. By the time you get six or seven feet away from the screen, reading anything other than fairly large type becomes difficult. And, you can make the reading process easier through the use of color, accent shapes, and so on.

Designing with Color

Color is an extremely important part of screen design, perhaps even the most important one. Compared to a black and white image, such as an overhead projector slide prepared with a standard black type printer, color images:

- Accelerate learning, retention, and recall by nearly 80 percent.
- Improve comprehension by more than 70 percent.
- Increase willingness to read by up to 80 percent.
- Improve selling efficiency by as much as 85 percent.

While color is important in your PowerPoint presentations, it is also important not to place too many colors on a single slide or screen. In general, five colors should be the maximum. Most of your screens probably will use even fewer colors than that, unless you are including a full-color photograph or drawn image.

Another way to look at color is to determine what the overall message of the screen or presentation is, then to choose a color appropriate to that message. For example, one study by the Wagner Institute for Color Research in Santa Barbara, CA, showed how people react to different colors in interior design.

The study showed that blue is a favorite color that elicits positive responses, while red triggers an emotional response. Green is a comfortable color and yellow gets attention more quickly than any other color. Gray says "exclusive" or "quality," while white projects a message of sophistication or refinement. Black, on the other hand, is not appealing to most viewers.

Some of the same general guidelines hold true for presentation material. Studies have shown that different colors cause different responses. Red, for example, is an emotional color that can actually make a person's heart beat faster. Red denotes excitement and may mean stop or danger, depending on the viewer and the context. It also takes longer for the eye to process red than any other color.

Dark blue, on the other hand, projects a stable, trustworthy, and mature message. It can encourage fantasy, but it also has a calming effect, so don't use blue if you want the audience excited or upbeat.

Light blue is considered youthful, masculine, and cool, while the message of green is growth, positive, organic, or go. Green can help people feel comfortable in unfamiliar places. Choose green carefully, however, because many of us carry a prejudice against institutional green—the green of classrooms and chalk boards.

White is a pure color that denotes the sensation of cleanliness, honesty, sophistication, refinement, or delicate things. Used properly with other colors, white can be useful in attracting an upscale audience.

Use black for serious topics or to project the concept of heaviness or death. You should use black carefully, but it can be useful, particularly for some backgrounds.

Gray is a color of integrity. It says exclusive, neutral, cool, mature. Creative people usually feel comfortable being around gray.

Brown is considered a wholesome color that is associated with organic themes and is unpretentious. Yellow, on the other hand, is emotional and positive. It can also denote the concept of caution. Yellow is interpreted by the eye faster than any other color. It can be a good choice for drawing attention to a slide or screen area, but it can also incite anger or irritation.

Another emotional color is orange. It evokes positive or organic feelings. Orange is also considered a neutral color that can help the viewer adapt to other colors. Orange and blue in combination denote strength. Gold is a conservative color, and is stable and elegant.

Both purple and pink are youthful colors. Purple is also considered contemporary in mood and pink is often associated with feminine or warm topics. In fact, all pastel colors are youthful and can be feminine. They also denote the concept of swiftness and sensitivity. Finally, any metallic color produces an image of elegance, wealth, and long lastingness.

Here's a more general way to look at color. Different colors usually are associated with specific feelings or moods. Cyan and blue are cool colors, while yellow and red are warm colors. Magenta and green, on the other hand, are transitional colors that can take on qualities of either warm or cool, though magenta is basically a warm color while green is a cool one.

As you design slides, you should generally use dark colors for backgrounds and lighter colors for text and illustrations, because the eye is naturally drawn to the lighter areas in the foreground. This is the same concept used by photographers and painters to focus attention within a scene. Notice especially people pictures printed by professional photographers. The faces—already lighter than the surrounding features—sometimes are made extra light to force attention on them. The same concept holds true when designing presentation slides. A dark background with light foreground helps keep the viewer focused on what is most important.

The Tektronix company is a leader in color printer technology. It advises that, from a viewer perspective, the most popular colors for backgrounds, in order, are:

1. Dark blue
2. Black
3. Gray
4. Brown
5. Red
6. Green
7. Purple

Also, if you design a chart that arranges items by color, or that uses color to code or flag certain concepts, you should consider arranging the items by color in the order in which the colors appear in the natural spectrum:

1. Red
2. Orange
3. Yellow
4. Green
5. Blue
6. Indigo
7. Violet

Your presentations should consist of logical groupings of color. You should use the same range of colors within a logical section of your presentation, and you should use colors that are close together on the color chart. If you switch color schemes too often or too suddenly it is jarring to the audience.

Using Photographs

I said earlier that you can use photographs to help the viewer relate the information on the slide to the real world. Look at the examples in Figures 3.10 and 3.11. The first illustration shows a bulleted list against a plain background. The second sample shows the same list against a photograph.

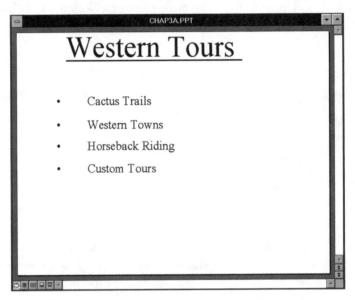

Figure 3.10 Bulleted List with Plain Background

The text information is presented in the same way in both cases, but the photographic background—even if only a hint of an item is shown—helps the viewer relate the textual information to something real. Also, a photograph can improve data retention.

A list that deals with automobiles could be placed over a picture of a car, for example. General sales information could be presented over a picture that suggests selling: a store interior, a shopping mall, or a cash register. If you don't have or can't get a photograph, use a graphic image as the next best choice. You can use something you have drawn from scratch or a clip art image.

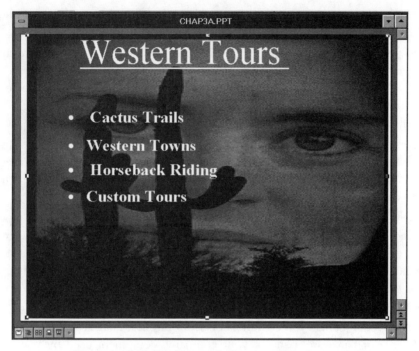

Figure 3.11 Bulleted List with Photograph Background
(photo by Tom DeMoss, Words and Pictures, Tucson, Arizona)

Where do you get photographs and other images for your presentations? There are many places to look, including:

- Company brochures, letter heads, business cards, or catalogs
- Annual reports, user manuals, sales aids, engineering reports
- Art used by other members of your organization in previous presentations
- Product samples, intra-company reports, letters
- Clip art, software samples
- Custom drawn art using a graphics package
- Video tape still frames

You can scan many of these images into the computer in a format that PowerPoint can use directly. Most scanners produce black and white images.

This works for presentations if you can either use colored text, place the photograph inside a color border, or colorize the image with a transparent overlay.

If you want a color image, or if you don't have access to a scanner, check your local telephone book. There are companies that offer scanning services. They will take your image, scan it, and return a computer .TIF, .PCX, or other file format compatible with PowerPoint.

There is a wide variety of sources for images to use with PowerPoint. Just be careful how you use images from outside sources. You can't legally scan an image from a magazine or a book, for example, and then use it for your presentation (without permission from the publisher, that is), though it might be tempting to do so.

One good source of still color images for your presentations is video tape or a video camera fed directly into a video capture board. Most video hardware includes some form of software driver to let you capture a still frame image. All you need to do is set up your camera on a tripod, light it to show what you want, and take a few seconds of tape. Then hook up your VCR player to the video capture board, take a snap shot, and you are ready to go.

This technique lets you capture shots from physical images such as computer keyboards or hardware, parts of your company, equipment used by your company, or scenes of your town or area. Once the image is captured and stored in a graphics file format, you can use it as a background or as a picture inside a window just as you would any other graphics image from your computer.

New technology from Eastman Kodak also makes it easy to insert high quality color photographs into your presentations. The Photo CD technology lets you take slides or negatives to your local drug store (or professional photo finisher) and send them away for translation to Photo CD format. Kodak and other companies supply software to convert these digitized photographs to .PCX, .TIF, and other graphics formats that you can use with PowerPoint.

Using Graphics

PowerPoint presentations are built around the concept of using graphics—either colored graphs that represent numerical data or clip art. As I have said, you can use photographs and other elements, but clip art or one of the PowerPoint internal graphs is an easy way to enhance a presentation.

PowerPoint is supplied with about 1,000 clip art images from a variety of categories. These images are designed to suggest a concept or idea, to add color and shape to your slides, and to provide the audience with images that help with data retention. In addition to the 1,000 or so clip art images, PowerPoint includes pre-formatted slides that reserve space for clip art. All you have to do is click on the clip art icon, and PowerPoint opens up the ClipArt Gallery display so you can choose the image you want that use. These are professionally designed slides that help you build quality presentations easily.

Do you want to present complex numerical data in a form the audience can easily interpret? The built-in PowerPoint graphing feature is there to help out. Use a graph any time you want the audience to understand concepts and trends instead of precise numbers. In fact, you might use a text chart of the real numbers coupled with a graph to provide the full picture.

Using Video

Motion video is still not the most common feature in presentations, mainly because the hardware and software to support it is still relatively expensive and rare. However, PowerPoint supports video and can help you enhance your presentations with interesting video clips.

Motion video is usually displayed in a small window that takes up only a part of your whole screen. One reason for using a small window within a screen display is storage limitations. Standard full-motion video presents information at a rate of 30 frames (screens) per second. Since each of these screens is a graphics image, storage requirements for this amount of information at full speed on a full screen can be staggering.

To get around this limitation, some full-motion video limits the size of the display screen and the resolution of the display. For many types of video, these limitations are not serious. After all, being able to see real-time, full-motion video as part of a presentation is probably worth a slight reduction in image quality.

Keep in mind that we remember things in picture form, not in words (and motion pictures are more lifelike than still pictures, which are more lifelike than drawings). Therefore, anytime you can use video as part of a presentation, you have increased the likelihood that the audience will remember the message you are trying to get across.

Remember, too, that the video component of a given slide doesn't have to carry the majority of the information. Just as you can use a background with a still photograph, you can place motion video so that it enhances other information. This can help the viewer focus on a topic or help the audience relate the data you are presenting to something in the real, physical world. (Use this technique carefully, however, as we all like movies and you don't want to pull the audience entirely away from what you are saying or what else you may be presenting on the screen.)

On the other hand, you can open a motion video window and let the person or the action in the sequence tell the whole story while the live presenter simply waits until the end. Such sequences should be short for a couple of reasons. Full-motion video requires a lot of storage space, so if you do very much of it during a presentation you may find yourself needing a larger hard disk than most budgets allow. And, any motion video sequence is there to augment or enhance the presentation, not to *be* the presentation. Use it for variety and to enhance interest, not to show a movie.

Testing the Presentation

Presentation testing is a fairly continuous process. As each module is completed, you probably will step through the slides and see how things fit. As you put modules together into a larger unit, you'll test them, and so on. If this is a one-time presentation to a small group, then you can probably view the show yourself and decide whether it achieves its goal. If the presentation will be used several times and you're looking for specific results, then the testing process needs to be somewhat more involved.

You may work alone during the initial design and production stages, but as you start building the final presentation you should get as many people as possible involved. If the show is for internal viewing, as with training or educational material, then you can use co-workers to view the presentation and offer critiques. You should schedule two or more showings to different audiences at different times and evaluate their feedback carefully.

Test audiences should feel free to tell you honestly how they react to your work, and you should be prepared to separate their comments and criticisms from personalities. Try to elicit honest opinions and use them in conjunction with your production expertise and what you know about the goals of the production to draw your own conclusions about the quality and value of the product.

One way to help test viewers open up is to prepare a questionnaire for them to fill out after they have seen the show. However, you have to be careful how you construct the questions in such a survey, and make sure they are not weighted in any direction. Another technique that may help a critical audience relax during a session is to make the presentation during a lunch break or over special refreshments during an afternoon break.

After you have received feedback, make whatever changes in the production you think should be made based on the comments received. Then schedule at least one more showing to see if the problems were corrected. Again, through personal contact, memos, or a pre-show presentation, make it plain that you appreciate everyone's involvement and that you have made changes in the show based on their previous comments. However, you should also make it clear that the previous comments were taken under advisement and the resulting changes were made on the basis of a variety of inputs, including that from other professionals.

Of course the final testing is done in the field, before a live audience. Always be aware of audience reaction during a presentation. If this show or another similar one will be used repeatedly, you may want to devise a questionnaire for each audience. Such regular evaluations, over time, can help you polish and refine a program, removing any unclear or unnecessary components.

To Sum Up

There's a lot of material in this chapter, from brainstorming about the overall design of a presentation to specifics on creating individual slides. You won't use all of these techniques in every presentation, of course, but the concepts in this chapter can help you to create professional and effective shows.

The important thing to remember about your presentation designs is that you have a message to impart to an audience, and the whole purpose of your PowerPoint presentation design is to help convey that message. Use the concepts in this chapter to help you do that. Hopefully some of this information will get you thinking in the right direction as you set out on your own to use the tools provided by PowerPoint to design a presentation.

In the next chapter I'll give you more detail on using PowerPoint Wizards, clip art, and templates.

if the life is bitch
; the bitch herself is
good doctor, so
the life is good
    Thanks

Using PowerPoint Templates, Clip Art, and Wizards

117

Computer software has changed in dramatic ways during the past few years. When I first started working with personal computers there was no software at all, just BASIC and Assembler that you used to develop your own applications. Those of us who came out of the minicomputer world longed for a real language—*COBOL* or *FORTRAN*—but that was years away.

Eventually, we started getting basic applications such as spreadsheets and databases. Even these were minimal programs that required a lot of configuring and programming by the end user. Some of us made a fair amount of money in those early days by taking what were marketed as finished applications and modifying them so that they did what the customer wanted, or, in some cases, so that they did anything at all. A lot of that early software didn't even work, believe it or not.

Today, we get quickly released software with a few bugs or shortcomings, but which works. This software includes useful tools to help beginners get a lot out of the program in a hurry. Microsoft's PowerPoint is one good example of this trend. Embedded within the program are a number of utilities, tools, and templates that make developing presentations easy. Not only that, the built-in features help beginners learn something about design so that they can avoid mistakes in the finished presentations.

This chapter explains how to use the built-in templates and utilities to produce your own slides and presentations.

Available Templates

A PowerPoint template is a pre-designed presentation in which the appearance of the masters (Slide Master, Outline Master, Handout Master, Note Master) and slide colors have been designed to achieve a particular look. You can start a new presentation with a particular template, or you can apply a template to an existing presentation. When you apply a template, the slide backgrounds, the appearance of the master screens, and so on, take on the look of the template.

NOTE To use a template with a new presentation, use File **New Template** and select a template from the list in the File Name window of the Presentation Template dialog. To apply a template to an existing presentation, use Format **Presentation Template...** and choose a template from the Presentation Template dialog.

In addition, any existing presentation can be saved as a template that can be used as the basis for the design of future presentations. If you are familiar with Microsoft Word 6, then you know how Microsoft uses templates to pre-design certain aspects of a word processor document. Presentation templates work in a similar way.

PowerPoint templates are grouped into three areas: black and white overheads (**bwovrhd** subdirectory), color overheads (**clrovrhd** subdirectory), and slide shows (**sldshow** subdirectory). You will find different templates and designs within each of these areas on the Presentation Templates dialog. All template files end in the **.PPT** file suffix or extension.

Although the total number of templates numbers over 150, there are actually only around 55 separate designs. These designs have slight variations in each of the major areas (black and white overheads, color overheads, and slide shows). If you study the file names you'll see that the same files appear in each of these subdirectories, but with slightly different names.

The basic black and white overhead with a shaded and boxed left border, for example, is in the **bwovrhd** subdirectory and is named **AZUREB.PPT** (see Figure 4.1). The companion template for color overhead projection is located in the **clrovrhd** subdirectory and is in the file **AZUREC.PPT**. This is essentially the same template shown in Figure 4.1, but it has a color background. The slide show file is in the **sldshow** subdirectory in the file **AZURES.PPT**. It, too, is very similar to the template in Figure 4.1, but it has a more complex color scheme than the template designed for overhead projection. The slide show template includes varying shades of color and more intense colors to take advantage of the extended resolution of the color screen and, if you wish, 35mm slides for projection.

Although it is a little difficult to see the differences among the templates in a black and white image, you can see in Figures 4.2, 4.3, and 4.4 how PowerPoint modifies a template for the different applications. Also, the precise colors you see on your screen will depend on the type of video display adapter and monitor you are using.

Figure 4.2 shows the **BLUDIAGB.PPT** template, which is designed for black and white overheads. Figure 4.3 shows the **BLUDIAGC.PPT** template, designed for color overheads, and Figure 4.4 shows the **BLUDIAGS.PPT** template, designed for slide shows. Notice that all of these templates have a similar design; it is the color scheme and the intensity of the color that differentiate one from the other.

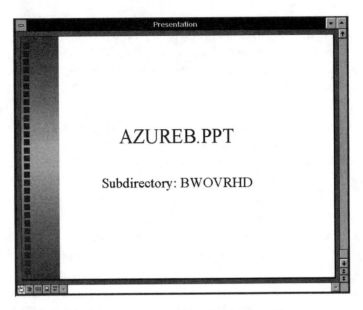

Figure 4.1 AZUREB.PPT Template Sample

Figure 4.2 BLUDIAGB.PPT Template

Figure 4.3 BLUDIAGC.PPT Template

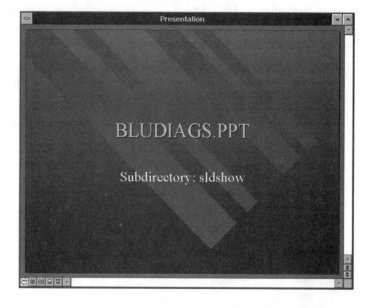

Figure 4.4 BLUDIAGS.PPT Template

In general, black and white templates use shades of gray with a light background, and the overhead versions use color with a white or light background. Slide show templates generally have darker colors and use graduated backgrounds that are black or dark.

In the next section I'll provide a quick reference to most of the templates supplied with PowerPoint. I'll give you the name of the template with a lower case **x** in the last position. This variable could be a **b**, a **c**, or an **s**, depending on the type of template you are using. Accompanying the template name is a screen shot of the black and white overhead template to show you how the template is designed. I've used the black and white template because it reproduces better in this book. You can create a new presentation (File **New**) or open an existing presentation (File **Open**) and then use Format **Presentation Template...** to display the Template Dialog. Select one of the templates on this dialog to view it on the screen. Remember that for a lightly-colored template, choose one from the **clrovrhd** subdirectory. For a deeply colored template, choose one from the **sldshow** subdirectory.

AZUREx

This template is designed to look like a printed award or certificate. It has a three-dimensional border with *drop shadow*. The color versions have a blue background and light buff center for added accent.

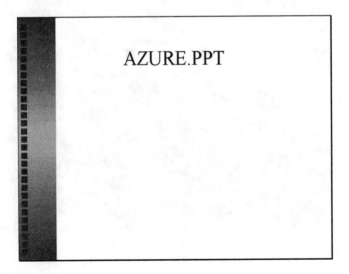

Figure 4.5 AZURE Template

BANNERx

The Banner template is similar to the Award template, but it does not include a 3-D border. The top of the slide is separated from the body of the slide by a shadow border. The color versions have a two-tone scheme with buff over dark green.

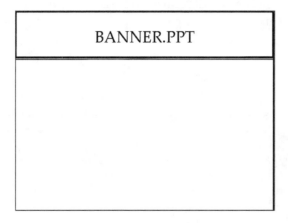

Figure 4.6 Banner Template

BEVELx

This template is basically the Award template with the addition of 3-D graphics on the four sides. Color versions add a light green background with shadows.

Figure 4.7 Bevel Template

BLACKx

This is a simple template with a graduated black strip down the left side of the screen. Use this template when you want to present a modern or clean-cut image. The color overhead slide has a gray vertical strip down the left side. The slide show version is designed in silver and black in graduated shades with yellow letters. All of these templates produce a modern, striking mood.

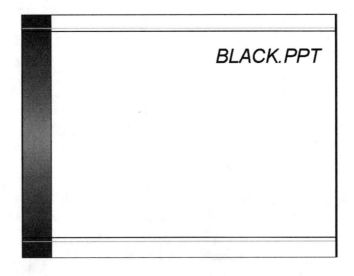

Figure 4.8 Black Template

BLSTRIPx

The Black Stripe template has a background of horizontal alternating dark and light stripes. The black and white version has gray and white stripes, and the color versions have alternating dark blue and black stripes.

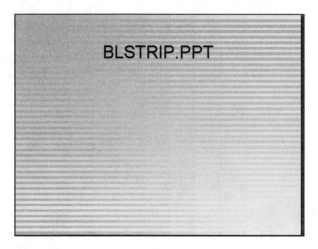

Figure 4.9 Black Stripe Template

BLUDIAGx

The Blue Diagonal template isn't blue at all in the black and white version, of course, but the color versions do present a pattern of dark blue diagonal lines on a lighter blue background. In black and white the pattern is a pleasant gray and white.

Figure 4.10 Blue Diagonal Template

BLUEBOXx

The black and white version of this template puts three gray boxes around the slide window. In the color version you get light and dark blue borders around the slide window and bright red shadowed lettering. This template offers a crisp, clean design that is particularly good for lists.

Figure 4.11 Blue Box Template

BLUEGRNx

This template places a wide line/thin line pattern behind the main slide window. In color versions these lines are light and dark green.

BRKNBARx

This template uses a wide bar followed by variable-width smaller bars to separate the title area of the slide from the body of the slide. The color versions use dark and light blue bars.

Figure 4.12 Blue Green Template

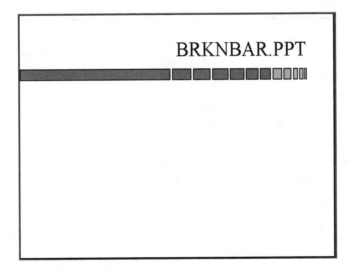

Figure 4.13 Broken Bar Template

BUBBLEx

For a light, party look to your slides, try the Bubble template. This could be a good choice for posters or announcements or any time you want to evoke a less-then-serious mood.

Figure 4.14 Bubble Template

CHECKSx

As the name implies, this template places a series of small squares or checks in a vertical bar at the left of the slide. The color overhead version of this template uses a very light, graduated green and white color scheme for a pastel look. The slide show version combines a graduated green with deep black accents and orange lettering for a modern, attractive scheme.

CHEERSx

This template uses a party motif with streamers scattered around the border of the slide screen. In color, this slide has a light and dark pink design with bright yellow text.

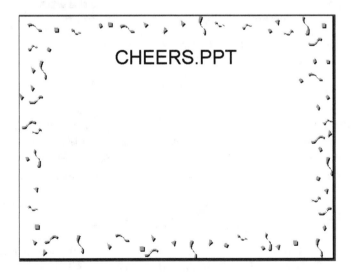

Figure 4.15 Checks Template

Figure 4.16 Cheers Template

COLORBXx

The Color Box template is a clean design with a small right angle of shaded boxes in the lower right-hand corner of the slide. In color templates, the boxes are various colors with a white background in the overhead version and a black background in the slide show version.

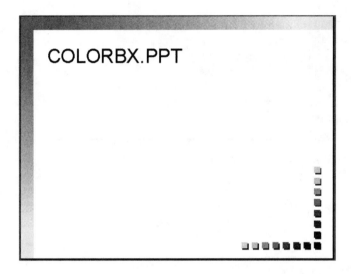

Figure 4.17 Color Box Template

CONFETIx

As the name implies, the Confetti template is based on a scattering of shaded color chips, which are placed around two edges of the slide screen. In color you get multi-colored chips on a clean, white background (overhead slide version) or multi-colored chips on a crisp, black background (slide show version).

DBLLINEx

The Double Line template is similar to the Banner template (see Figure 4.6), except that the separating line is graduated. In color, this line is purple, green, and black with either a white background (overhead) or a black and violet background (slide show).

Figure 4.18 Confetti Template

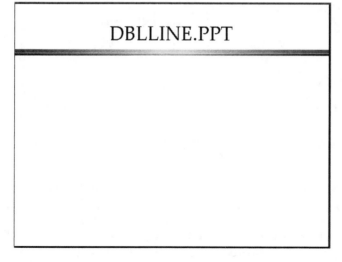

Figure 4.19 Double Line Template

DIAMONDx

The Diamond template is simple and clean. It has a single three-dimensional diamond shape in the upper left corner of the screen. The lettering overlays the diamond. The slide show version of this template is particularly interesting, with a graduated black to pastel green background, a blue diamond, and yellow text.

Figure 4.20 Diamond Template

DROPSTRx

This template evokes a diplomatic mood, with a shaded vertical ribbon terminated in a three-dimensional star. In color, the template uses a multi-hued green strip with a white background on the overhead version, and a deep black background in the slide show version.

EMBOSSDx

The Embossed template has a modern design composed of straight lines accented by an integral square in one of the horizontal lines. The color versions are based on a light and dark green color scheme, which is pastel in the overhead slide version and has a metallic look in the slide show version.

Figure 4.21 Drop Strip Template

Figure 4.22 Embossed Template

FIESTAx

As you might expect, the Fiesta template has a party feel similar to the Cheers template (see Figure 4.16). The black and white version is, in fact, very similar to the Cheers template. The color versions use a blue, brown, and green color scheme instead of the pink tints of Cheers.

Figure 4.23 Fiesta Template

FLAGx

The Flag template is based on a flowing, flag-like pattern behind the upper area of the slide. In black and white the mood is muted with shades of light gray and a white background for the body of the slide. The overhead slide maintains the light gray flag and white background, but adds blue text. The slide show template uses a gray background instead of the white of the overhead template.

FORESTx

Not exactly a primitive forest design, but the little trees in the border do hint at a forest theme. Probably not for serious environmental topics, but useful when you want to suggest a forest theme.

Figure 4.24 Flag Template

Figure 4.25 Forest Template

GRIDWRKx

The Grid Work template uses a three-dimensional series of linked squares around the top and left side of the slide window. In color, this pattern is in deep blue.

Figure 4.26 Grid Work Template

INTLx

This is a simple template that uses a world globe in the lower right-hand corner of the slide window. The black and white slide is in shades of gray, while the color versions use dark blue and white.

ISLANDx

A northern coast mood seems to be the intent of this template. In black and white the slide is a little flat, but in color versions shades of dark green add some interest.

Figure 4.27 International Template

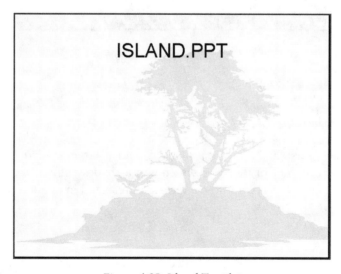

Figure 4.28 Island Template

LINSBLUx

This is a relatively simple template, but it can serve you well as a background for lists or simple graphics. The graduated grays or blues (on the color versions) present a clean image that should be particularly useful for high tech topics.

Figure 4.29 Lines Blue Template

MARBLEx

This template uses shadow effects heavily, with a large shaded block in the upper left-hand corner of the slide screen and a shadow effect around the bottom and right edges. In color, these effects are presented in red and pink.

MEDICALx

This design uses a caduceus as a shaded background, in gray on the black and white design and in pastel purple and blue in the color versions.

Figure 4.30 Marble Template

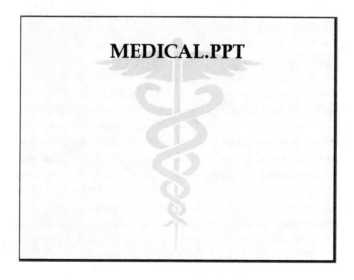

Figure 4.31 Medical Template

METLBARx

This is a modern industrial design that can be used to good advantage for high tech or manufacturing topics. The black and white version is a metallic gray design, whereas the color templates use shades of blue and silver.

Figure 4.32 Metal Bar Template

MOVNGLNx

This is another modern template based on crisp horizontal lines. The black and white version uses heavy black lines against a white background, while the color versions use red lines and blue text.

MULTBARx

This template uses a series of shaded metallic-type bars to frame the left and top section of the slide screen. In color these bars add a deep blue and red accent to the metallic gray.

Figure 4.33 Moving Lines Template

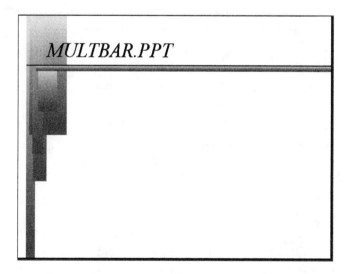

Figure 4.34 Multiple Bar Template

MULTBOXx

This template is based on a series of shaded boxes in the upper left and lower right corners of the slide window, accented by a shadowed box in the center of the display. In color the slide uses shades of lavender, green, and blue for a pastel fifties mood.

Figure 4.35 Multiple Box Template

MUSICx

This template has a musical theme. It places the text on top of a music staff accented by musical notes. In color this template uses red notes and staff with a blue background.

NEONLITx

The Neon Lights template is another design that evokes memories of the fifties. In black and white the mood is good for manufacturing themes. The grid background accented by graduated shaded boxes on the right of the slide present a clean design. In color, these templates use purple, green, and blue shades.

Figure 4.36 Music Template

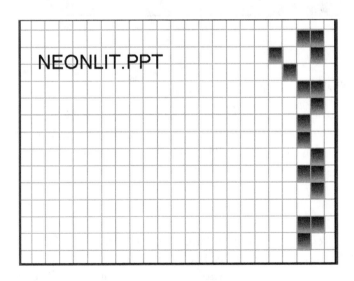

Figure 4.37 Neon Lights Template

PASTELx

A basic design, the Pastel template should serve well for educational topics or any time you want the slide itself to jump out from the template. The color versions use graduated violet-to-gray shades with either a very light violet or a light green background.

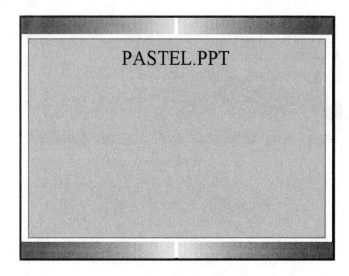

Figure 4.38 Pastel Template

PATCHWKx

Patch Work is a busy design that plays better in color than in black and white. The sharp triangular border can be distracting, so use this design only for strong slides that stand well on their own merits. The color slides use strong shades of black, red, yellow, and blue, but are still potentially distracting.

REDLINEx

The Red Line template is a design based on horizontal lines. In black and white, the template uses graduated gray lines separated by white space. In the overhead color version the lines are red and the separating space is black. In the slide show version, the overall mood is more muted with dark red lines and lighter accents.

Figure 4.39 Patch Work Template

Figure 4.40 Red Line Template

SEASHORx

The Seashore template offers a seashore theme with a hint of sand dunes and sea grass. The color versions replace the light gray images with dark blue.

Figure 4.41 Seashore Template

SHADBARx

The slides using this template have graduated, shaded bars at the top and bottom, with clean left and right margins. The black and white versions use graduated gray and black, while the color templates use purple and sand (slide show) or blue and red (overhead).

SIDEBARx

One of the simplest templates, Side Bar uses a single thin horizontal line under the title, with the remainder of the slide plain. The color versions remain clean and simple. The overhead slide version colors the horizontal line blue; the slide show version uses yellow text, a pink bar, and a blue background.

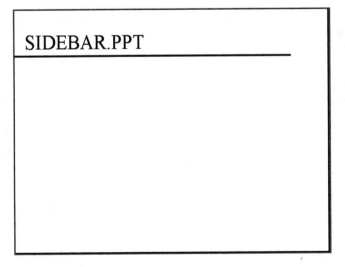

Figure 4.42 Shaded Bar Template

SIDEBAR.PPT

Figure 4.43 Side Bar Template

SIDEFADx

This template uses a wide graduated vertical bar at the left of the slide window and a horizontal double line at the top. The effect is crisp and clean, offering a good accent for presentation material. The color overhead template is presented in shades of green for a cool, pastel effect. The slide show template uses darker tones of sand and black for a metallic look.

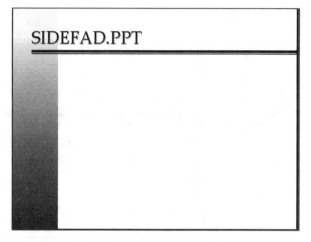

Figure 4.44 Side Fade Template

SOARINGx

This template uses a unique graphic shape as a background for your slides. A sweeping, wing-like shape moves from the lower right corner to the upper left corner of the slide window. In black and white the shape is a light gray. In color the shape is in shades of light and dark blue. The slide show template adds a dark blue background with graduations to black, offering a futuristic background for your information.

SOUTHWSx

The Southwest template uses a Western U.S. Indian design on the left border and as a background. The black and white template uses a black vertical bar with white accents on the left of the slide with shades of gray as the background. The overhead color template uses fluorescent green and orange as accent colors against a light gray background. The slide show version, on the other hand, changes the vertical bar to pastel earth colors with a black background.

Figure 4.45 Soaring Template

Figure 4.46 Southwest Template

SPARKLEx

A bright star in the upper left-hand corner of this template is accented by double horizontal bars under the title. Use this slide effectively for accenting information, especially with short lists and uncomplicated slides. The color versions use metallic blue shades for emphasis.

Figure 4.47 Sparkle Template

SPLATx

Like splotches of paint splashed randomly across the slide, the Splat template adds interesting shape and color to your slides. This is particularly suited for color applications. The color overhead template uses magenta and green against a white background. The slide show template splashes magenta and green color against a dark, cobalt blue background.

TABLETx

Clean, simple lines can help you enhance your slide displays without distracting shapes or colors. The three-dimensional shadow border of the Tablet template helps your slides jump out of the screen. The color versions add a light green shade for accent.

Figure 4.48 Splat Template

Figure 4.49 Tablet Template

THEATREx

Add ancient Egyptian symbols to a movie-screen-like box for your slides, and you have an accent that can help promote your information. This design is best used in color. The overhead version adds a green border to the white background, while the slide show template adds a graduated green-to-black background and a gold border.

Figure 4.50 Theatre Template

TOPLINEx

One of the simpler templates, this one places a wide black line across the top of the slide. In color, you get a graduated blue background with a magenta line in the overhead version. The slide show template has a bright and catchy black and blue background.

Figure 4.51 Topline Template

TRAVELx

A boat and a plane accent this template, which is effective in black and white as well as in color. The color overhead version has shades of blue against a white background, while the slide show puts black images against a cobalt blue background.

Figure 4.52 Travel Template

TRIDOTSx

This combination of triangles and tiny dots gives a modern, even futuristic feel. This could be a useful template for side-by-side lists and sequential display lines.

Figure 4.53 Triangles and Dots Template

TRIUMPHx

This template places an Olympic torch along the left margin of the slide against a gray or red background.

TROPICx

This template offers a tropical theme with palm tree silhouettes and a setting sun. Use this one in color for best impact.

Figure 4.54 Triumph Template

Figure 4.55 Tropic Template

TWINKLEx

This template is similar to the Diamond template (see Figure 4.20), except that it uses a twinkling star or sparkle symbol on top of the diamond. The color versions add shades of violet and blue or green and black.

Figure 4.56 Twinkle Template

VIVIDLNx

A clean center area is accented by a group of horizontal lines about three-fourths of the way from the top of this slide format. The title is in a shadow box. The color versions use red and yellow lines.

WATERCOx

This is a fun template, especially in the Slide Show version. It consists of a light background flanked by multi-colored flecks along the right and left borders. Use it anytime you need a light-hearted mood for your presentations. The black and white version is rather flat.

Figure 4.57 Vivid Line Template

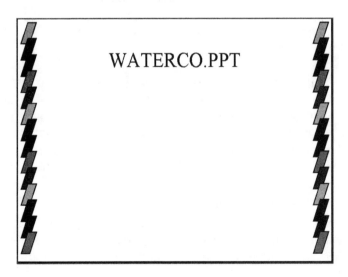

Figure 4.58 Water Color Template

WORLDx

The World template places a watermark of a flat global map as the background of the center of the slide. This can be quite effective in black and white or in color.

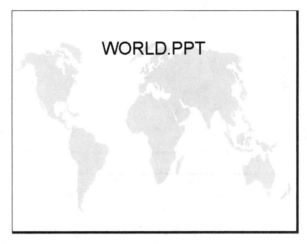

Figure 4.59 World Template

Using Templates

Now you know which templates are available. In this section I'll show you how to use them. As I mentioned earlier, you can apply a template by simply using the Format **Presentation Template...** command. You can also click on the **Template** button at the right corner of the Status Bar (bottom of the screen). Try to match the template you use to the topic or mood of your presentation. As you can see from the reference section earlier in this chapter, some of the templates tend toward the frivolous, while others are more serious. Some are colorful and bright, and others are muted and plain. So it is with the topics you'll cover.

You might choose a bright template to liven up a dull subject—sometimes that helps. But use this technique carefully or you will trivialize the subject. Although there are no hard and fast rules, try to consider the relationship between the topic you are covering in your presentation and the mood the template you use presents.

When you apply a template, any slide design you choose from the New Slide dialog contains the color scheme and the images that are part of the template design. In other words, a template applies to an entire presentation, giving it an overall mood or look. You can't apply templates to individual slides. You probably wouldn't want to do this because part of creating a successful presentation is developing a look that carries throughout the presentation.

You can format individual slides within a template design, if you wish. You could select a different background for specific slides, for example, or change the color scheme for part or all of specific slides without changing the template design for the rest of the presentation. Do this by displaying the slide you want to change, then by using the Format **Slide Layout...**, Format **Slide Background...**, or Format **Slide Color Scheme...** commands to reformat the slide. This is useful for emphasis or to introduce a new section of the presentation.

Remember that you don't have to use a pre-formatted template for your presentations. You can start with a blank presentation and design the slide color and pattern on your own. In addition, once you have a presentation design you like, you can use the presentation as a custom template. Notice that templates are saved as **.PPT** files. These are Presentation files that are saved without text or clip art.

You can use an existing file as a template simply by specifying the file name from inside the Template dialog. Notice that PowerPoint shows you a full directory and path display within this dialog with the files inside the Template subdirectories displayed as a default. To use another file as a template, simply step up the directory structure to where the file you want to use is stored. When you load a file as a template, the data that goes with the presentation is stripped away and only the background and other formatting are used with the new presentation.

Available Clip Art

Text, backgrounds, and designs aren't the only things that make up a presentation. PowerPoint comes with about 1,000 clip art images that can be used to enhance individual slides in your presentation. Some slide layouts include areas for clip art, making it easy to drop in one of these images as part of your slide design. A clip art image is a simple drawing that can be used to suggest a topic or to enhance a list or other text display. You can use photographs or other images with your presentations, of course, but the simplicity of clip art sometimes has an advantage.

The clip art supplied with PowerPoint is grouped into several categories to make it easier to select an image for a particular application. There are far too many clip art images to show them all in this book. However, in the following sections I'll show you the opening screen of the ClipArt Gallery for each of the categories. That'll help you visualize what is in each section. To see these images on the screen for yourself, simply open the ClipArt Gallery (Insert ClipArt...) and choose the category you want to view from the Category window at the top of the dialog.

The individual clip art screens on your system may vary from these. The ClipArt Gallery utility can scan your computer and install other images it finds. Use the Options button the Gallery dialog to customize your ClipArt Gallery.

Academic

Use clip art from the academic collection to accent school or education topics. (You used three of these images in the sample presentation about this book in Chapter 2.)

Figure 4.60 Academic Clip Art

Animals

This collection of 20 or so animal pictures includes farm animals, domestic animals, and creatures from the wild. As with most clip art, these are suggestive pictures and don't provide a lot of detail. However, when you need a suggestion of a particular animal or type of animal, one of these pictures should work for you.

Figure 4.61 Animals Clip Art

Buildings

There are about 40 clip art symbols you can use to suggest buildings and other structures, from skyscrapers to oil derricks, from churches to palladium windows.

Figure 4.62 Buildings Clip Art

Backgrounds

Use the clip art backgrounds to set an overall mood for your presentation. You can use the same background on all slides within a presentation, or simply to add emphasis to one or more slides. Of course these are standard clip art images, so they don't have to be used as backgrounds if you have another use for them.

Figure 4.63 Backgrounds Clip Art

Business

The 30 or so business selections give you material for suggesting business equipment, ideas, or operations. This section includes copiers and printers, computers and computer paper, disks and chips.

Cartoons

These are humorous images, mostly of people, that can be used to suggest a mood or an action. Choose from computer operators, cavemen, mountain climbers, light bulbs, and more.

Figure 4.64 Business Clip Art

Figure 4.65 Cartoons Clip Art

Communication

The communication clip art could have been placed under business, but by separating out telephones, modems, telephone wires, and billboards, you get a collection of images for more specialized applications. This section also includes drawings such as sound waves and radio broadcasting.

Figure 4.66 Communication Clip Art

Currency

When you talk about budgets, sales figures, exchange rates, or anything having to do with money, you can choose from one of these currency drawings. This group includes stacks of bills, coins, and money bags, plus domestic and foreign currency symbols ($, Cz$, etc.).

Figure 4.67 Currency Clip Art

Electronics

This group contains a wide range of images with an electronic focus, including video cameras, radios and tape players, and tape. These images are mostly in black and white.

Figure 4.68 Electronics Clip Art

Energy

The concept of energy can mean many different things to different people, so this collection is wide ranging. It includes power lines and oil wells, shovels of coal and water wheels, windmills and power meters.

Figure 4.69 Energy Clip Art

Entertainment

Hockey players, a magician's hat, playing cards, presents, microphones, and spotlights are only part of what you can find in the entertainment group of clip art.

Figure 4.70 Entertainment Clip Art

Flags

Any time you are dealing with international topics, one or more of these flag clip art symbols might be an asset. These are full color drawings that can enhance an overhead or 35mm projected image.

Figure 4.71 Flags Clip Art

Plants

Trees and flowers, cacti, and seeds are included in this color and monochrome collection.

Figure 4.72 Plants Clip Art

Gestures

These cartoon drawings of hands can be used to suggest concepts from applause to handshake deals to numbers and direction.

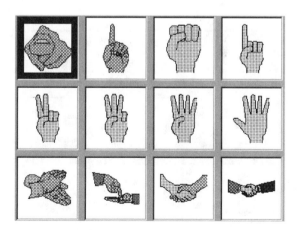

Figure 4.73 Gestures Clip Art

Hardware

Use one of these tool and hardware images to suggest carpentry, home improvement, automobile, or industrial topics.

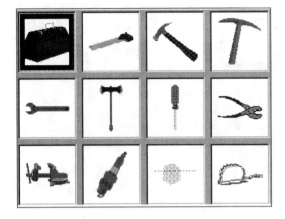

Figure 4.74 Hardware Clip Art

Household

The household collection is a large collection which includes everything from food to coffee cups, from cleaning supplies to keys. Most of these images use some color.

Figure 4.75 Household Clip Art

Landmarks

You'll recognize most of these landmarks as famous images from well-known American and foreign cities. This collection includes the Statue of Liberty, the Capitol dome, the Saint Louis arch, the Eiffel tower, and more.

Figure 4.76 Landmarks Clip Art

Maps—International

International maps can be used to suggest a location or to add interest for any international topic. You won't find everywhere here, but enough of a selection to be useful. The maps are generally in green and earth tones.

Figure 4.77 Maps—International Clip Art

People

This collection is a series of drawings, but they are not cartoons. Although the images are simple sketches, you see real people doing real things such as business meetings, walking to work, speaking at a lectern, studying a blue print, and more.

Figure 4.78 People Clip Art

Science and Medicine

When you need images of body parts and skeletons, medical instruments and symbols, this is the group to select. You'll also find a small group of scientific images here, including the solar system, beakers, Bunsen burners, and instruments.

Shapes

This catch-all group includes arrows, circles, lines, and shapes. Use these symbols to indicate direction, relationships, and more.

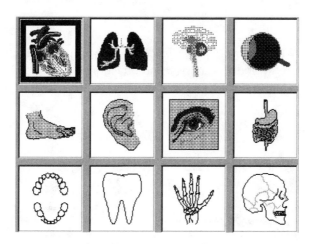

Figure 4.79 Science and Medicine Clip Art

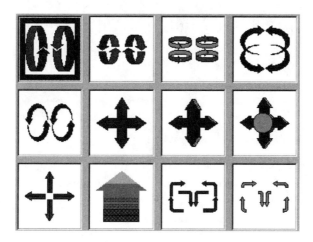

Figure 4.80 Shapes Clip Art

Signs

These are mostly black and white silhouette images that suggest stop signs, international service symbols, warnings, and directions.

Figure 4.81 Signs Clip Art

Sports and Lesiure

You can find some sports images in the entertainment category, but there are more here. From golf clubs to dart boards, from runners and bowlers to swimmers and cyclists, you can find something to suggest just about any sport. Many of these images are stick figure silhouettes.

Technology

Look to the business category for some computer and technology symbols, and to this group for even more. This collection is slanted toward computers and computer equipment, but also includes CDs and CD players, telephones, and other items.

Figure 4.82 Sports and Leisure Clip Art

Figure 4.83 Technology Clip Art

Transportation

Cars and trucks, boats and planes, trains and tanks are just part of what you'll find in this group. Most of these images carry a high level of detail and many are in color.

Figure 4.84 Transportation Clip Art

Maps–U.S.

This collection includes state maps in addition to some complete U.S. maps. Use individual maps of states to talk about sales territories, travel, and so on.

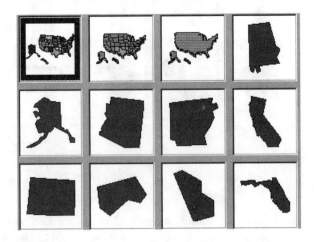

Figure 4.85 Maps–U.S. Clip Art

Using Clip Art

To use clip art with a layout that includes space for it, simply double-click inside the clip art area to display the ClipArt Gallery dialog, shown in Figure 4.86.

Figure 4.86 ClipArt Gallery Dialog Main Screen

Select the category of clip art you want to use and step through the displayed images inside that category until you find what you're looking for. You can either double-click on the image you want, or select it by clicking on it once and then clicking on **OK**.

You can add clip art to any slide, whether or not it contains a pre-formatted area for art or objects. Simply make the slide to which you want to add clip art current, then use the Insert **Clip Art...** command to display the ClipArt Gallery. PowerPoint will reserve a place on the slide for the clip art. When you choose the image you want to use, it will be inserted into this location. The size and position may not be what you want, but you can adjust it after you exit the Gallery display.

When you return to your slide, the clip art image you just inserted is selected. You can tell this by the presence of handles around its parameter. You can grab any one of these handles and drag that side of the image to change the size. Also, with the image selected you can place the mouse pointer anywhere inside the image, then hold down the left mouse button and drag the picture anywhere on the slide screen. This combination of sizing handles and the ability to drag the entire image anywhere you want it on the slide gives you a lot of flexibility in slide design. You can also size and move the clip art you inserted on a pre-formatted slide.

To select a different image for a given location, simply double-click on an existing image to display the ClipArt Gallery dialog. When you select a new image, it replaces the existing one. If you have resized the existing image, the new image is inserted into the same location and at the same size as the previous one.

Be careful resizing images. Obviously if you shrink a piece of clip art top to bottom, then everything in it shrinks. You can get some strange looking people, places, and things this way. Try to shrink left-to-right at about the same ratio as you shrink top-to-bottom to keep the aspect ratio of your image the same as the original. Be aware of how the pictures inside an image border change when you start resizing it, and use good judgment in adjusting the borders.

Available Wizards

You could think of a Wizard as a smart template. In reality it is an interactive macro (small program) that steps you through some of the tasks associated with creating presentations in PowerPoint. Two Wizards are supplied with PowerPoint: the Pick a Look Wizard and the AutoContent Wizard. I'll describe each of these Wizards in this section.

Pick a Look Wizard

The Pick a Look Wizard helps you select a template to use with your presentation, and it asks you questions so you can decide what additional appearance features you want to use. This Wizard helps you insert automatic page numbers, for example, and it prompts you for the name of your company and other information that can appear on each slide.

For a hands-on example of using the Pick a Look Wizard, refer to the sample presentation you created in Chapter 2.

You can select the Pick a Look Wizard when you begin a new presentation, or you can complete the basic presentation material and create the look you want by starting the Pick a Look Wizard at any time. If you later decide you'd like a different style, simply run this Wizard again to make the changes.

AutoContent Wizard

The AutoContent Wizard goes beyond the Pick a Look Wizard in helping you design a presentation style and content. Through a series of interactive screens, this Wizard helps you select slide layouts that communicate a particular message, such as selling a product or idea, recommending a strategy, or communicating bad news.

The interactive dialogs ask you questions about the topic of the presentation, the name of the presenter, and the type of presentation. Then the Wizard suggests an outline based on the topic and presentation type. A set of slides is created with some information already inserted. A template is chosen based on the type of presentation. You can work with the outline to insert information specific to your presentation, or switch to slide view to work with the slides. Figure 4.87 shows the suggested outline for a presentation designed to recommend a strategy.

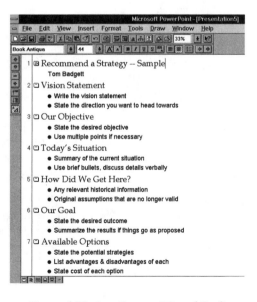

Figure 4.87 AutoContent Wizard Outline

Of course you can choose a different template if you wish, and you can change the basic slide titles, but the Wizard gives you an excellent place to start based on professional design criteria. A good way to see what the Wizard did in creating the presentation is to view it in the Slide Sorter, as shown in Figure 4.88.

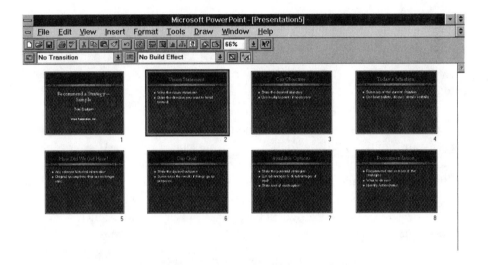

Figure 4.88 AutoContent Wizard Presentation in Slide Sorter

Using Wizards

As I said, you can use the Pick a Look Wizard when you start a new presentation design, or at any time during the design process. The AutoContent Wizard, on the other hand, starts a new presentation for you when it is launched.

You can pick either Wizard from the New Presentation dialog (see Figure 4.89). You can access this dialog with File **New** or by clicking on the **New** icon on the Standard toolbar. You can also select a Wizard directly from the Standard toolbar. (See Figure 2.15 for a close-up view of the Standard toolbar.)

Figure 4.89 New Presentation Dialog

In addition, you can select the Pick a Look Wizard from the Format menu (Format **Pick a Look Wizard...**), since you can use it simply to format an existing presentation. The AutoContent Wizard is only available from the toolbar or the New Presentation dialog, however.

When you place a presentation in Slide Show view, you can click the right mouse button to insert a pencil icon at the lower right corner of a slide. Select this tool with the left mouse button to place temporary drawings on any displayed slide. This is helpful during a presentation to help the audience focus on a particular section of the slide. When you advance to the next slide, this new drawing is removed.

To Sum Up

You can use this chapter as a reference during presentation or slide design. The images of individual templates and clip art will help you plan your presentations even when you don't have access to your computer and PowerPoint (as when you are at home and your computer is at the office). In fact, as you can see from the material in this chapter, PowerPoint is so rich in material that it may take you a while to become familiar with all of its features. I urge you to use the information in this chapter as a jumping off place for further study. Use the computer and PowerPoint's screens to teach yourself even more about this useful program.

In the next chapter I'll give you additional information about designing individual slides in PowerPoint, and I'll offer some suggestions on using PowerPoint for on-screen and projected slide shows.

Computer Slide Shows with PowerPoint

If you have read the previous sections of this book and have tried at least some of the things I have suggested, you have a firm foundation in PowerPoint. You know how to use the preformatted templates and interactive Wizards to produce a slide show or presentation.

In this chapter I will show you in more detail how to design individual slides—apart from the templates and Wizards—and how to use the screens to actually produce a computer-based slide show. In later chapters I'll show you how to take the basic on-screen material and turn it into overhead projection foils, printed pages, graphics files, or 35mm slides.

Designing Slides

I've already talked about slide design considerations in Chapter 3. These general guidelines will help you choose the proper typeface, type size, and colors for a particular application. In this section I'll show you how to use PowerPoint tools to create your own slide designs, either from scratch or by starting with a template and editing it for your own needs.

N O T E Review the information on templates in Chapter 4. Also, remember that you can use any presentation you design as a template for future presentations.

Let's start with a blank slide, no template, no design. Do this with the File **New** (**Ctrl+N**) command from the main PowerPoint menu. In the New Presentation dialog, specify **Blank Presentation** and choose a blank slide from the New Slide dialog. (This is the last slide on this dialog. Use the scroll bars beside the AutoLayout window to display this blank.) Your screen should look like the one in Figure 5.1.

Now let's put some text and graphics on that blank slide. This time we'll use the manual features of PowerPoint instead of the automatic and pre-programmed features.

Adding Text

First we'll add a title to the blank slide. Obviously you could choose one of the *AutoLayout* slides in the New Slide window to help with this design, but I want you to understand how these slides are formatted. That way you'll be able to start with a blank slide or an AutoLayout slide and edit it to achieve the look you want.

Figure 5.1 New Presentation with Blank Slide

To add text, simply click on the text tool on the Drawing toolbar at the left of the PowerPoint slide window. The mouse cursor should change to a downward-pointing arrow. Move this cursor to the location on the slide where you want the text to begin, then click the left mouse button. That fixes the beginning of the text cell so you can simply type from the keyboard the text you want to insert on the slide. PowerPoint places a small shaded box around the cursor, indicating that a text window has been opened and is ready for input.

Type one line of text. I've used **This is a Title** for the example and I've placed it at the top of the slide in a title position (see Figure 5.2).

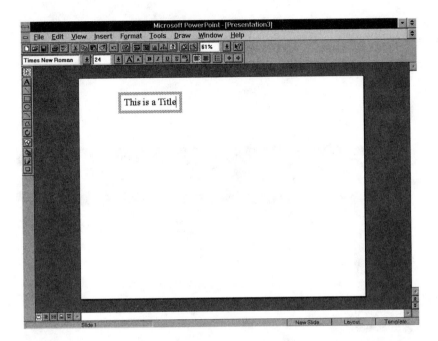

Figure 5.2 Sample Slide with **This is a Title** *Inserted*

As you can see from Figure 5.2 and your own typing, PowerPoint selected a font for these letters for you. Like a word processor, PowerPoint has some preset defaults that apply unless you change them.

Specifying Font and Size

For text, the default font is Times New Roman 24 point. Times New Roman specifies the typeface—the particular design of the characters—while 24 point specifies how big the characters are. A 24-point letter is about one-third of an inch tall, because it takes 72 points to make a character one inch high.

When you type a business letter or a report on a word processor, you will likely use 10- or 12-point type. That's about the right size for most standard text. When you are using text in a presentation, however, the letters generally need to be much larger than those used on a normal printed page. In fact, the 24-point default in PowerPoint is much too small for a main slide title. If you use one of PowerPoint's AutoLayout slides, the text in the title portion of the slide is preformatted at 44 points (0.61 inches). That is large enough for projected slides, but may be too small if you are using the computer screen itself.

Here's how to enlarge text. We'll leave the Times New Roman typeface because it produces good general purpose text that is easily read. Use the mouse to select the text you just entered. Do this by placing the cursor to the right or left of the text, holding down the left mouse button, and highlighting all of the text. You could also place the insertion point at the beginning or end of the text, hold down the **Shift** key, and then use the cursor movement keys on the keyboard to select the block.

· Click on the **Increase Font Size** button on the Format Bar. Notice that the font size increases from 24 points to 28 points. Each click on this button increases the size of the selected text by 4 points.

If you are using very large fonts, the **Increase** or **Decrease Font Size** button will change the font size by much more than 4 points. If you start with a 4000 point font, for example, the change is 364 points with each click.

Click four more times on the **Increase Font Size** button to raise the size of the title text to 44 points, PowerPoint's default for preformatted slides.

You can see that this is the new point size by looking at the Font Size window beside the Font name on the Format Bar. Each time you click on the **Increase Font Size** button the number in this window increases by four points. You can see the size of any text on the screen by placing the insertion point within any word and then looking at the number in the Font Size window.

Is a 44-point title big enough for your application? That depends on how you will use the slide or presentation you are creating. You can try a larger font size by simply clicking more times on the **Increase Font Size** button. You can also pull down a list of standard font sizes by clicking on the down-pointing arrow beside the Font Size window, as shown in Figure 5.3.

Try a 72-point (one inch) font for this title by using the scroll bars to the right of the pull-down font size list. This produces a large font that can be seen easily, even on a computer screen presentation. For a larger font, select 96 points (1.3 inches), which is the last standard font on the list.

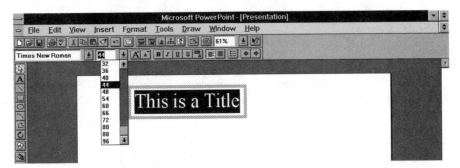

Figure 5.3 Font Size Pull-Down List on Format Bar

Want a REALLY big font for a short title? Select the font size displayed in the Font Size window of the Format Bar and type in the font size you want to use. The standard pull-down list contains fonts that range from a very small nine points to a relatively large 96 points. However, you can type in font sizes from 1 point (too small to see) to 4,000 points (about 55 inches). Obviously you have to adjust the size of the text you're using to fit the application. You can't see a 55-inch character on a 14-inch computer screen, but you might be able to print it if you have a large plotter that can handle images that large. Use **Slide Setup** (File **Slide Setup...**) to set the paper size if necessary and use **Printer Setup** (File **Print Printer...**) to select the plotter to which you want to print.

Setting Text Position

I've shown the text on this slide as a top-of-slide title. However, you can place text anywhere on the slide. Simply select the text tool (as described above) and click on the slide where you want to start entering text.

Now, suppose you want to position the text in a different orientation than horizontal, left to right. Let's say you want to position the previously-entered title as a corner banner at the upper right-hand area of the slide (see Figure 5.4).

PowerPoint's built-in utilities make this an easy process. Here are the steps:

Select the text by clicking anywhere within the title. PowerPoint places a box around all of the text. Click on the box to place handles around the title (see Figure 5.5).

Grab the title box and drag it toward the middle of the slide. This is to give you room for the rotation of the text. Use Draw **Rotate/Flip** to display the Rotate/Flip menu shown in Figure 5.6.

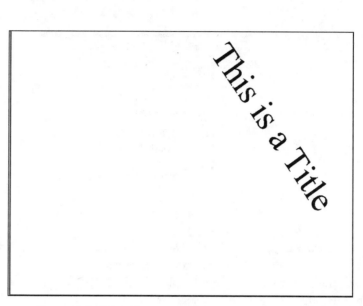

Figure 5.4 Slide Title Positioned at Upper Right Corner

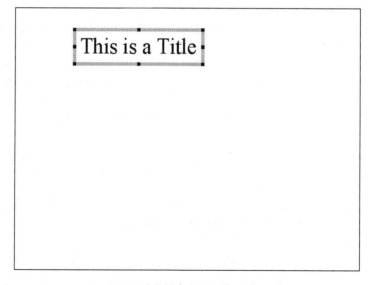

Figure 5.5 Title Text Selected

Figure 5.6 Pull-Down Draw Rotate/Flip Menu

Choose **Free Rotate** from this menu. The mouse cursor changes to a double circular arrow, indicating that you can rotate the selected text freely in any direction. Move the cursor to one of the handles on the selection box around the title text. The cursor changes again to a small square.

Grab the handle by pressing and holding the left mouse button. Now you can rotate the box around a center point by moving the mouse. Turn the box until it is approximately 45 degrees relative to the upper right-hand corner of the slide. Don't worry if you don't get the angle exactly right. You can change the angle later if you need to. Click anywhere outside the text box to turn off rotation. The mouse cursor changes back to a pointer and the selection box around the text is removed.

Click anywhere inside the text once more to re-select the text. Now you can grab the box as before and move it to the upper right corner of the slide. If the rotation isn't exactly right, use Draw **Rotate/Flip** again to adjust the angle so the text will fit into the corner of the slide. The finished results should look like Figure 5.4.

Another way to change the orientation of text is to enter it in a vertical line instead of horizontally. You could use a short line of vertical text to call attention to a graphic or to help the viewer focus on a different area of the slide. You can enter a vertical line of text easily. Simply select the text tool and position the cursor where you want the first letter in the line of text to appear. Type the first letter, then press **Enter**. Now enter the second letter and press **Enter**, and so on. Press **Enter** twice between words to separate them.

You can select this vertical line of text by clicking anywhere inside the line and then dragging the entire box where you want it on the screen. You could rotate this line of text as well, but it can be difficult to read rotated vertical text. I'm not saying you shouldn't rotate a vertical line, but that you should use good judgment in how much you rotate it, and you should keep the amount of text to a minimum.

You should choose the typeface for vertical text carefully. A large bold font is a good choice, perhaps a *sans serif font* (one without serifs) such as Impact or Helvetica. Also, it is a good idea to keep the number of words in a vertical line small. It is relatively difficult to read text with one character on top of another. In fact, a single word for emphasis is the best choice, but you can use several words. Just be aware that it may take slightly longer for the audience to assimilate multiple words in a vertical format than it would take if the text were conventionally placed. Figure 5.7 shows how you might use a single vertical word to emphasize an idea also presented by clip art. Figure 5.8 shows rotated vertical text.

Figure 5.7 Vertical Text with Clip Art

Figure 5.8 Vertical Text Rotated for Emphasis

Changing Text Color

You can do other things with text besides changing its size and moving it around the slide. For one thing, you might want to change the color of text if you are designing a presentation for projection, for conversion to 35mm slides, or for color printing on overhead foils.

To select a different text color, first select the text either by holding down the left mouse button and highlighting the text you want to change, or by clicking anywhere inside a line of text to select it all. If you select a single word or a single character by highlighting, you can change colors on a character-by-character or a word-by-word basis. If you place a text selection box around a block of text by clicking anywhere inside the line, you'll change the color of everything inside the box at once. Either way, change text color by popping up the **Text Color** selector from the Format Bar. Click once on the **Text Color** symbol to display the selector shown in Figure 5.9.

Figure 5.9 Text Color Selector from Format Bar

 You can also change text color with the Format **Font Color** command sequence. This procedure displays the Font dialog and then pops up the Text Color Selector box inside this dialog.

N O T E

To change the color of any selected text, simply click once inside the square of the color you want to choose from the Text Color Selector box.

Placing Text Inside Objects

What else can you do to format text? You could place text inside a colored object, for example, or you could enter text and then place an object over or behind it. Suppose you want a colored rectangle with text inside it. In fact, you could use multiple rectangles on a slide to hold different text components. Consider the slide in Figure 5.10.

Figure 5.10 Slide with Multiple Text Boxes

This slide incorporates several text formatting features of PowerPoint: underlining, text color, text over an object, and parallel positioning. Here's how to re-create the slide in Figure 5.10.

Start with the clip art. I've used a computer image from the technology clip art group. You can select something else for this exercise if you'd like. Use Insert **Clip Art** to place an image within the slide. PowerPoint places the selected image at about the middle of the slide and at a pre-formatted size. For this slide design, however, neither the default size nor the default position is what we want.

PowerPoint places handles around the edges of the image. Drag the image to the left side of the slide, then use the handles to resize the image so that it has a generally vertical orientation.

NOTE Use care in resizing clip art, photographs, or other images. If you shrink the image horizontally (narrowing the width) without also changing the height, you change the *aspect ratio* of the image. You can determine the proper aspect ratio by looking carefully at the image as you resize it.

Now insert the text. Select the text tool and click in a clear area on the slide. Type the first block of text. If you are re-creating the sample slide, type **Improved Sales!** Click on the box that surrounds the text to select it as a block. PowerPoint places selection handles at each corner and in the middle of each side of the text box. Now you can move the text, size it, and change its attributes.

Click on the **Increase Font Size** button on the Format Bar until the size of the text increases to 32 points, as shown in the Font Size window of the Format Bar. Drag the text box to where you want it to appear on the slide. In our example this text goes at the upper left of the slide above the clip art image.

Select the rectangle tool from the Drawing toolbar and use this tool to draw a rectangle around the block of text. Do this by placing the pointer to the left and above the text box. Hold down the left mouse button to nail down the upper left corner of the rectangle, then drag the box to the lower right edge of the text box. When you release the mouse button, PowerPoint creates a colored box on top of the text. Unless you have changed PowerPoint's defaults, the box is blue and covers up the text. The blue box is selected (you can tell this because there is a line around the box and selection handles on it).

Use Draw **Send to Back** to move the colored rectangle behind the text. This makes the text visible. Now you should see black text inside a dark blue rectangle. Click on the text inside the colored box. PowerPoint places a white box around the text and opens the block of text for editing. You could type additional text or delete text inside the box at this point, but we don't want to edit the text. We want to change the text's color and its attributes. Click on the box that PowerPoint has drawn around the block of text. You can tell the whole block is selected because PowerPoint places handles on it. Now you can manipulate all of the text as a block without having to select it by marking a block in the conventional way.

Click on the **Bold** button on the Format Bar to change the text to boldface. (You can also use the Format **Font** command to display the Font dialog. You can select the bold attribute from this dialog.) Also select the underline attribute, either by clicking on the **Underline** button or by using the Font dialog.

Open the Text Color Selector box either from inside the Font dialog or by clicking on the **Text Color** button on the Format Bar. Choose the white color box from inside this display to change the text color to white. This produces a blue box with bold underlined white text inside it.

Create two additional text boxes with the same attributes—one which says **Lower Prices** and one which says **Flexibility** (or other text if you are designing your own slide instead of following my example). Position these text boxes where you want them on the slide.

 Although the colored boxes and text seem to be single objects, they remain separate. You can reposition them by moving the text, then dragging the box over it. Or, you can group the text and box, making

N O T E   it easy to move them together. Click on a colored box to select it, then hold down the **Shift** key and click on the text. Now additional "star" handles show that both text and box objects are selected. Use Draw **Group** to join the two. Now you can move them as a single object.

Finally, add the initials to the computer screen that is part of the clip art. Select the text tool, position the cursor where you want each letter on the screen, then click and type the letter. As before, select each letter and set the attribute to bold. Change the text color from the black default to white so that the letters will stand out more sharply on the screen.

Positioning Text

One more text feature needs to be discussed. Notice the two text boxes at the right of the slide. They are lined up one on top of the other, and they start in the same relative position, left to right. This can be difficult to achieve when you have different blocks of text that you are trying to keep aligned. Fortunately, PowerPoint includes a tool to make this job easier.

In Figure 5.11 I have added a ruler display to the left and top of the screen. You can do this with the View **Ruler** command.

Figure 5.11 Text Box Slide with Ruler Display

As you move the mouse, you can track the vertical and horizontal position by noting the position of the pointers on the two rulers. Notice that the center of the slide is at 0,0. In conventional screen addressing, the upper left-hand corner is usually 0,0.

To make sure that two text boxes are lined up on the same vertical line (they are the same distance from the left of the slide), place one box where you want it. Next move the mouse pointer onto the left edge of the box and note the horizontal position on the top ruler. Now you know where to position the next box. Grab the next box and drag it to a position where the left edge is on the same vertical line as the first one. Obviously you can use the same technique to position a series of objects along a horizontal line by using the vertical ruler at the left of the PowerPoint screen.

In addition, you can use these rulers to help you align text or other objects in a block. When you activate a block of text by clicking inside the text, the ruler changes to show the area of the slide occupied by that block. Notice how the rulers have changed in Figure 5.12. Duplicate this display by clicking on the text in the Lower Prices block on the sample slide. You can see the width and height of the block by referring to the spaces defined on the two rulers.

Figure 5.12 Rulers Showing Height and Width of Text Block

Remove the rulers with the View **Ruler** command sequence. This is a toggle command, so the first time you use it, a check mark is placed beside the Ruler menu item and the rulers are displayed. The second time you use the command, the check mark is removed and the rulers disappear.

Creating Bullet Lists

Another format in which you can use text is the *bullet list.* You've seen these previously in this book. Here I want to show you how to create your own list outside the preprogrammed PowerPoint slides. Try building your own list by first inserting a new slide. (Click on the **New Slide...** button at the bottom of the screen or use Insert **New Slide....**) Again, choose the last slide in the AutoLayout list—the one with no preformatted sections for title, lists, and clip art.

Select the text tool and click on the slide where you want to start the bullet list. Type the first line of the list. Now you can either press **Enter** to create a list as a single object, or you can click outside the text block to close the box. If you do the latter, then you must select the text tool again, reposition the insertion point, and type the next line of text. If you want more flexibility in positioning items in the list, make each line a separate object. If you are satisfied with the order and don't plan to move individual items to different areas of the screen, then enter the bullet text as a single list.

A basic list of single-line text items is shown in Figure 5.13. I've added a title to this slide as well, and I've enlarged the type from the PowerPoint defaults.

Using Bullet Lists

Lists summarize data

Lists focus audience attention

Lists organize presentations

Lists add visual impact

Figure 5.13 Basic Text List without Bullets

Now you can add standard PowerPoint bullets to the list. Select the first text block (or the only block, if you've entered the list as a single object). Click on the **Bullet List** button on the Format Bar. PowerPoint adds a standard bullet to the beginning of each text line within the selected block. If you have more than one block, repeat the process until you have each line bulleted, as shown in Figure 5.14.

Using Bullet Lists

•Lists summarize data

•Lists focus audience attention

•Lists organize presentations

•Lists add visual impact

Figure 5.14 Beginning Bullet List

Notice that PowerPoint doesn't place any additional space between the bullet and the text. Normally you want to format a bulleted list as a hanging indent paragraph. In PowerPoint, however, you so rarely have a multi-line bullet that a simple tab between the bullet and the first character in the text line is sufficient.

To insert a tab after the bullet, click to the left of the first character in each line to place the insertion point between the first character and the bullet. Click on the **Bullet List** button to remove the bullet temporarily and press **Tab**. Now, place the insertion point at the beginning of the line and click on the **Bullet List** button to re-insert the bullet. As you can see from Figure 5.15, the list is more pleasing and easier to read with spaces after the bullets.

Using Bullet Lists

- Lists summarize data
- Lists focus audience attention
- Lists organize presentations
- Lists add visual impact

Figure 5.15 Bulleted List with Spaces

You have used the PowerPoint default bullet settings to create a bulleted list. What if you want to use another character for the bullets? This is easily done. Select a block of text by clicking anywhere in the line. This is like selecting a paragraph in Microsoft Word or other word processors. Now use the Format **Bullet** command to display the Bullet dialog shown in Figure 5.16.

Figure 5.16 Bullet Dialog

Notice that the default bullet is highlighted, and the Use a Bullet button is selected. (This is because you previously inserted a bullet into this line of text. If the selected text did not have a bullet already, then this button would be blank.) The Normal Text font is in the Bullets From window of the dialog. There are several interesting choices for bullets on this screen, including boxes of various shapes, special symbols such as the copyright (©) or registered trademark (®), and foreign characters. But that's not all. There are a number of typeface groups from which to choose bullets. To find out what's out there, click on the down arrow beside the Bullets From window to display a list of typefaces, as shown in Figure 5.17.

For some interesting choices, use the scroll bar beside this pull-down list to find the **Wingdings** entry. Select this entry to display the bullet choices shown in Figure 5.18.

These symbols look fairly small in the Bullets dialog. To get a better look at any one symbol, just click on it. PowerPoint enlarges the symbol, as if it were placed under a magnifying glass. You can insert any bullet at the beginning of a line of text either by double-clicking on the bullet, or by clicking on **OK** after selecting the bullet you want to use.

Figure 5.19 shows the bullet list with smiley faces as bullets instead of plain black dots. Obviously this is just one of many choices for unconventional bullets for your lists. If you want card suit symbols (diamonds, spades, etc.), for example, select the **Symbol** typeface from the pull-down list instead of Wingdings.

Figure 5.17 Bullets from Typeface List

Figure 5.18 Wingdings Bullets

Using Bullet Lists

    ☺   Lists summarize data

    ☺   Lists focus audience attention

    ☺   Lists organize presentations

    ☺   Lists add visual impact

Figure 5.19 Bullet List with Smiley Faces as Bullets

Don't forget that you can change the color of the text lists, including the bullets. I showed you how to do that earlier in this chapter.

Adding Clip Art, Pictures, and Graphs

As you've already seen, effective slides aren't built from text alone. Although text blocks may carry the majority of the information in a slide, other objects can help to emphasize the message of the text, or to augment it in different ways.

Using Clip Art

In the previous chapter you learned how to insert a clip art image from the ClipArt Gallery, and also how to move and resize the image. Clip art won't solve all of your graphics needs in PowerPoint, but it can go a long way toward helping you design and create powerful, effective presentations. PowerPoint comes with about 1,000 images, and you can find clip art within other applications such as Microsoft Word, WordPerfect, Parsons Technology Announcement, various calendar, card, and banner programs, as well as drawing programs.

PowerPoint clip art is stored in compressed files under the various categories you see in the ClipArt Gallery. You can list these files using DOS. Issue this DOS command to change to the directory that holds the clip art files:

```
CD \POWERPNT\PCSFILES
```

Now type **DIR** and press **Enter**. You will see a list of files that end in the **.PCS** extension. The names are the same as those you see in the ClipArt Gallery dialog when you insert clip art into a PowerPoint slide.

Using Pictures

You don't have to limit yourself to PowerPoint clip art. As I have mentioned, clip art images are frequently supplied with other applications. These are standard format graphics files that may end in **.PCX**, **.TIF**, or another file format extension. You can insert these images into a PowerPoint presentation with the Insert **Picture...** command sequence from the main menu. This command displays the Insert Picture dialog shown in Figure 5.20.

Figure 5.20 Insert Picture Dialog

The default directory will be the current directory or the last directory you used to insert a picture. PowerPoint automatically lists files of known graphics types that it can convert and import. In the File Name window of this dialog you can see the file types PowerPoint expects to see:

> *.wmf, *.wpg, *.drw, *.dxf, *.hgl, *.cgm, *.eps, *.tif, *.pcx, *.pic, *.gif, *.pct, *.adi, *.cdr, *.plt, *.pcd, *.tga, *.bmp, *.dib

That's a comprehensive list of graphics files. If you want to narrow the list to a specific type of file—such as *.pcx or *.tif, common formats with scanners and many graphics programs—then simply type *.pcx or *.tif in the File Name window. The list of files will change to reflect the new file name specification.

Use the scroll bar, if necessary, to step through the list of files, and double-click on the one you want to import into the current slide inside your presentation. You can change directories by clicking on the parent directories listed in the Directories window of this dialog, then stepping down through the list to the directory you want.

Double-click on the file name you want to import, or select the name and click on **OK** to import it into PowerPoint. Once the image is imported into your current slide, you can move it or size it just like the clip art you experimented with earlier in this chapter.

The ability of PowerPoint to import graphics images from a variety of drawing and graphics programs lets you use images created by almost any popular application inside your PowerPoint presentation. If you're using a drawing program to prepare graphics elsewhere in your company, or your business involves CAD design, it is probable that you can use native images from these applications directly inside PowerPoint presentations. Many applications can export files in other than native format, so if a particular program doesn't use a file format that is compatible with PowerPoint import filters, chances are that you can export files into a format that PowerPoint will support.

Using Graphs

As I mentioned in the previous section, you can import images and files from a wide variety of programs. This lets you use powerful graphics, drawing, and image programs to help you support presentation design in PowerPoint. However, PowerPoint itself contains features that can handle many, if not most, of your image needs.

You can import a *spreadsheet* graph from Excel or 1-2-3, for example, and this is what you may want to do if the data on which the graph is based is complex or if you merely want to avoid entering the data a second time. However, if you are dealing with raw data that you want to represent as a graph, you can use PowerPoint's built-in graphing facility.

Click on the **New Slide...** button at the bottom of the PowerPoint display. Select the third slide (the first slide in the third column at the right) in the

AutoLayout display. This slide is preformatted with a title and space for a graph. Your screen should look like the one in Figure 5.21.

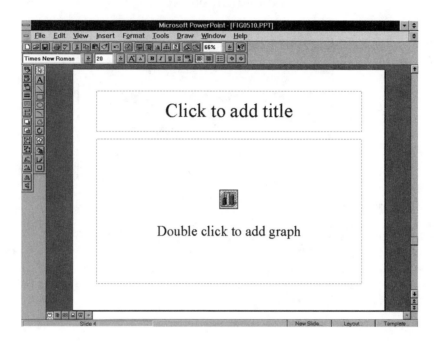

Figure 5.21 New Slide with Graph AutoLayout

Although we are using a preformatted AutoLayout slide in this example, you can add a graph to any slide, whether or not it has a section set aside for one. The graph image works like any other object such as clip art or pictures. Once on your slide, you can move or size a graph image just as you can clip art.

Add a title to the sample slide, if you wish, by clicking in the indicated area and typing the text for a title. I've used the title **Sample Graph Slide** for this example. Double-click on the graph symbol to open the PowerPoint graphing utility (*Microsoft Graph*) shown in Figure 5.22.

Notice that PowerPoint inserts the graphing utility screen inside the current slide, and that it includes sample data that is used to present a sample graph. The graph utility window looks like a portion of a spreadsheet window. You can enter new labels and data to replace the existing information and create your own graphic display of raw data.

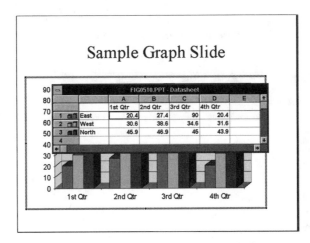

Figure 5.22 PowerPoint Graphing Utility

Suppose you want to compare the number of endangered species in the U.S. with those in foreign countries in a graphical form. (This is data right out of the *1994 World Almanac*. Your information might be different, but you can see from this example how to present numerical data as a graph.) Here is the raw information to be graphed:

Table 5.1

Group	U.S. Only	U.S. & Foreign	Foreign Only
Mammals	37	19	249
Birds	57	16	153
Reptiles	8	8	64
Amphibians	6	0	8
Fishes	55	3	11

To use PowerPoint's graph utility, simply re-create the list inside the graph utility. Replace the East, West, North titles with Mammals, Birds, Reptiles, Amphibians, and Fishes, and enter the numbers in the appropriate columns. Replace existing data by selecting it and typing in the new information. PowerPoint automatically updates the graphs in the window based on the new data you enter. Figure 5.23 shows how the screen looks after the raw information has been entered into the graphing utility.

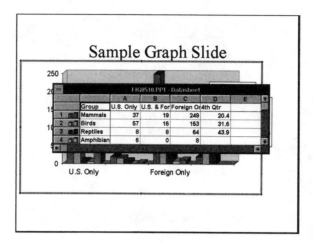

Figure 5.23 Raw Endangered Animal Data in Graph

Notice that there are some problems with the display in Figure 5.23. You are probably having the same problems with your graph display, unless you are familiar with Microsoft Excel and have corrected the problems as you entered the data. (Microsoft Graph behaves in many ways like Excel, although it lacks many of its features.)

First, we have entered three columns of data, but the sample graph includes four columns. You can remove this last column by moving the cross hair cursor onto the **D** at the top of the fourth column, then clicking once to select the whole column. PowerPoint will set the column in reverse video to indicate it has been selected. Press **Del** once to remove the data in that column.

Now only data you want to display is in the spreadsheet, but some of the cells are too narrow to hold the information. You can widen the cells easily by moving the cross hair cursor into the top of the column. As you move the cursor over the vertical line that divides the columns, the shape of the cursor changes from a cross to a doubled-ended arrow. Try this with column **B**. When the shape of the cursor changes to the double-ended arrow, press and hold the left mouse button and drag the dividing line between columns **B** and **C** to the right, widening the entire **B** column. Drag the line far enough to make room for the whole title, **U.S. & Foreign**.

Repeat this process for the **C** column, making room for the **Foreign Only** title. Notice how the data window and the graph window have changed. PowerPoint redrew the graph as you entered new information into the data window. You can get a look at the graph without closing the data entry window by dragging the data entry window off of the top of the graph. This gives you a picture like the one in Figure 5.24.

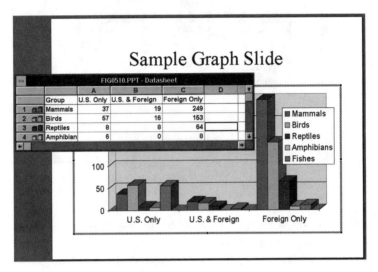

Figure 5.24 Graph with Data Entry Window to Side

If you need to edit the data you've entered, simply click inside the cell you want to change and type the new data. When all the titles and numbers are correct you can close the data entry window, leaving the newly-created graph inserted on the current slide. To close the data entry window, click on the **control panel** button at the upper left corner of the data entry window, and either choose **Close** or press **Ctrl+F4**. The result is the slide shown in Figure 5.25.

Notice that the graphic representation of the data can be much easier and quicker to interpret than numbers. Creating a graph with PowerPoint's built-in graphing feature makes the process automatic and easy.

Using Other PowerPoint Objects

Because PowerPoint is well-integrated into the Microsoft Windows environment, you can insert a number of other types of objects into your slides. To insert something into the current slide, use the Insert **Object...** command to display the Insert Object dialog shown in Figure 5.26.

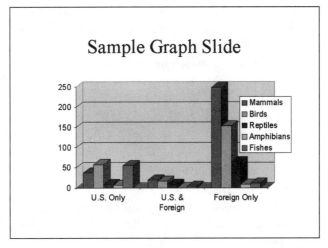

Figure 5.25 Finished Graph Slide

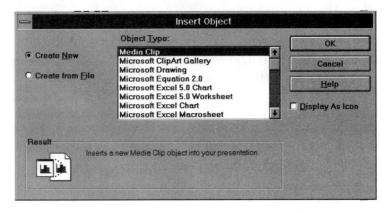

Figure 5.26 Insert Object Dialog

The object types that appear in the Insert Object dialog depend to some extent on what other resources you have installed on your system. Many Microsoft products are installed with common components in subdirectories within the Windows subdirectory. In general, however, you should find choices for Media Clip, Microsoft Drawing, equations, graphs, Word documents, WordArt, and a range of other objects from Microsoft applications. Just how these objects behave on a PowerPoint slide depends slightly on what the object is, but you can generally expect to insert an object, size it, and move it just as you would clip art or pictures.

I've shown you already how to use AutoLayout slides to create a particular style of slide. The AutoLayout dialog includes sample slides with placeholders for text, clip art, charts, and so on. You can start with one of these designs and change the placeholder type if you want to build a show of slide types before you insert the actual images. Do this by selecting the placeholder and then clicking on the type of image on the Standard toolbar that you want to use. You can also use the Insert **Object...** command to display the Insert Object dialog. When you choose an object type, PowerPoint inserts a placeholder for that object in place of the previous one.

If you are starting with a slide that does not have a placeholder, use Insert **Object...** and click on the **Display as Icon** button on the Insert Object dialog. Then when you select an object type, it will be inserted on your slide as an icon. You can double-click on this icon to launch the utility that lets you insert an object of this type.

Adding Organizational Charts

I showed you in Chapter 2 how to use the Organization Chart utility in PowerPoint. I'll just review the process here, and add more information to the basics already provided. Click on the **New Slide...** button at the bottom of the PowerPoint screen. Notice that the second slide down in the third column of the AutoLayout window has a section set aside for an organizational chart. If you choose that slide, you can add an organizational chart by simply double-clicking on the slide's organizational chart symbol. For this example, however, select the last slide in the third column—the blank slide. This will show you how to format your own slide and how to find the Organization Chart utility without the AutoLayout prompt.

With a blank slide on the screen, choose the text tool from the Drawing toolbar and create a title for this slide. I used the title **Organization Chart Sample Slide**. Increase the size of the title font to 54 points and underline it. (See the text section earlier in this chapter if you need help remembering how to do this.) Your slide should look like the one in Figure 5.27.

You can insert an organizational chart by clicking on the **Insert Organization Chart** symbol on the Standard toolbar, or by using the Insert **Object...** command and choosing **Microsoft Organization Chart** from the Insert Object dialog. Either way, the Organization Chart utility screen, shown in Figure 5.28, is displayed.

OrgChart Sample Slide

Figure 5.27 Organization Chart Sample Slide with Title Only

Figure 5.28 Organization Chart Utility Main Screen

This utility is similar to the graphing utility. You use a separate application closely tied to PowerPoint to create the organizational chart, then you insert the final image into your slide at a predetermined location at the center of the screen. After the image is inserted, you can size it or move it as with clip art and other objects.

The Organization Chart screen contains a predefined organizational chart with a title line and two organizational levels—one top-level box and three boxes at the second level. Each box contains dummy entries for name, title, and two comments. You can see only the name and title lines when Organization Chart opens. To open an entire box, click on one of the dummy lines of text inside a box. Organization Chart expands the box to show all four lines of dummy text, as you can see in Figure 5.29.

Figure 5.29 Organization Chart with Left Box Opened

Notice that a toolbar beneath the Organization Chart menu bar lets you add text to the area around the chart boxes and add more boxes to the chart. Study the toolbar carefully and you can see that each button has a connective line attached at a different location on the box icon. You choose the appropriate icon to add a box at a specific location on the chart.

To change the dummy text on any Organization Chart box, click on the box to activate it and use the mouse to select the text you want to replace. When you start typing, Organization Chart replaces the selected text with what you type.

Organization Chart includes several formatting features to help you design the precise type of organizational chart you want. These features are accessed from the Organization Chart menu bar. For example, when you click on the Styles menu, Organization Chart displays the organizational chart formats shown in Figure 5.30. If you first selected an entire existing chart—such as the default sample chart—you can change the style of this chart by clicking on one of the designs in the Style dialog.

Figure 5.30 Style Dialog from Main Organization Chart Menu

Select an organizational chart by holding down the left mouse button and drawing a box around the chart or chart portion you want to modify. Organization Chart changes the color of the selected chart or chart portion. Now you can use the Styles menu to re-arrange the existing boxes. For example, if you click on the second style in the Style dialog, a top-down subordinate design, the Organization Chart default chart looks like the one in Figure 5.31. Use this design to create deeper subgroups under a main level.

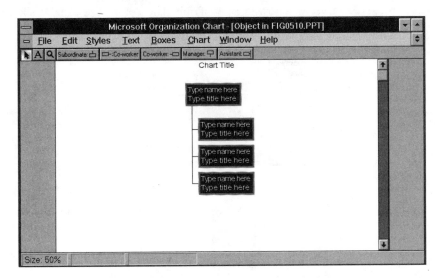

Figure 5.31 Top-Down Organizational Chart

Another way to change the appearance of an organizational chart is to change the borders around the boxes or the color or style of the lines between boxes. Make these changes, and others, with the Boxes menu, shown in Figure 5.32.

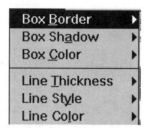

Figure 5.32 Boxes Menu from Organization Chart Main Menu

With these menu selections you can add or remove borders, change the thickness of the lines, change line style and color, or add shadows around the boxes. Use these formatting features to add emphasis to part or all of your organizational charts. You can tell by the right arrows beside each of the Boxes menu entries that additional menu choices are behind each of these selections.

After you have added the text and formatting you want to an organization chart in Organization Chart, use File **Update** to place the image into the current slide. Then use File **Exit** to return to PowerPoint. The completed sample slide is shown in Figure 5.33.

Figure 5.33 Completed Organization Chart Sample Slide

You can return to the Organization Chart utility at any time by double-clicking on a chart inserted into a PowerPoint slide.

Editing and Building the Presentation

In the previous sections of this chapter you have built a small presentation or slide show. Now it is time to learn how to manipulate these images into a final presentation.

Using the Slide Sorter

The best way to get an overview of a presentation is to turn on the Slide Sorter view. Do this by clicking on the **Slide Sorter** icon at the bottom of the slide display, or by using the View **Slide Sorter** command sequence from the main PowerPoint menu. Figure 5.34 shows the sample presentation we built in this chapter in Slide Sorter view.

Figure 5.34 Sample Presentation in Slide Sorter View

There are seven slides in Figure 5.34. (You may have a couple more or less, depending on how you followed the samples earlier in this chapter.) This view of your presentation shows how the various slides are positioned, and it gives you the opportunity to move them around if you wish. This is also a good place to start when you want to add new slides to a presentation.

Notice that PowerPoint places a large insertion point or cursor within the Slide Sorter view. This shows the current location of the slide pointer. You can use the mouse to place this pointer anywhere in the presentation. You can click on an existing slide to select it and make it the current slide, or you can click in the space between slides to insert a new slide in that location. Once a slide has been selected, you can use the mouse to drag it to any position within the Slide Sorter. Try that now. Move slide number 7, the organization chart, to position 2, right after the **This is a Title** slide. Your Slide Sorter screen should look like the one in Figure 5.35.

Figure 5.35 Slide Sorter with #7 in #2 Position

Notice that as you drag a slide, the pointer changes to a packet or envelope to indicate that you are carrying an object. The entire slide won't move until you place the insertion point in the new location and release the mouse button.

This view is also a good place to try templates or other formatting to get an overall effect for the show. You can click on the **Template** button at the bottom of the screen to open the Template dialog. Choose a template and PowerPoint will update all of the slides with the new information. Figure 5.36 shows the Slide Sorter view of this presentation with the **LINSBLUS.PPT** template as an example.

Figure 5.36 Sample Presentation with LINSBLUS.PPT Template

Adding Transitions

After you have the slides in the order you want and you have inserted any new slides, you are ready to work on *transitions*.

If you are designing a presentation for overhead projections or for conversion to 35mm slides, you don't need to worry about transitions. If you will use the presentation as an on-screen slide show or will project the computer images to a large group, then transitions can enhance the presentation.

A transition setting specifies how PowerPoint will make the change from one slide to the next. You might specify a *fade*, for example, or a pattern that dissolves across slides. Such effects smooth the transition between slides. You should either choose an effect and stick with it through most of the presentation, or use *straight cuts* except when you want to emphasize a slide or idea. Too many different types of transitions can be distracting, especially when the slides are changed frequently. Properly used, however, transitions can give you some time between slides for narration and can help guide the viewer and indicate that a slide change is taking place.

To specify a transition, select a slide and then use the Tools **Transition...** command sequence from the main PowerPoint menu. This displays the Transition dialog, shown in Figure 5.37.

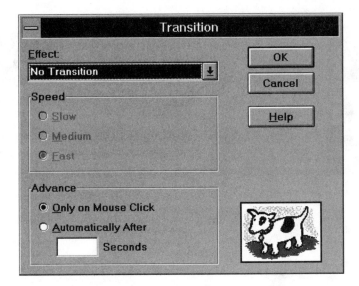

Figure 5.37 Transition Dialog

You can see from this figure that No Transition is the PowerPoint default. That means that when you enter Slide Show mode and press a key or click the left mouse button, the current slide is removed and the next slide is presented without any transition effect between them.

To view a list of possible transitions, click on the down facing arrow to the right of the Effect window. Your display should look like the one in Figure 5.38. Use the scroll bar to display the rest of the list, which contains at least 45 transition types.

To specify a transition, first select a slide, then choose a transition type from this pull-down list. You can also specify whether the transition is to occur at a fast, medium, or slow rate. When you make these specifications, PowerPoint demonstrates the transition on the small slide at the lower right-hand corner of this dialog. To see the example again, just click on the Speed button that you want to review. Even if the button is already selected, you can click on it and get a preview of how the transition will take place.

When you choose a transition you are specifying how the current (selected) slide will be presented, not the next slide. If slide #2 is the current slide and you choose a slow *dissolve*, for example, then slide #2 will appear after displaying slide #1 or slide #3 (if you are backing up through the show) with a slow dissolve.

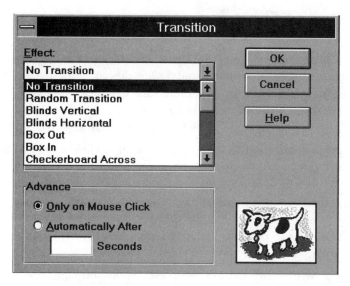

Figure 5.38 Pull-down Effect List in Transition Dialog

Try specifying a transition for slide #2. Pull down the Effect list and use the scroll bar to locate the Random Bars Vertical transition. Click on **Slow** in the Speed section of the dialog and observe the sample transition. Some of these transitions are reminiscent of techniques used in videos or movies, including dissolves, wipes, pattern dissolves, and so on. Experiment with various transition effects to find one (or several) that seem to fit the mood of your presentation.

One possible choice—especially as you are designing a presentation—is Random Transition, which is the first transition choice in the Effect list. If you specify Random Transition for every slide, then as you work with the slides you can view several different types of transitions. This may help you locate one that works best. You could leave Random Transition specified for your actual presentation and it might work fine. However, as I mentioned earlier, too many different effects can become distracting. As with any special effect or formatting, try it out, be aware of your subject and your audience, and use what works for you.

You may want to specify slow transitions for all slides until you have decided on what the final effects will be, then you may want to switch to medium or fast. In general, you want the effects to simply take you from one slide to the next, not get in the way of the show.

Presenting the Show

Now you're ready to present the show, or at least to step through it and practice your narration, evaluate transitions, study slide design, and so on. The more complex your presentation design, the more time this stage of design and building will take. It won't take long to step through our simple show, but the same techniques I'll show you here will work for any presentation you design.

To view the presentation as a slide show, simply click on the **Slide Show** icon at the bottom of the screen or use View **Slide Show...** to present the images in full-screen mode. PowerPoint will display the current slide and then wait for you to press a key or click the left mouse button before going on to the next slide. By starting in the Slide Sorter view and then launching the Slide Show view, you can begin the presentation anywhere you wish by selecting the starting slide from the Slide Sorter.

To advance to the next slide in the presentation you can press one of the following keys: the space bar, **Enter**, the **N** key, down arrow, page down, or right arrow, or you can click the left mouse button. To back up one slide, either click the right mouse button, hold the **Ctrl** key and press the left mouse button, or press one of the following keys: left arrow, the **P** key, up arrow, page up, or **Backspace**.

If you need a reminder of what keys do what during a presentation, press **F1** to display a help dialog that shows major keyboard and mouse functions (see Figure 5.39).

Notice that you can jump directly to any slide within the show by entering the slide number and then pressing **Enter**. To jump directly from slide 3 to slide 7, for example, simply press **7** on the numeric keypad or at the top of the keyboard and then press **Enter**. The slide in the number 7 position will appear, using whatever transition you have specified for that slide.

You can also use the Outline view or the Slide Sorter to jump to a specific slide. Click on **Outline View** or **Slide Sorter**, select the slide you want to view in the Slide Show view, then click on the **Slide Show** icon to restart the slide show.

Figure 5.39 Slide Show Help Screen

Adding Slide Notations

There's another PowerPoint feature that can be extremely useful during a live presentation. When you are in Slide Show view, PowerPoint places a small pencil icon at the lower right corner of the screen, but not until you move the mouse pointer after the slide is displayed. You won't see this icon if you use the keyboard or if you just click a mouse button to change slides. After a slide is displayed, however, you can move the mouse pointer to make the pencil icon appear.

Click once on this icon and the mouse pointer changes to a pencil. You can move this pencil anywhere on the slide and then hold down the left mouse button to draw on the slide. What you draw lasts only until you change slides, and it doesn't affect the slides stored on disk. This tool can help you emphasize some data or a feature displayed on the screen. Figure 5.40 shows one of the sample slides with drawings on it that were created during a presentation.

Figure 5.40 Sample Slide with Hand Drawings for Emphasis

Exiting a Slide Show Presentation

Press **Esc** at any time during a presentation to return to the screen that you were viewing prior to starting the slide show. If you were viewing the slides in Slide Sorter view before starting the slide show, you will be returned to the Slide Sorter if you press **Esc** during a show.

If you decide that one or more slides should not be used for a given presentation, don't delete the slide(s). Instead, select the slide you don't want to use, then use Tools **Hide Slide** to avoid displaying this slide in Slide Show view. It will still appear in the Slide view, the Slide Sorter, and the Outline.

Using a Build Slide

Another PowerPoint feature you may want to use with presentations is the Build or Progressive Disclosure slide. Although you can use successive slides to reveal information in a list, there may be times when you want to keep the same slide on the screen but have each item in the list appear when you need it.

You will probably use a Progressive Disclosure slide as part of a bullet list. Let's add a slide to the sample presentation we've used in this chapter and create a bullet list as the basis for a Progressive Disclosure slide. In general, to create a Progressive Disclosure slide you first design a slide that includes a list of information, such as a bullet list. Then you convert the slide to display each item in the list sequentially. I'll show you the steps for completing a build slide in this section.

 To create a Progressive Disclosure slide, your list must be constructed with one of the bullet list AutoLayout forms provided with PowerPoint.

N O T E

First open the presentation to where a bullet list slide exists, or create a new bullet list slide. Let's add a bullet list slide to the existing presentation as the last slide.

Click on the **Slide Sorter** icon at the bottom of the presentation screen to enable Slide Sorter view. Click in the space after the graph (slide #7 in our sample presentation).

Click on the **New Slide** button at the bottom of the screen. PowerPoint displays the New Slide dialog. Choose the second AutoLayout slide (the first slide in the second column), which has a title and bullet list layout. A blank slide is inserted. Double-click on the blank slide to open it for editing in Slide view. Your screen should look like Figure 5.41.

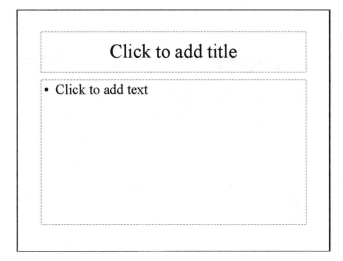

Figure 5.41 New Bullet List Slide in Slide View

Add a title by clicking in the title area of the slide. I used **Progressive Disclosure** as the title. Add several lines of bullet text by clicking on the **Click to add text** prompt. Press **Enter** between lines. My finished slide looks like Figure 5.42. This slide gives you a summary of the process for creating a *build* or Progressive Disclosure slide.

Figure 5.42 Finished Bullet List Build Slide

Now use Tools **Build...** to display the Build dialog, shown in Figure 5.43.

Figure 5.43 Build Dialog

Click on the **Build Body Text** button. Next, click on the **Dim Previous Points** button if you want previous lines of text to dim as each new line of text is added to the slide. If you select this option, also pull down the color dialog beneath this choice and specify which color, if any, you want to use for the dimmed material.

Click on the **Effect** button and pull down the list of special effects for displaying each line of text on the slide. Fly From Left is the default, but you have the same choices here as for slide transitions.

Click on **OK** to close the Build dialog. The current slide is now programmed for single-line display. You can check it by clicking on the **Slide Show View** button at the bottom of the screen (or by using View **Slide Show** from the main menu). PowerPoint will display the slide without any of the bullet list items. To add a new line of text, click the left mouse button, press the space bar, or use any of the other keys you normally use to advance to the next slide.

Adding a Blank Slide

When you advance past the last slide in a presentation, you will be returned to the previous presentation view. You may wish to add a blank slide to the end of the presentation so that when you step past the last slide in your show, a blank screen is displayed instead of the Slide or Slide Sorter view of the presentation.

Here's how to create a blank slide to go at the end of your show. Make the last slide in your presentation the current slide. Click on the **New Slide...** button at the bottom of the screen and choose the blank slide from the AutoLayout list (this is the last slide in the list).

Use Format **Slide Color Scheme...** to display the Slide Color Scheme dialog. Double-click on the **Background Color** button to display the Background Color dialog. Choose **Black** and click on **OK**. Click on **Apply** to close the dialog and return to Slide view with the black slide displayed.

N O T E

Be sure to save your work often as you build presentations in PowerPoint. After you have saved a file for the first time, you can use File **Save**, the disk icon on the Standard toolbar, or **Ctrl+S** on the keyboard to save the current file to its original file name.

Creating a Play List

A play list is another feature you might find useful as you present on-screen or projected presentations from within PowerPoint. You can create a text file called a play list, and then have PowerPoint or the PowerPoint Viewer load one or more presentations and play them in sequence.

To create a play list, use your word processor, the MS-DOS Editor, or any text editor that can save text files. Place the name of each presentation you want to display on a line by itself, including the **.PPT** extension. To play three presentations, one after the other, your text file would look something like this:

```
PRES01.PPT

PRES02.PPT

PRES03.PPT
```

However, instead of **PRES01.PPT**, you would enter the name of the first presentation you want to run. In place of **PRES02.PPT** you would enter the second file name, and so on. If you have files named **MISPRESS.PPT**, **JOBS.PPT**, and **SALES.PPT**, for example, you could run these presentations in sequence with the following play list:

```
MISPRESS.PPT

JOBS.PPT

SALES.PPT
```

After you have entered all of the names of the presentations you want to include in the play list, save the file in text (ASCII or DOS) format with a file extension of **.LST**. You could save a file as **SHOW.LST**, for example. You can put the file anywhere, but it probably is best to place it inside your PowerPoint subdirectory.

Now you can play the file by opening it from inside PowerPoint as you would a presentation. Use File **Open** from the main PowerPoint menu. When PowerPoint displays the file list, you can select the file you are using for the play file, or you can select another directory to locate the proper file.

When you double-click on the file name or select the file and click on **OK**, PowerPoint scans the file for the presentation names you have entered, loads them into PowerPoint in the order you specified, and begins playing the first slide. Each presentation is presented in the way that it normally would be. If you have set up a presentation for automatic slide advance, that's the way the program plays. On the other hand, if you have established manual slide advance, you must use the mouse or the keyboard to move to each successive slide.

You can also play any script file from within the PowerPoint Viewer (which should be installed as part of your PowerPoint installation). The Viewer icon (see Figure 5.44) may be in your Microsoft Solutions, Microsoft Office, or PowerPoint application window, depending on how you installed PowerPoint. If the Viewer icon is not in one of your application windows, you may not have installed it when you installed PowerPoint. Locate the VIEWER diskette that is part of your PowerPoint package. Insert it into one of your floppy drives and use the File **Run** command from the Microsoft Windows Program Manager. Enter the name **VSETUP** when the Run dialog asks for the name of the file you want to run.

PowerPoint
Viewer

Figure 5.44 PowerPoint Viewer Icon

When the first presentation on the list is complete, PowerPoint loads the next presentation and lets you step through those slides, and so on.

You can also launch a presentation from within the Program Manager if you have installed the PowerPoint Viewer. Use the File Manager to link your play files to the viewer. Then you can use File **Run** from the Program Manager to run the list files. You can also simply launch the viewer and enter the file name when the Viewer dialog asks for it.

To Sum Up

I can't possibly tell you everything there is to know about formatting slides or presenting slide shows in PowerPoint. There simply isn't enough room in this book. However, we have looked at PowerPoint's major features and I've shown you how to access all of its menus. You can go beyond what I've shown you in this chapter by exploring the menu and toolbars in PowerPoint on your own. A good technique for learning is to set up a simple presentation like the one I used in this chapter. It shouldn't be one you really hope to use so that you don't feel hesitant about experimenting with it. Then you can add slides, edit slides, move slides around, and play with PowerPoint features until you feel comfortable using them. Don't forget the help feature, which is a strong asset of this product. (I'll show you more about using PowerPoint help in Chapter 9.)

In the next chapter you'll learn how to set up a printer and how to print presentation data from PowerPoint. Then in Chapter 7 we'll look at ways to create presentation quality output such as overhead projection foils, video tape, and color slides.

Printing from PowerPoint

227

You may never print a presentation from PowerPoint. After all, the object of this program is to help you prepare slides for display on the computer screen, for projection directly from the computer, for the creation of 35mm slides, or for use with overhead projectors. If your presentations are relatively simple and informal, you may not need to print any of the presentation components.

However, PowerPoint supports more than just presentations. It also supports outlines, speaker notes, audience handouts, and so on. Even if you don't print the presentation itself, you may want to print some of the support material that PowerPoint produces along with it.

As I have suggested before, you may want to use PowerPoint to design report covers, section dividers, charts, and other visual material to use in a printed report. Although PowerPoint is primarily designed as a live presentation tool, printed material is a presentation too. And PowerPoint can support these efforts very well. Whatever the reason, if you want to print from PowerPoint, this chapter will show you how to approach it.

Configuring the Printer

When you install PowerPoint, it becomes part of the Microsoft Windows environment. That means that it can use common features of Windows that are available to all Windows applications. This includes the installed printers and other output drivers. In addition, PowerPoint installs a *driver* to facilitate the production of 35mm slides from your presentation art. This is the Genigraphics Driver, which you will see in your Windows Printer Setup or your PowerPoint Printer Setup dialog. I'll talk more about how to use this driver—and others—in Chapter 7.

For conventional printer output you will use whatever standard printer you normally use. The majority of business computer installations today have some type of laser printer available, and perhaps a dot matrix impact printer as well. If you are using PowerPoint on a network, you may have several printers at your disposal.

To find out what printers you can use to print PowerPoint information, use File **Print** to display the Print dialog shown in Figure 6.1.

Figure 6.1 PowerPoint Print Dialog

This is the dialog you'll use to actually print from inside PowerPoint. I'll tell you more about that later. To configure or choose a printer to use, click on the **Printer...** button on the right of this dialog. This displays the Print Setup dialog shown in Figure 6.2.

Figure 6.2 Print Setup Dialog

This is essentially the same printer setup dialog you would see from inside the Windows Control Panel. Again, because PowerPoint is a Windows product and is well-integrated into that environment, the printers installed for use by Windows are the same printers you will access from inside PowerPoint. Figure 6.3 shows the Printer Setup dialog from inside Windows on the same machine I used to create Figure 6.2. This is just to show you the printer list and the available options on the dialog. For the remaining discussions in this section, refer to Figure 6.2.

Figure 6.3 Microsoft Windows Printer Setup Dialog

The system from which this screen shot was taken has six printers available. Actually, there are three printers (Apple LaserWriter II NTX, HP LaserJet III, IBM Graphics) and two non-printer drivers (Genigraphics Driver, Microsoft At Work Fax).

You have the same printer configuration options with PowerPoint as you do with Windows. You can specify paper source, for example, or you can specify an encapsulated *PostScript* file.

Notice that each of these printer names is associated with a computer *port*. The Apple LaserWriter II NTX, for example, is set up to print on *LPT1*, the standard printer port, as is the IBM Graphics printer. The HP LaserJet III also is installed for output on FILE. This is not another printer, but merely another porting of the same LaserJet printer.

Normally, once you have selected a printer from this list, you won't use this dialog again until you change printers on your computer or until you want to create a printer file on disk to send to another site for printing or for conversion to 35mm slides. Of course if you are working on a network you may change printers fairly often, depending on the type of printing you want to do or which printer is busy.

Suppose you have an HP LaserJet connected to your local computer, but you want to use the features of a PostScript printer located on the network. You have previously selected the HP LaserJet and perhaps have used it for printing before. To specify a PostScript printer—such as the Apple LaserWriter II NTX— use File **Print...** to display the Print dialog. Then click on the **Printer...** button on this dialog to display the Print Setup dialog. From there you can double-click on the Apple LaserWriter II NTX printer listed in the Printers window. If you want to establish this new printer as the default printer, click on the **Set As Default Printer** button. Now, whenever you load PowerPoint, this is the printer that will be used instead of the original printer.

You can also select another printer by using the cursor movement keys to highlight the printer you want and then pressing **Enter** or clicking on **OK**. In addition, you can select the printer you want with the mouse and then click on **OK** to choose it.

With the new printer selected, PowerPoint returns you to the Print dialog. From this dialog you can specify how much of the presentation to print and how to print it.

Specifying What to Print

The default output is slides without builds. When you print slides, PowerPoint configures the output in a *landscape* format (slides wider than they are tall), one image per page. Slides are printed in a 10- x 7.5-inch frame. To specify another type of output, click on the down arrow beside the Print What field of this dialog. You'll see the choices in Figure 6.4.

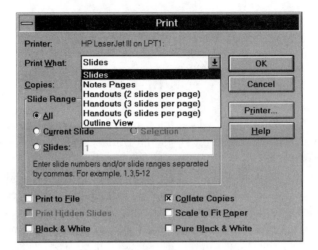

Figure 6.4 Print What Pull-Down Menu on Print Dialog

You have the following choices for PowerPoint printer output: Slides (with Builds), Slides (without Builds), Notes Pages, Handouts, and Outline View. Let's look at additional details of each of these output choices.

 If your presentation does not include any build slides (slides with Progressive Disclosure), you are not given the option of printing Slides with Builds. The first option in this dialog would be simply Slides.

Slides (with Builds)

This option prints each phase of the build slide as an individual page. If you have six bullet items in a build list, for example, PowerPoint prints six slides—each one showing an additional item in the list. If you have only one build slide in the presentation, then only one slide is expanded in this way; the remainder of the slides are printed with all of the information for each slide on a single page. Slides are printed in a 10- x 7.5-inch landscape format.

Slides (without Builds)

This option prints all slides in the presentation without builds. If you have a slide with six items in a bullet list in build format, this option prints the slide once, showing all of the entries on the bullet list. Slides are printed in a 10- x 7.5-inch landscape format.

Notes Pages

This option prints the speaker's notes pages for the slides specified in the print range. Notes Pages show one slide at a time in a reduced size at the top of a *portrait*-format page. Each page has room at the bottom for notes to accompany the slide. You can use the Notes Pages to help you organize a presentation or to use during the presentation to help you remember the main points you want to cover while the slide is displayed. Figure 6.5 shows how a Notes Page prints and is displayed on the screen. PowerPoint defaults to 12 point text on this screen. If this is too small to read comfortably, click on the font size arrow on the Format Bar and choose a larger font.

Figure 6.5 Sample Notes Pages Screen

Handouts

Handout pages are designed to provide the audience with material about the presentation. You can print handouts with two, three, or six slides per page. When you specify two slides per page, PowerPoint prints two slides, one above the other in portrait format. When you specify a three-slide handout format, PowerPoint places three slides on a portrait page, one above the other. A six-slide format produces a printout with two columns of three slides each on a portrait page.

> **NOTE** If your presentation includes more slides than will fit on a couple of handout sheets, you should include slide numbers with the slides. Use View **Master Slide Master** to display the Slide Master screen. Then use Insert **Page Number** to place a page number symbol on the slide. Grab the number box and place it on the slide where you want it to appear in the show and on the handout sheets.

Outline View

When you specify Outline View on the Print dialog, PowerPoint prints the outline for the current slide show instead of the slide images themselves. The Outline View includes the slide title and any bullet list text that was inserted from an AutoLayout slide.

Special Printing Considerations

There's more to printing a PowerPoint presentation than specifying whether to print slides, presentations, handouts, or outlines.

Specifying Number of Copies

You can specify more than one copy of the items you are printing. Obviously, if you are preparing audience handouts, you may want to print more than one copy. Select the **Copies** field and type the number of copies you want to print, or use the up and down arrows beside the Copies field to select the number of copies to print.

Specifying Slide Range

The default slide range to print is All, which prints all of the slides in the current presentation. You can print a single slide by clicking on the **Current Slide** button. This will print the slide that is selected or is being displayed when you start the print routine.

To print a range of slides—from one slide to all of the slides in the presentation—click on the **Slides** button and enter a range of slides in the field beside this prompt. You can enter slide ranges in a number of ways:

X-Y	Print slides **X** through **Y** inclusive
X-	Print slide **X** and all of the slides that follow it
A-B, X-Y	Print slides **A** through **B** inclusive and **X** through **Y** inclusive, but omit the slides between **B** and **X**
X-X	Print only slide **X**

Selecting Slides to Print

You can print a selection of slides by choosing the slides to print before launching the Print routine. The easiest way to select a range of slides is to display the presentation in Slide Sorter format. Then hold down the left mouse button and drag a box around the slides you want to print.

Specifying Print Options

There are six print options that you can select on the Print dialog. Two of these—Print Hidden Slides and Collate Copies—are selected by default. You can also specify Print to File, print in Black & White, Scale to Fit Paper, and Pure Black & White. These print options are chosen in addition to the Slide Range, Copies, and Print What selections.

Print to File

Use this option to create a file of printer commands that can be used to print the specified selection to any printer of the same type specified in the File Print Printer... dialog. If you are using an HP LaserJet printer, for example, then the print file that results from choosing the Print to File option will contain Hewlett-

Packard printer commands to print the specified part of the current presentation. If the selected printer is a PostScript printer, then the file created by PowerPoint will be PostScript commands.

After you click on **OK** on the Print dialog, PowerPoint asks for the name of the file you want to use to store the printer commands. Creating a print file in this way lets you print a PowerPoint slide or presentation on a printer not attached to your computer or on a computer that does not have PowerPoint installed. To use a print file, enter **COPY filename PRN**, where **filename** is the name of the print file.

If you have problems printing a file in this way, add the **/B** (for binary) switch after the copy command. This tells DOS to pass the characters through to the printer exactly as they appear in the file.

Print Hidden Slides

PowerPoint prints hidden slides by default, but you can turn off this default by clicking on the **Print Hidden Slides** button. You may want to hide one or more slides in a presentation that are not appropriate for a given audience, without removing the slides from the presentation. However, if you want to print all of the slides in a presentation—even those marked hidden—you can do this by accepting PowerPoint's default. To avoid printing the hidden slides, click once on this button and none of the slides marked hidden will print.

Black & White

This option prints all slides in black and white, turning all fills on objects to white, or to black and white if the fill uses a pattern. Unbordered objects that don't include text appear with a thin black frame.

Collate Copies

This option—a PowerPoint default—keeps the pages of a presentation together when you print multiple copies. If you print three copies of a ten-page presentation, PowerPoint prints all ten pages of the presentation in order three times. Without Collate Copies selected, PowerPoint prints three copies of page one, three copies of page two, three copies of page three, and so on until the print job is completed.

Scale to Fit Paper

The Scale to Fit Paper option causes PowerPoint to print all slides so that they fit the paper selected with your printer.

Pure Black & White

Pure Black & White printing goes beyond the Black & White option. This option turns all fills to white, converts all text to black, adds outlines (borders) to all filled objects, and reproduces pictures in grayscale. You may want to choose this option for draft output on a color printer or for more readable output on a black and white printer.

Configuring the Presentation

In addition to specifying what parts of a presentation to print, you can make changes to the format of the presentation that affect the way your slides print. By default, PowerPoint prints slides in landscape format in a 10- x 7.5-inch frame. You can use the Slide Setup dialog to make additional specifications about the way PowerPoint slides print. Use File **Slide Setup...** to display the Slide Setup dialog shown in Figure 6.6.

Figure 6.6 Slide Setup Dialog

Setting Slide Size

The PowerPoint size default is for on-screen presentation. You have other choices for slide size, including standard letter paper, A4 paper, 35mm slides, and custom sizes. You can see these choices by pulling down the list in the **Slides Sized for** field of the Slide Setup dialog. Click on the arrow beside this field to see the list in Figure 6.7.

Figure 6.7 Slides Sized for List on Slide Setup Dialog

In the following sections I'll give you more information about each of these choices.

On-Screen Show

This choice sets the size of presentation slides to a width of 10 inches and a height of 7.5 inches. This is an aspect ratio of 3:4.

Letter Paper (8.5x11 in)

The Letter Paper choice is basically the same as On-screen Show. This setting assumes a landscape orientation specification. When you print a slide on paper, the slide prints sideways so that you look at the slide with the long portion of the paper oriented horizontally. (You can change the orientation on the Slide Setup dialog.) This is also an aspect ratio of 3:4. It is the most common selection for printing overhead transparencies.

Genigraphics Corporation
Products and Services
1994

The title slide sets the mood for the show, giving the audience a first impression of your topic and of your company.

This slide shows poor formatting: too-large text, too much white space at the bottom, no color. You have up to 16 million colors at your disposal. Use them!

. . . .

Genigraphics Corporation

Products and Services
1994

. . . .

Reduce white space and make the text smaller, less overwhelming. This slide uses layout space more efficiently.

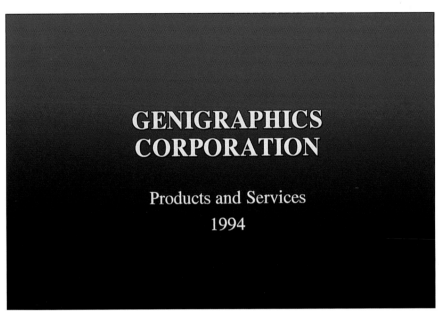

Use a standard company font for titles to promote consistency. This slide also adds a background treatment for atmosphere and depth. To establish the show and confirm the company image, a creative title slide can stay on the screen as the audience enters and leaves.

Genigraphics' Joey Schroth used the drawing tools to produce a company logo. He created the sweeping arcs with the arc tool to add impact to this slide.

Other strong points: simple and succinct copy; a limited number of typefaces; a dark background with a light foreground; three simple colors that don't distract from the message.

Note that the subdued design elements focus attention on the content which fills 3/4 of the background area.

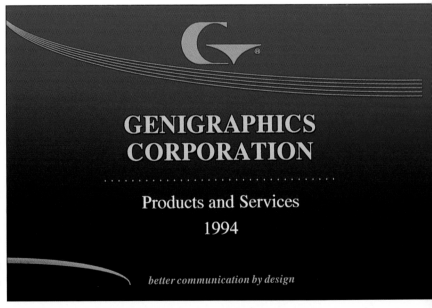

TIP: Add a company jingle or slogan for multimedia presentations.

TEXT CHART EVOLUTION

Genigraphics Corporation Is The Leading Supplier Of Visual Communications, Providing Presentation And Marketing Support Materials To Companies And Organizations

Genigraphics was the first company to use computer graphics for production of color presentation and marketing materials. In the 1970's, Genigraphics automated the production of 35mm slide presentations by employing their own computer systems and software. In the 80's, as specialized computer technologies and companies took on more of their own graphics production in-house, Genigraphics again led the way with highly automated imaging services.

In the 90's, as the lines between presentations, desktop publishing and marketing collateral have blurred, Genigraphics has broadened it's scope, applying over two decades of experience in the design and production of graphic communications in all areas of marketing communications. Genigraphics continues to provide the best value without any compromise in their commitment to meet customer deadlines.

This slide contains too much information and too little white space. Break the title into a title and subtitle. Use succinct words and phrases, and enlarge text. Finally, add color or art to help the audience remember the message.

· · · · · · · · · · · ·

· · · · · · · · · · · ·

This slide is better because: the content is basic, more succinct; the title stands out; the subtitle is associated with the title by proximity; the body copy is to the point; the presenter can elaborate each point; the text is large and pronounced, yet comfortable.

Genigraphics Corporation
A Computer Graphics Pioneer

1970s - 1st to use computer graphics for production of color presentation and marketing materials

1980s - Automated Imaging Services

1990s - The Total Solution - Presentation and marketing materials

Genigraphics Corporation
A Computer Graphics Pioneer

- **1970s - 1st to use computer graphics for production of color presentation and marketing materials**
- **1980s - Automated Imaging Services**
- **1990s - The Total Solution - Presentation and marketing materials**

Color with the MOVNGLC.PPT template creates interest and adds impact. Remember, color increases recognition by 78%, and increases comprehension by 73%. Bullets on the list help the audience focus on the topics while the choice of fonts provides emphasis.

. . . .

Genigraphics Corporation
A Computer Graphics Pioneer

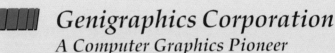

- 1970s - 1st to use computer graphics for production of color presentation and marketing materials
- 1980s - Automated Imaging Services
- 1990s - *The Total Solution*
  - » Presentation and marketing materials

. . . .

You can enhance basic templates. In this slide the computer is from the Clip Art Gallery, and the screen image is a drawing. Additional text formatting improves impact. In addition, you should use consistent colors and layout.

DATA CHART EVOLUTION

Current Presentation Market - Material Overview

Two-thirds of all presentations are given inside the firm. These presentations are almost by definition, informal meetings where people are presenting in a conference room. Twenty-two percent of presentations are delivered in someone's office. This means that presentation graphics programs are being used for one-on-one and one-on-two discussions, not just for podium presentations to large audiences.

Most presentations are in the conventional media: overhead, and paper. Seventy-three percent of all presentations were made on black and white paper and overheads, with twelve percent being color. Once again, evidence that most presentations are informal. Seven percent of media usage consists of 35 mm slides. This number is expected to stay about the same over the next few years. Electronic presentations are growing -- even though they represent only eight percent of all presentations made, some twenty plus percent of all users now give electronic presentations.

This slide is too dense and communicates the specifics of data values poorly. Everything in this copy is important, but it is difficult to interpret in this form.

. . . .

Presentation Market Overview

■ Usage

Outside Firm	36%
Your Office	22%
Conference Room	42%

■ Media

Paper & Overheads	85%
35mm Slides	7%
Electronic	8%

. . . .

Use lists whenever possible. Lists reduce text and enhance retention. This data type is a Column Chart. The MOVNGLNC.PPT Template adds color and helps the audience focus on main points on the display.

Use charts and graphs t aid data interpretation. Ba charts give side-by-sid comparisons and pie char give comparisons of th whole. In general, graph are visually appealin and communicate dat more effectively.

Three dimensional charts have more impact. Five to ten colors per visual are enough. Too much information is still included in this sample so make two slides. This image is well suited for either a color overhead or 35mm slide presentation. Avoid using red and green together since they can be hard to differentiate. Avoid red because in financial data it has negative connotations.

Africa:
Total Annual Precipitation and Average Annual Temperature

Station	Precipitation in	mm	Temperature °F	°C
Agadir	9	229	66	19
Cairo	1	25	72	22
Cape Town	26	660	63	17
Harare	30	760	64	18
Kinshasa	60	1,524	77	25
Nairobi	36	914	64	18
Yaundé	60	1,524	75	24

Even with its many numbers this slide works because of the pleasing color scheme and the background treatment. The clip art map and subtle colors reinforce the African theme. The subdued tone could let the slide stay on the screen relatively long to give the audience time to study the numbers.

. . . .

. . . .

The strength of this slide is in its simplicity, creative layout, and good use of color. The template is BLSTRIPC.PPT. The shuttle clip art was enhanced with clouds and exhaust that were created with the drawing tools. The dark background and sharp contrast enhance this slide's impact.

Microsoft PowerPoint
What You See Is What You Get

- No more previewing!
- Directly manipulate graphics, text, colors – even complete slides

Even with its high concentration of data, this design presents data clearly. Clip art flags enhance the association of data. The LINSBLUS.PPT template offers a dark background brightening and enhancing the colors in the clip art.

. . . .

. . . .

PowerPoint helps you communicate data relationships clearly with a flow chart. The METLBARS.PPT template enhances the crisp, graphic nature of this design. Extra space around boxes lends clarity while the bold attribute helps emphasize necessarily small text.

A4 Paper (210x297 mm)

This choice is for European-sized paper. It sets the slide image size to 26 cm wide (10.83 inches) and 18 cm high (7.5 inches). The aspect ratio is between that for On-screen Show and 35mm Slides.

35mm Slides

For 35mm slides, PowerPoint sets the width to 11.25 inches and the height to 7.5 inches, for an aspect ratio of 2:3.

Custom

The Custom setting is what the name implies. When you choose this setting, you can click on the up and down arrows beside the Width and Height boxes on the Slide Setup dialog. In fact, you can force the Custom selection by clicking on one of the up or down arrows with any setting visible in the Slides Sized for window. PowerPoint automatically jumps to Custom when you change the height or width from the pre-set values for any standard slide size.

Changing Orientation

PowerPoint selects landscape orientation for slides of all sizes. The support material—outlines, handouts, and speaker's notes—prints in portrait orientation. However, you can change these defaults by clicking on the proper button in the Orientation section of this dialog. Simply click on **Portrait** to change the slide default from **Landscape**.

Figure 6.8 shows the standard landscape orientation for an on-screen display, while Figure 6.9 shows how the display changes when you switch to portrait orientation.

Notice that many parts of a slide can change when you change orientation. In our sample, part of the text is obscured when the width of the display area is reduced by the portrait orientation setting. With other slides you may not see such a dramatic change. You may only notice a narrowing of some of the objects. If your application requires portrait orientation, you should specify that setting before you design the slides.

Figure 6.8 On-screen Show in Landscape Orientation

Figure 6.9 On-screen Show in Portrait Orientation

One application where you may want to change these defaults is when you are printing overhead projection foils. Although many projectors can handle landscape or portrait orientation, some do a better job in portrait orientation.

In addition, you may want to use landscape orientation to print handouts, especially if you are putting six slides on a page. A landscape orientation for a page this full may make it easier for the audience to use, depending on the type of slides your presentation includes. You can test the orientation for handouts by choosing landscape. Then, from the Print dialog, specify only the current slide. PowerPoint uses the current slide as a starting point and prints the number of slides you specify in the Print What field of the Print dialog.

Setting Slide Numbering

PowerPoint automatically numbers the slides in your presentation beginning at one with the first slide. You can change this default numbering scheme by clicking on the up arrow beside the **Number Slides From** field on the Slide Setup dialog. Or, you can select the default number in this field and type a new number on the keyboard.

Normally, when your presentation stands alone as a separate presentation, you will leave this default setting alone. However, there may be times when you want to put two or more presentations together as a single show. In this case you might start numbering the second set of slides after the last slide in the first show; the third show would start numbering after the last slide in the second show, and so on.

NOTE Even if you specify a slide numbering scheme, PowerPoint won't include a number on the slides unless you have specified slide numbers on the Slide Master. Use View **Master Slide Master** to display the Slide Master screen. Then use Insert **Page Number** to place a number where you want it on the slide master. Then numbers will appear on all slides in your presentation, beginning with the number you specify in the Number Slides From field on the Slide Setup dialog.

Solving Printing Problems

Printing presentations from inside PowerPoint should be straightforward and you should encounter no problems. There are a few situations that may cause some head scratching, however. The best general advice for solving printing problems is to check all of the settings in the Print dialog and in the Slide Setup dialog. If these are correct, then your presentation should print as you expect. If you encounter any of the situations listed in the following sections, perhaps the suggestions included will help.

Nothing Prints

Suppose you seem to be doing everything right and you get no error messages, yet nothing comes out on the printer. There are some very common causes of this problem.

Wrong Printer

Probably the most common cause of nothing printing, if you are connected to a network, is that you have specified the wrong printer. The slides you're printing are coming out, but not on the printer you're watching. In this case, check the printer definition on the Print Setup dialog (File **Print Printer…**).

The same thing can happen if you have specified the wrong printer driver even if you're not on a network. If you are using a PostScript printer, for example, and you send it non-PostScript commands, the printer may print nothing. If you've sent the wrong commands to a printer one or two times, you may have to turn the printer off and then back on again to get it to print correctly, even after you change the printer definition inside PowerPoint.

Previous Printer Problem

In the Windows environment you don't actually print directly to a printer. Instead, the Windows *Print Manager* grabs the output from an application and spools it to disk. That clears the print operation quickly and lets Windows manage printing in the background. Also, you can send printer output from multiple applications without waiting for the previous print job to finish. Multiple print jobs—whether from a single application or from several applications—stack up in the Print Manager and are sent to the printer in turn.

However, suppose one of these print jobs encounters a printer error. Perhaps the printer ran out of paper, or you sent work to the printer and forgot to turn on the printer. Whatever the cause, the print job that encountered the error is stalled, waiting for the printer problem to be corrected.

You can find out if your printer is stalled because the Print Manager is waiting for problem resolution by following these steps. Shrink PowerPoint (click on the **Minimize** button at the upper right corner of the screen). Locate the Print

Manager icon, shown in Figure 6.10. If your printer is stalled, the Print Manager icon is probably on the *desktop*, indicating that the utility is running minimized. If you don't find it on the desktop, open the Program Manager and locate the Print Manager icon in the Main applications window.

Print Manager

Figure 6.10 Print Manager Icon

Double-click on this icon to open the Print Manager. You should see an error message similar to the one in Figure 6.11. Note that this Print Manager screen came from Windows for Workgroups. If you are running standard Windows, your Print Manager will look different.

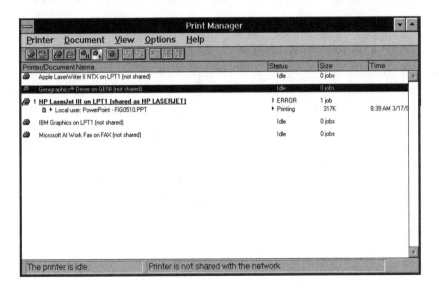

Figure 6.11 Print Manager with Print Error Message

You will get an error message such as this any time the Print Manager can't complete the print job. To correct the problem, turn on the printer, add paper, or correct any other problems (such as a paper jam). Then click on the printer name in the Print Manager to select it. Finally, use Printer **Resume Printer** from the main Print Manager menu (or click on the **Resume** button on the Print Manager toolbar) to restart the print process.

N O T E You may have a Print Manager error even if you think you have corrected a printer problem. When the printer runs out of paper, for example, the printer stops printing until you add paper. As soon as the printer senses that it has paper, printing resumes as the printer continues to dump the contents of its internal print buffer. It looks as if everything is okay. However, only the information that remains in the print buffer is printed. The data that remains in the Print Manager *print spooler* won't resume printing until you open the Print Manager and use the **Resume Printer** command.

You can also make room for later print jobs by selecting the document that is stalled in the Print Manager, then using the Document **Delete Document** command (or pressing **Del** on the keyboard). This will remove the partial document from the Print Manager and will move the next document up in the queue.

Garbled Output

Suppose you print a slide or a presentation and the printer seems to work, but you get only a partial printout or garbled data on the page. This probably means you have selected the wrong printer driver. Depending on the particular printer you are using and the driver you have specified, an incorrect driver may cause no output at all, or it may cause the printout to be unreadable.

One common problem is getting a series of text lines on the page instead of the picture you expected (see Figure 6.12). This probably means you have chosen a PostScript printer driver in PowerPoint, but your printer is a LaserJet or other non-PostScript device.

The solution to the problem is to check the settings in the Print Setup dialog (File **Print Printer...**) to make sure you have selected the proper printer driver for your printer.

```
▯%!PS-Adobe-3.0
%%Creator: Windows PSCRIPT
%%Title: PowerPoint - FIG0510.PPT
%%BoundingBox: 14 9 597 784
%%DocumentNeededResources: (atend)
%%DocumentSuppliedResources: (atend)
%%Pages: (atend)
%%BeginResource: procset Win35Dict 3 1
/Win35Dict 290 dict def Win35Dict begin/bd{bind def}bind def/in{72
mul}bd/ed{exch def}bd/ld{load def}bd/tr/translate ld/gs/gsave ld/gr
/grestore ld/M/moveto ld/L/lineto ld/rmt/rmoveto ld/rlt/rlineto ld
/rct/rcurveto ld/st/stroke ld/n/newpath ld/sm/setmatrix ld/cm/currentmatrix
ld/cp/closepath ld/ARC/arcn ld/TR{65536 div}bd/lj/setlinejoin ld/lc
/setlinecap ld/ml/setmiterlimit ld/sl/setlinewidth ld/scignore false
def/sc{scignore{pop pop pop}{0 index 2 index eq 2 index 4 index eq
and{pop pop 255 div setgray}{3{255 div 3 1 roll}repeat setrgbcolor}ifelse}ifelse}bd
/FC{bR bG bB sc}bd/fC{/bB ed/bG ed/bR ed}bd/HC{hR hG hB sc}bd/hC{
/hB ed/hG ed/hR ed}bd/PC{pR pG pB sc}bd/pC{/pB ed/pG ed/pR ed}bd/sM
matrix def/PenW 1 def/iPen 5 def/mxF matrix def/mxE matrix def/mxUE
matrix def/mxUF matrix def/fBE false def/iDevRes 72 0 matrix defaultmatrix
dtransform dup mul exch dup mul add sqrt def/fPP false def/SS{fPP{
/SV save def}{gs}ifelse}bd/RS{fPP{SV restore}{gr}ifelse}bd/EJ{gsave
showpage grestore}bd/#C{userdict begin/#copies ed end}bd/FEbuf 2 string
def/FEglyph(G )def/FE{1 exch{dup 16 FEbuf cvrs FEglyph exch 1 exch
putinterval 1 index exch FEglyph cvn put}for}bd/SM{/iRes ed/cyP ed
```

Figure 6.12 PostScript Commands on Printer Output

To Sum Up

Printing from inside PowerPoint is a relatively simple process. For the most part you will accept the program's default settings for page size, orientation, and printer. If you need to adjust the settings for a particular output need, or if you have problems with your printer, then the suggestions in this chapter should help you get on the right track.

In the next chapter we will look at some additional presentation output considerations, including producing 35mm slides and videos.

Roland

Think life

Ahead? Compare

the Past

Creating Presentation Output with PowerPoint

In the last chapter I showed you how to print the various components of a PowerPoint presentation. But there is more to using PowerPoint than just printing the output as slides, outlines, notes, or handouts on a standard printer. You can also use PowerPoint to create slides that you can use for live presentations, or to create 35mm slides or videos.

In some ways you can improve your PowerPoint results by considering the output first. Will you be printing PowerPoint images in color? Is the final output for projection—either 35mm slides or overhead transparencies? Who is the audience? What type of images will you produce?

Before creating any graphic images with PowerPoint, decide what form of media will be used to present the images. Based on the type of media, different rules should be followed. For example, if the final images will be printed on a laser printer, and included as black and white images within a business report, there is no need to take advantage of PowerPoint's colors when creating the image. On the other hand, if the images will be converted into some form of color media, such as 35mm slides or overhead transparencies, then color is a vital component of the finished image.

You should consider these questions for each series of drawings you produce in PowerPoint. This will help you visualize the output before you start image design and production. In this chapter, I'll give you some insight into using PowerPoint for these applications.

35mm Slides

Once you have created a presentation that you can show on your computer screen, you can also create 35mm slides as another way of presenting your show.

You can create 35mm slides from any PowerPoint presentation, but the results will be better if you establish 35mm format for your slides before they are designed (use File **Slide Setup...**). This ensures better sizing and formatting.

A slide version of your presentation offers several advantages over computer projection or overhead transparencies. For one thing, you don't have to carry a computer with you when you make the presentation. Moreover, almost any hotel, convention center, or company conference room is equipped with a slide projector. However, you may have trouble finding a computer of the type you need, especially with projection equipment.

Slides offer much higher resolution than the computer monitor. If you have a slide reproduced by a slide service, you can get 3500–4000 lines of resolution. Some of these services will enhance the basic computer display to take advantage of this resolution. You'll also find it easy to rearrange a slide show once the slides are produced. You can use a simple hand-held viewer or light table and sort slides at home, at your hotel, or even on an airplane.

Many professional presenters also find that 35mm slides help the speaker make a good impression on the audience. When a speaker arrives for a presentation with a set of slides, it is obvious that considerable time has been spent preparing for the show.

NOTE Even if you design a slide show for multiple presentations, a good technique is to prepare a custom title slide for each presentation. That way, when your standard show opens, the audience sees the name of their company or conference, the date, and the topic right at the start. This enhances your image as one who prepares carefully, and it improves audience acceptance of your material.

Besides designing the images for the slide format, there are additional guidelines that can help you prepare a successful presentation:

- Prepare at least two copies of the slides for each presentation. This lets you use some slides more than once, either for emphasis or to fill in weak spots that you discover later. It also gives you a backup set of slides in the event that you lose the primary one.

- Plan on enough slides to carry the show. A good rule of thumb is two to three slides per minute of presentation. If you leave one slide on the screen too long, the audience loses interest and your show loses momentum.

- Learn as much as you can about the room where your presentation will be made. If it can be made totally dark, you can be more creative in slide design. For general designs or where you aren't sure about the location, use dark backgrounds and light letters on your slides. That way, if you have to present in a relatively light room, the material will still be visible.

- Have someone else proofread your slides on the computer or from a printout before you have them converted to film. Don't proof your own slides; it is too easy to miss spelling and other errors. Reenie Feingold, who is the owner of Visual Horizons in New York and is a professional presenter, recommends three steps to slide proofing:

  1) Read first for content.

  2) Read the second time word-by-word looking for spelling errors.

  3) Read the third time from the rear to the front and from the bottom to the top. That way you will evaluate each word as it stands alone without the influence of context. Also check numbers in reverse order.

- Get professional help in slide design. PowerPoint helps you overcome the mechanical problems of creating presentations, but we all can use some professional design help in telling specific stories. The more complex or the more important your presentation, the more valuable professional advice will be. Remember, you may need only one person in your audience to change their mind, to modify their buying habits, or to say yes to your proposal to make the expense of preparing a professional presentation cost-effective.

- Rehearse your presentation alone and in front of a group. You can learn your presentation in the same way you learn to type or to play the piano. Your mouth seems to remember the right words if you have enough preparation time.

Obviously, if you are designing a presentation for 35mm slide display, you'll need some way to convert the slide images from the computer display to slides. There are two basic ways to create 35mm slides from a computer display. You can either take a picture of the screen or you can send the slides to a file for conversion by a slide service.

Using a Screen Camera

You can hire a slide service to produce film slides from your computer images (see the following section for more information). However, if most of the work you do with PowerPoint involves producing slides, then it may be more cost-effective to produce the slides yourself with a screen capture camera. These cameras consist of a high resolution black and white or color television monitor, a light mask, a camera mount, and an electronic interface to your computer. Depending on the device design, you may plug in a circuit board to serve as a custom interface between your computer and the camera display, or you may attach the camera directly to your computer's video display adapter or cable. When you display an image on the computer screen, the connection to the screen capture camera displays the same image on the camera display.

You then take a picture of the screen with a quality 35mm camera. The camera may be part of the camera system, or you may purchase the camera separately or use a camera you already have. Usually these devices include electronic control of the camera. The camera—although it looks in many respects like a standard 35mm camera—may not include a standard viewfinder and other features you usually associate with modern cameras.

The LFR film recorder from Lasergraphics is one example of this type of device. It is capable of 4,000 line resolution. You can use it with either standard 35mm or Polaroid film packs. The LFR attaches to your PC through a custom bus-level interface that includes a graphics co-processor to speed up operation. For more information, contact Lasergraphics, Inc., 17671 Cowan Ave., Irvine, CA 92714, 714-727-2651.

Similar devices include the offerings of Polaroid Corporation and Agfa. In fact, Polaroid offers a number of output options for computer presentation, including multiple file recorders and projection devices. The Polaroid CI-3000S and CI-5000S devices, for example, use a special interface to attach to your computer. Then you can use Polaroid or conventional cameras to capture screen images to film (see Figure 7.1). For more information, contact Polaroid at 565 Technology Square, Cambridge, MA 02139, 617-386-2000.

Agfa also offers a range of products to support desktop publishing and computer-based presentation. You can get more information from Agfa at 200 Ballardvale Street, Wilmington, MA 01887, 508-658-5600.

Using a Slide Service

A number of companies will produce these slides for you. This is the way to go if you only need an occasional slide or slide show. Generally, the procedure is to create the images you need in PowerPoint. Then you either mail a diskette to the company, or you send the image files over a modem directly to a computer or through an electronic mail store and forward service such as CompuServe.

Figure 7.1 Polaroid Film Recorders

Most slide production companies can load up the graphics image, edit it, add backgrounds, change the color, and make other minor changes before producing a high resolution 35mm color slide for you.

NOTE For a text slide, never fill up more than 75 percent of the slide with text. Many slide services recommend that no more than twenty words be used in a title or text slide. When creating images with PowerPoint, be sure that the information being depicted in the slides will not be misunderstood by the audience. Misunderstandings can easily occur if too much information is included within the image, or if part of the graphic image does not pertain to the point being conveyed.

Color has a major impact on the visual appeal of graphic images that are created with PowerPoint and converted into slides or overheads. Lines, text, and all graphics should contrast with the background color being used. In most cases, dark backgrounds with light-colored text and graphics work best for slides. The opposite is true for overhead transparencies. Many of the borders and color clip art images available for use with PowerPoint can be edited. This means that the colors of the border or clip art images can be changed to maintain color continuity throughout the presentation.

For more detailed information about putting together a 35mm slide presentation, consider an Eastman Kodak book titled *Slides: Planning and Producing Slide Programs*, which covers the basic rules for developing slide shows. This book does not specifically cover the use of computer generated images. However, much of the information in this book is applicable.

Many of the service companies will go beyond simply producing slides from your computer images. They can consult on slide design, write scripts, produce custom backgrounds, do color correction, and more. You can also find companies that will produce your initial slides for free so that you can learn about their services and receive suggestions about your presentation. Visual Horizons, for example, offers three free slides from your software. The images will be finished in about three days and returned via first class mail.

When it is time to produce your entire show, you can choose from a variety of slide services and service times. In fact, Visual Horizons, like many other slide service providers, offers 24 hour service for a premium price. This company, and others, can also produce overhead projection slides from your computer files.

In general, when you use a slide service, the company can either use native files from PowerPoint or they may send you additional software that converts PowerPoint data to a format compatible with their equipment. This software may operate as a stand-alone application, or it may simply install as a printer driver in the Windows Control Panel. Then, when you want to prepare material for conversion by the service, use File **Print Printer...** to choose the proper driver and send the information to a disk file.

In fact, one such driver is shipped with PowerPoint. You can see it in the Print Setup dialog as **Genigraphics Driver on GENI**. The following sections provide a brief summary of the services available from a few selected service providers.

Genigraphics

Genigraphics is one of the multi-function service providers that is specifically targeted at PowerPoint. It was Genigraphics that designed the templates for the new version of PowerPoint. The Genigraphics Driver supplied with PowerPoint lets you print a presentation to a disk file complete with job instructions, billing information, delivery requirements, and other data, then send it to Genigraphics electronically. It will be processed at one of Genigraphics' locations and most likely transmitted to Memphis, TN for final production. The Genigraphics office in Memphis is across the street from the Federal Express distribution center, which means that if you submit a job to Genigraphics today you can get finished slides on your desk via Federal Express tomorrow.

To submit a PowerPoint presentation to Genigraphics, start by loading the presentation and making it current. Then use File **Print** (**Ctrl+P**) to display the PowerPoint Print dialog, shown in Figure 7.2. (If you are specifying 35mm slides, review the information on formatting presentations for 35mm slides in the previous section of this chapter).

Figure 7.2 PowerPoint Print Dialog

Click on **Printer...** to display the Print Setup dialog shown in Figure 7.3.

If you have installed PowerPoint correctly, you should see the Genigraphics Driver as one of the printer choices. Select this driver and click on **OK** to return to the Print dialog. Make any changes necessary on the Print dialog (such as what to print), and click on **OK** to start the interactive Genigraphics print process. The first dialog is the Genigraphics Job Instructions dialog, shown in Figure 7.4. Note that all of the slides in the current presentation will be sent to the Genigraphics file. To print a selection of slides, copy the ones you want to a new PowerPoint presentation.

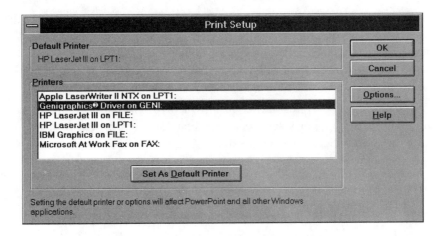

Figure 7.3 Print Setup Dialog

Figure 7.4 Genigraphics Job Instructions Dialog

Specify information about how you want the presentation returned in the **Copies** section of this dialog. Notice that you have the choice of 35mm slides in plastic or glass mounts, 8 x 10-inch overhead foils, or 8 x 10-inch color prints. Especially if this is a presentation that is likely to be repeated several times, you should have at least two copies of whatever media you specify. This gives you the freedom to use one image at least twice, and it can cover you in the event that one set becomes lost or damaged.

Select whether you will send the finished file over a modem or via diskette in the **Send Via** section of this dialog. Specify how you want the finished slides returned. Courier means Federal Express, Mail means U.S. Mail, and Hold for Pickup means you live close enough to one of the Genigraphics offices that you (or someone in one of your offices) can retrieve the finished job in person.

If you want to specify custom services (which you have ideally already coordinated with a Genigraphics service representative), click on **Custom >>**. This displays the Custom Services window shown in Figure 7.5.

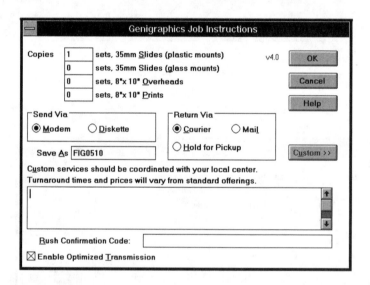

Figure 7.5 Custom Services Window on Genigraphics Job Instructions Dialog

If you specify Hold for Pickup in the Return Via section, for example, you can specify which service center you want to hold the finished job for you.

When the information on the Genigraphics Job Instructions dialog is complete, click on **OK**. PowerPoint displays the Genigraphics Billing Information dialog, shown in Figure 7.6.

Enter the required information on this screen, including the shipping and billing addresses, credit card information (if applicable), and a tax exempt ID number if you have one.

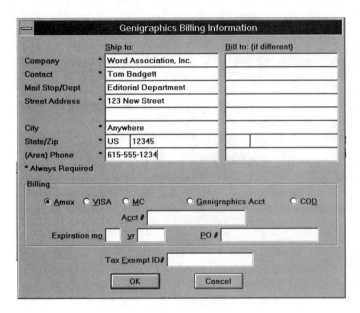

Figure 7.6 Genigraphics Billing Information Dialog

If you choose credit card or Genigraphics account billing, you must enter a valid account number for the print process to proceed.

N O T E

When the information on the Billing Information dialog is complete, click on **OK**. The PowerPoint presentation and the associated billing and shipping information will be saved to a file in the GENI subdirectory within the System subdirectory in Windows (C:\WINDOWS if your Windows software is installed on the C: drive in the conventional directory). The file will have the same name as the name of your presentation, but with the **.GNA** extension.

If you chose modem transmittal (the PowerPoint default), then the reminder to use GraphicsLink to transmit the file will be displayed (see Figure 7.7).

When you have finished printing a presentation to a Genigraphics file, be sure to use **Printer...** from the Print dialog to return the default printer to your physical printer. Otherwise future printouts from **N O T E** PowerPoint will assume you want to create a Genigraphics package instead of a hard copy printout.

Figure 7.7 Use GraphicsLink Program Prompt

To run GraphicsLink, return to the Windows Program Manager and locate the applications window that holds the PowerPoint icons. Double-click on the GraphicsLink icon shown in Figure 7.8.

GraphicsLink

Figure 7.8 GraphicsLink Icon in Program Manager

The opening GraphicsLink dialog is shown in Figure 7.9.

The files you have saved into the GENI subdirectory are listed, along with status (sent, unsent), the date each file was last modified, and the approximate transmit time. You can access job instructions and billing information from this dialog by clicking on the appropriate button.

The first time you use this facility, use File **Communications Setup...** to display the Communications Setup dialog. This dialog tells GraphicsLink what type of modem you are using, where it is located, and so on (see Figure 7.10).

The Communications Setup dialog lets you choose which Genigraphics office you want to use and lists their phone numbers. You can add to or edit this information as Genigraphics adds or changes facilities. To change the information about an existing facility, highlight the facility name and click on **Change...** to display the Change Entry dialog shown in Figure 7.11.

Figure 7.9 Opening GraphicsLink Dialog

Figure 7.10 Communications Setup Dialog

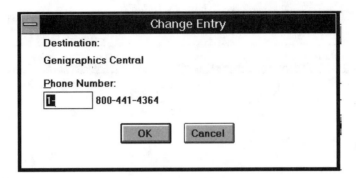

Figure 7.11 Genigraphics Change Entry Dialog

To add a new Genigraphics facility, click on the **Add...** button to display the Add Entry dialog shown in Figure 7.12.

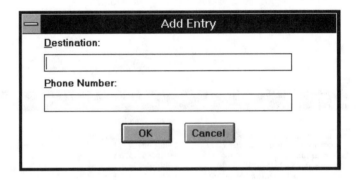

Figure 7.12 Genigraphics Add Entry Dialog

Click on **Port** to pull down a list of available communications ports. Select the port where your modem is installed.

 Even if you are using an internal modem, it must be installed to use one of the computer's standard ports. You may have to refer to the modem's instruction or setup manual to determine which port is being used. If you can't figure out which port, try **COM1** or **COM2** and try sending a file. If it doesn't work, change the port assignment. You can specify **COM1–COM4** on this dialog.

Click on **Settings...** to display the Settings dialog shown in Figure 7.13. This dialog lets you specify baud rate (communications speed) and other data for the specified communications port.

Figure 7.13 Settings Dialog

Finally, click on **Modem...** to display the Modem dialog shown in Figure 7.14.

Figure 7.14 Modem Dialog

This dialog lets you specify the type of modem you are using. It also enables you to set the dialing type (rotary or tone) and, if you are using a non-Hayes modem, the initialization string as well as the dialing and disconnect commands.

If you are using a Hayes or Hayes-compatible modem, you can probably accept the default settings on this dialog. On the other hand, many Hayes-compatible modems include extended features that you may want to turn on with a custom initialization or dialing string. In this case, select **Other** from the **Modem Type** pull-down list. This will enable the additional fields and let you type in the specific information you want.

Click on **OK** to close the Modem dialog and return to the Communications Setup dialog. Click on **OK** again to close the Communications Setup dialog and return to the GraphicsLink window. With setup complete and the file you want to send selected, click on **Send** to initiate the send process.

Genigraphics Corporation, Two Enterprise Drive, Suite 305, Shelton, CT 06484, 800-638-7348.

Graphexec Visuals

Graphexec Visuals offers custom presentations or straight slide conversions from PowerPoint as well as a variety of other packages. You can supply the company with a rough idea of your presentation and let their professionals design slides for you. A proof will be sent for your approval if time permits.

You can either mail diskettes with PowerPoint slides for conversion to film, or you can use the Graphexec bulletin board to upload the files. If you have access to a modem this is the best choice. You save shipping charges, the images arrive at the Graphexec offices immediately, and there is less chance of losing your files.

In addition to preparing 35mm slides and overhead foils, Graphexec can supply full color prints from your PowerPoint disk. You can use these prints for inclusion in printed reports, as section dividers, or for report covers.

As with many presentation services, Graphexec can also scan your color or black & white images so you can insert them into a PowerPoint presentation. Services such as these let you access the images you need without the expense of purchasing a high-end scanner.

Graphexec Visuals, 1991 Highway 54 West, Fayetteville, GA 30214, 404-487-2165.

Visual Horizons

Visual Horizons offers one of the most complete ranges of services in the industry. You can send completed PowerPoint presentations and have Visual

Horizons convert them to 35mm slides or overhead foils. If you'd like to try this company's services, send three images to get three free slides as a sample. The company's Transgraphic software helps you set up images for conversion, asks about deadlines and special requirements, then calls up Visual Horizons and uploads the images. Then you can choose from a variety of services and deadlines.

In addition, you can send Visual Horizons an outline or ideas about your presentation and have their professionals help you design the slides and offer suggestions on presentation design. In fact, this company will pick up your presentation at just about any point in the process and step you through the rest of the procedure to complete the package. You can let them add colors or backgrounds, insert graphics, and more. Visual Horizons also supplies helpful booklets that show you how to design and proof your presentation for a professional result.

Visual Horizons, 180 Metro Park, Rochester, NY 14623, 716-424-5300

Overhead Projection

In addition to 35mm slides, PowerPoint is excellent for creating either black and white or color overhead transparencies. Since an overhead transparency is similar to a typical 8.5 x 11 inch piece of paper, but will be projected onto a wall or screen to be seen by many people, the rules for creating transparencies are a cross between printing a hard copy of the final PowerPoint image and developing a slide image. As with slides, the key to creating an effective overhead is to keep the message simple.

To create a black and white overhead, the printed PowerPoint image can be copied onto overhead transparency stock using almost any copy machine. Many office supply stores and computer stores sell overhead transparencies that may be used with a copy machine or with a laser or dot-matrix printer. If you use the transparency material directly in your laser printer, make sure your printer can use it without damage.

Although you should be able to use copy machine transparencies in your laser printer, your particular machine may have problems with it. Some office supply stores and discount houses offer laser machine transparency material that is known to work with most printers; your best bet is to use this stock instead of the standard copy machine variety.

The NEC LC-890 technical manual, for example, cautions that transparencies for use with this LED printer must be able to withstand the high fusion temperatures of up to 170 degrees C (338 degrees F). In addition, only transparencies that are 0.10 mm or thinner and have been treated to prevent static buildup should be used.

The user manual for the Hewlett Packard LaserJet III includes the caution **Use only overhead transparencies recommended for use in laser printers.** In addition, HP recommends that you use a straight exit path for the transparency sheets. HP LaserJet printers turn the printed page once at the end of the print cycle so that it exits the printer face down, collating the sheets. You can bypass this step by opening a rear exit door on the printer. This reduces the possibility of curling, which can be caused by that final sharp turn while the transparency material is hot from the printer.

You should also watch your printer carefully as the transparency sheets exit. Remember, they are extremely hot and may tend to stick together when they stack up. To avoid this possibility, print one page at a time. Or, you can simply take care to remove each page as it is printed so the pages don't stack up in the printer output tray.

These guidelines are probably good ones for most modern page printers. Check your printer manual and your printer supplier. Many printer manufacturers will sell you transparency material as well as other specialty output material, either through approved distributors or through a division of their own company.

Creating color overhead transparencies is slightly more complicated. Unless a color laser printer (or other color output device) is used, the PowerPoint image must be sent to a company such as Visual Horizons for conversion to color transparency. There is a growing number of color printers available to handle your color output. Whereas a full color printer used to cost anywhere from $5,000 to $20,000, you can get acceptable color output today for under $3,000. In fact, there are a few color printer models available at slightly less than $500 that might do all the color output you need for your presentations.

Hewlett-Packard offers at least two relatively low-priced color printers. In addition, the Fargo Electronics Primera Color Printer, a dye-sublimation device, is priced under $1,000. You can use wax-based inks for medium quality draft and proof output, then change to dye-sublimation when you want photo quality output. All you need to do is change paper and ribbon. You could take color prints from printers of this type and create overhead transparencies by simply running them through a color copier at your local copy center. Compared to the

$5 to $10 the service bureaus charge for overhead foils, the $1 to $2 for an over-head slide done this way is a real bargain. Besides, you can use these color pages directly in annual reports and other printed documents.

Computer Projection

Many of the presentations you make with PowerPoint will be displayed right on the computer screen. If you have a small group that can sit around a table or a desk, all you need is the standard 14-inch computer screen for everyone to see the material.

When you want to use the computer as a presentation platform for larger groups, however, you need a way to enlarge the image so everyone can see it. One way to do this is to convert your computer's signal to a television signal. Once that is done, you can attach your computer to projection TV devices or large screen monitors, or you can dub to video tape. See the discussion on using video tape later in this chapter for details on how to do this.

Another way to project your computer image is to connect the computer display to a projector that enlarges the image and projects it onto a wall or a screen. There are a number of devices that can do this, but they all work in gen-erally the same way. Figure 7.15 shows a conceptual diagram of a computer pro-jection device.

Figure 7.15 Typical Computer Projection Diagram

In general, a projector connects to your computer's video adapter and then projects the information onto the wall or screen. These devices may include their own projection hardware, or they may make use of projectors integral to other equipment. For example, a projector adapter may display the computer's image on a small flat screen that can be positioned on top of an overhead projector. The overhead projector then projects the screen image onto the wall.

The quality of a projected image may not be as good as an on-screen image, and it may not even be as sharp as a computer image converted to video (television). This depends on the technology used to make the projection, but there are times when there is no reasonable substitute for this approach. Figure 7.16 shows a typical computer projector that can help you enhance your computer-based presentations.

Figure 7.16 Typical Projector

The following list includes sources for computer projection hardware.

Boxlight Corporation
17771 Fjord Drive, NE
Poulsbo, WA 98370
206-779-7901

Eiki International, Inc.

26794 Vista Terrace Drive

Lake Forrest, CA 92630

714-457-0200

Proxima Corporation

9440 Carroll Park Drive

San Diego, CA 92121

619-457-5500

Sharp Electronics Corporation

Sharp Plaza

Mahwah, NJ 07430-2135

201-529-8731

Spectrel International

1308 Bayshore Highway 100

Burlingame, CA 94010

415-343-5987

In addition to straight projection, some companies—such as Proxima Corporation—offer control devices that help you concentrate on the audience and the topic instead of the mechanics of manipulating the computer and the presentation. The Proxima Cyclops interactive pointer system, for example, lets you stand in front of an audience and control your PC-based presentation with an infrared pointer (see Figure 7.17).

Whatever projection and control system you choose, make sure it functions properly with your computer and that it provides the quality and control features you need. Without a doubt, this kind of hardware gives you more freedom in designing PowerPoint presentations. You can take advantage of the sound, video, and other computer-based features of PowerPoint, which you can't do if you elect for overhead or 35mm slide projection.

Figure 7.17 Proxima Cyclops Interactive Pointer System

PowerPoint and Multimedia

It is getting more and more difficult to separate multimedia from conventional computing. The majority of new computer packages today include at least a CD-ROM drive and interface, and an increasing number of off-the-shelf machines include audio boards and speakers. These two components—CD-ROM and audio—offer a level of capability those of us with several years of computer experience couldn't even imagine just a short while ago.

CD-ROM Drive

With a CD-ROM drive you have access to over 600 megabytes of read-only storage that can include high resolution pictures or drawings, motion video, clip art, utility programs, and sound. Figure 7.18 shows a typical external CD-ROM drive with the caddy that holds the CD platter itself. Other designs fit inside your computer in place of a 5.25-inch floppy drive. In addition to storing images and digitized sound, many of these CD-ROM players will play back standard audio CDs with the addition of a software control package.

Figure 7.18 Typical CD-ROM Drive and Carrier

These features are important to PowerPoint users because they open up a variety of image types and a wider variety of images that can be made a part of your PowerPoint presentation. You can purchase photographs, clip art, music, sound effects, drawings, movie clips, and more on CD-ROM at reasonable prices for inclusion in your PowerPoint productions. (I've listed a few suppliers of these and other support products at the end of this section).

Sound Card

A sound card offers the same kind of enhancement for your PowerPoint presentations. You can attach a microphone, CD player, or other audio source to record digitized sound into disk files. These files can then be attached to individual PowerPoint slides to be used as background sound, music, or narration. Combined with video tape output (see the discussion on using video tape later in this chapter), PowerPoint slides with sound and narration can produce a self-running instructional presentation.

Refer to the information with your sound card for details on recording and playing sound. Once you have a **.WAV** or a **.MID** file recorded to disk, you can insert the file into your PowerPoint presentation fairly easily. First, load an existing presentation or start a new one. Make the slide to which you want to add audio the current slide. Use Insert **Object...** to display the Insert Object dialog shown in Figure 7.19.

Figure 7.19 Insert Object Dialog

Click on the **Create from File** button at the left of this dialog. This tells PowerPoint that you want to use an existing sound file, and it opens the File Selection window shown in Figure 7.20.

Figure 7.20 File Selection Window on Insert Object Dialog

You can create new sounds on the fly by accepting the **Create New** default in PowerPoint. If you accept this default, PowerPoint loads the Media Player utility to let you record a new sound for use on the current slide. I prefer to create the sound files first.

Either enter the path and file name of the sound file you want to use, or click on **Browse...** to open the Browse dialog shown in Figure 7.21.

Figure 7.21 Browse Dialog from Insert Object Dialog

Choose a directory and a sound file from the Browse dialog. Double-click on the file name or select it and click on **OK**. PowerPoint inserts the path and file name into the Insert Object File dialog.

 If you want to experiment with sound and you haven't recorded your own, use one of the .WAV or .MID files from the Windows subdirectory. There are several files there that you can use as trials.

 If you are using short sound effects or music bridges, you will probably use .WAV files. These are digitized recordings directly from a microphone or other sound device. For longer background music, consider .MID (MIDI) files. These are programmed files that require a fraction of the storage space of .WAV files. You could use a relatively small .MID file to provide background music throughout an entire presentation, for example. A .WAV file of that duration would require more disk space than you're likely to have.

By default, PowerPoint displays .WAV files as a microphone icon and .MID files as the Media Player icon. If you'd like to specify your own icon to represent sound files on your slides, click on **Display As Icon** on the Insert Object dialog. This displays the default icon and adds a **Change Icon** button (see Figure 7.22). Click on the **Change Icon** button to display the Change Icon dialog shown in Figure 7.23.

Figure 7.22 Insert Object Dialog with Change Icon Button

Figure 7.23 Change Icon Dialog

Notice that the current and default icons are shown. You also have the option of selecting another icon from a file on disk. If you click on the **From File** button and then the **Browse...** button on this dialog, PowerPoint again opens a file selection dialog so you can specify a directory and file from which to select the icon.

N O T E   Many executable (program) files include icons. You can use their icons by specifying the particular file name. The Windows **PROG-MAN.EXE** file includes a number of icons. Later versions of Windows also include a file named **MORICONS.DLL** that includes another good selection of icons. And, you can look through the Windows and other directories for any file ending in **.ICO**. (You can purchase collections of icon files from a variety of sources.)

When you have selected the icon you want to use, click on **OK** to return to the Insert Object dialog. The new icon appears on the dialog under the Display As Icon prompt. Click on **OK** once more to close the Insert Object dialog and return to your document. PowerPoint inserts the icon you have specified at the center of the current slide. You can leave it there or grab it and drag it to another position. To play the sound, double-click on the icon.

If you insert a .MID file with a long playing time, you can play another sound file—such as a sound effect—on top of it. For example, you could insert a .MID file on one of the first slides and start it playing to provide background music. Then, on that and subsequent slides, use additional sound inserts for sound effects or narration.

You may have your own sound and music to include with PowerPoint presentations. If you need help with sound effects or music, contact one of the vendors in the list below. This is by no means an exhaustive list, but it will get you started.

Creative Support Services

1950 Riverside Drive

Los Angeles, CA 90039

213-666-7968

800-468-6874

Killer Tracks

6534 Sunset Boulevard

Hollywood, CA 90028

213-957-4455

800-877-0078

Multimedia Arts, Inc.

3900 West Alameda Avenue

Suite 1700

Burbank, CA 90068

818-972-2625

800-468-9008

The Music Bakery

660 Preston Forest Center

Suite 300

Dallas, TX 75230

800-229-0313

The Music Library

80 South Main Street

Hanover, NH 03755

603-643-1388

800-545-0688

Valentino, Inc.

500 Executive Boulevard

PO Box 534

Elmsford, NY 10523-0534

914-347-7878

800-223-6278

Motion Video

In addition to inserting music and sound into your PowerPoint presentation, you can make use of full motion video in a PowerPoint slide window. This is another impressive benefit of PC-based multimedia. Use the same technique as with sound to insert a motion video clip into a PowerPoint slide. Access the Insert Object dialog (Insert **Object...**) and click on **Create from File** to open the File Selection window. Either enter the name of the motion video file or use the **Browse...** button to locate the file you want from the directory and file name display.

The video and sound component of PowerPoint uses the Windows Media Player utility, so it is capable of accessing any files the Media Player can play. What files are supported depends on what hardware and software drivers you have installed. You can learn something about what to expect by opening the Control Panel in the Main applications window, then choosing **Drivers** from the Control Panel display. Figure 7.24 shows the main Control Panel display with the Drivers icon visible. Figure 7.25 shows the Drivers window open.

Figure 7.24 Windows Control Panel Display

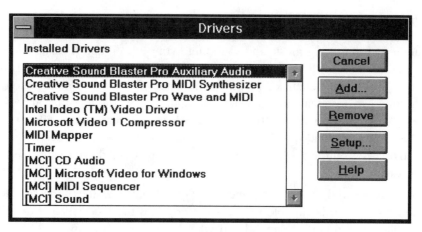

Figure 7.25 Control Panel Drivers Window

For motion video, you may find files with various extensions. One common extension is **.AVI**. Locate a file with an .AVI extension from inside the PowerPoint Insert Object dialog. When you double-click on the file, PowerPoint inserts an icon containing the file's first video frame onto the current slide. The icon in Figure 7.26 comes from a sample video file that ships with SnapIt Pro version 3, one of the products I used for the screen captures in this book.

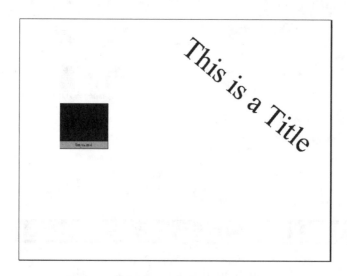

Figure 7.26 Sample Video Icon on PowerPoint Slide

As with sound files, you can play a video clip inserted onto a PowerPoint slide by double-clicking on the icon. PowerPoint launches the Media Player in the background, and opens another window on top of your slide. (Notice that this second window opens. The icon that represents the video clip does not play.) Figure 7.27 shows how the Media Player launches and plays the video represented by the icon on the slide.

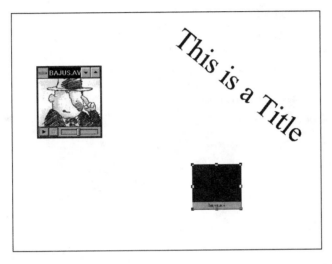

Figure 7.27 Media Player Video Clip on PowerPoint Slide

The video clip window is opened as a very small square. While the clip is playing, you can click on the **Maximize** button at the upper right-hand corner of the video window to enlarge the window. Because of the video technology used with the standard player, you won't get a full-screen display even when you click on the **Maximize** button. You can make this motion video segment a part of a video tape presentation of slides as well. See the Video Tape section later in this chapter for information on how to do this.

Just as you can purchase canned audio—sound effects and music—for use in your presentations, you can also purchase film clips on CD or video. These range from stock footage designed for presentation applications to historical film fragments. I've listed a few suppliers of stock footage below. Contact one or more of these companies to get help in enhancing your PowerPoint and other computer-based presentations.

Alpha Technologies Group, Inc.

6921 Cable Drive

Marriottsville, MD 21104

410-781-4200

Archive Films

530 West 25th Street

New York, NY 10001

212-620-3955

Bliss Interactive Technologies

6034 West Courtyard Drive

Austin, TX 78730

512-338-2458

BMUG, Inc.

1442a Walnut Street, Box #62

Berkeley, CA 94709

510-549-2684

Jasmine Multimedia Publishing, Inc.

1888 Century Park East

Suite 300

Los Angeles, CA 90067

310-277-7523

800-798-7535

Mediacom

PO Box 36173

Richmond, VA 23235

804-794-0700

Video Tape Library, Ltd.

1509 North Crescent Heights Boulevard

Suite 2

Los Angeles, CA 90046

213-656-4330

Video Clips, Inc.

22 Fisher Avenue

Wellesley, MA 02181

617-235-5617

WPA Film Library

5525 West 159th Street

Oak Forest, IL 60452

708-535-1540

800-777-2223

Other Presentation Types

The variety of methods available to you for presenting information created with PowerPoint is almost unlimited. In addition to conventional PC-based presentations, projecting your PC images, and using 35mm slides, you can use custom presentation hardware, convert your show to video, and more. I'll discuss a few of these options in this section. However, as you work with PowerPoint and become more comfortable with designing and giving presentations, keep your ears, eyes, and mind open to other options that can enhance your message and keep your audience interested.

VideoShow

One of the many ways to present PowerPoint images is with General Parametrics Corporation's VideoShow. This is a stand-alone presentation system that uses PC-compatible disk files to produce an electronic slide show similar to projecting a presentation from the PC (see Figure 7.28). VideoShow is essentially a video projector, except that you don't use your computer. It is a stand-alone device that uses disk files created by your computer to present video slides.

Figure 7.28 VideoShow

PowerPoint files can easily be transferred into VideoShow format by installing a Windows driver and printing the show or individual slides to a disk file after selecting the VideoShow driver. Press **Enter** with the Print dialog displayed, and the file name will be translated into VideoShow format and placed in whatever subdirectory PowerPoint image files are saved in. VideoShow files can be placed in any subdirectory by entering the appropriate path when the file name is entered.

Using VideoShow, PowerPoint files can be displayed on any RGB video monitor or video projector. Files can be linked together using special effects, and exciting presentations can easily be developed. VideoShow uses PowerPoint files that are saved on floppy disk. To use the product, a computer is not required (after the images are created). VideoShow is similar to a VCR (both in size and in function) for displaying computer images. After you insert a floppy disk containing graphic files, VideoShow will display the files in any order, and will let you add different types of effects for enhancing the presentation. VideoShow can be programmed to provide a self-running presentation, or, with the use of a remote control unit, VideoShow can be used as a visual aid during a speech.

General Parametrics offers another interesting product to support presentations—the VideoShow Presenter. This is a hand-held computer-compatible video screen with a control pad. A cable connects the Presenter to your PC, and the 4-inch color display in your hand helps you manage the show. From the control panel you can access any image in the show instantly, privately preview any image without showing it on the screen or projector, or review speaker's notes on the screen.

For more information about VideoShow or VideoShow Presenter, contact: General Parametrics Corporation, 1250 Ninth Street, Berkeley, CA 94710, 800-223-0999 or 510-524-9954.

Video Tape

Once you have your PowerPoint presentation planned and produced, you can show it to your audience in a variety of ways. With today's computer technology, the option of converting your show to video tape is relatively easy and inexpensive. All you need is a plug-in board or external interface to convert your computer's display to video format. Then you can attach a standard video recorder to the output of this converter and step through your presentation, recording it to tape. Figure 7.29 shows a typical connection diagram for attaching your computer to a VCR.

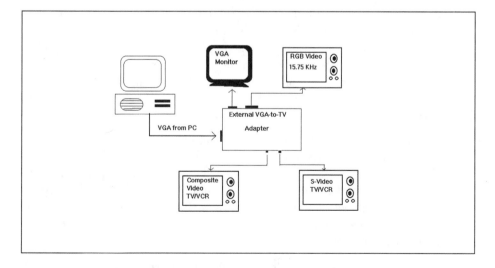

Figure 7.29 Typical Computer-to-VCR Connection Diagram

If you are using a sound card with your computer and have attached sound or narration to your PowerPoint presentation, you can also output the audio portion of your show to the VCR to create a stand-alone, self-running presentation that anyone can view. Of course you can also record audio information on video tape after you convert the PowerPoint images to video. There are numerous video service companies (one is probably located in or near your town) that will add music and narration to your basic slide show for a reasonable price. If you are working for a relatively large company, there are probably video production facilities available to you to help you enhance your PowerPoint/video production.

The hardware available for PowerPoint to video conversion is varied in function and in price. Many products available to do the job are part of a more comprehensive package designed to support full desktop video editing. If you intend to expand to more advanced video work, this kind of product is a good investment. On the other hand, if all you really want to do is convert your PowerPoint shows to video, then you can use a simpler (and lower priced) unit. In the following sections I'll give you a summary of a few of the available products to help you use video with PowerPoint. Obviously there are other products available. Ask your local computer dealer and check the mail order advertisements and magazines for more choices.

Notice that you can use these devices not only to produce video tape, but also to enable you to show your computer shows on a standard television monitor. This is a good choice when you are presenting PowerPoint shows in a location that is wired for television instead of computer video projection. Many conference rooms have a number of large screen television monitors around the room, or are equipped with a large screen projection TV. Using a VGA-to-video interface lets you plug directly into these display devices to present your PowerPoint show to a large audience directly from your computer.

Bravado

The Truevision Bravado encoder is more of a multimedia device than a presentation device, but the two applications are beginning to merge in today's high-end software such as PowerPoint. Bravado is a multi-function board that supports composite or S-Video output as well as audio. This multimedia board also lets you display a variety of components on your VGA monitor, including text, graphics, and video windows. Bravado supports live motion video as well as static computer displays.

Like many other video output boards, the Bravado includes standard VGA circuitry, so you don't need a separate VGA adapter. The Bravado accepts two stereo or four monaural inputs. Amplified audio output lets you use the audio portion of the board with standard speakers without the requirement of a separate amplifier. Line outputs to carry audio to a video recorder or amplifier system are also available.

Truevision, Inc., 7340 Shadeland Station, Indianapolis, IN 46256, 317-841-0332.

Genie and VINplus

Jovian's VINplus is a low-cost hardware/software combination that handles the VGA-to-TV conversion for your PC. You connect the external box to the VGA port and install the required software to output composite or S-Video signals for video recording or television monitor display.

For about three times the cost of VINplus you can purchase the Jovian Genie, a hardware-only device compatible with PC or Apple computers. In fact, you can connect PC and Apple computers to the Genie input simultaneously and convert their outputs to TV signals one at a time. Separate NTSC and PAL models are available for Genie and VINplus.

Jovian Logic Corporation, 47929 Fremont Boulevard, Fremont, CA 94538, 510-651-4823.

PC-TV Encoder Box

The PC-TV Encoder is a small, flat box that sits outside your PC and converts standard VGA signals into television signals. It supports displays up to 640 x 480 resolution in full color, and it can display on a television monitor and VGA display simultaneously. Television outputs include S-Video and composite signals. PAL and NTSC models are available. No separate software driver is required. You simply connect your VGA signal to the input, and a television monitor, recorder, or other television device to the output. A separate encoder card that plugs inside your PC also is available if you prefer to have the converter inside the computer instead of outside.

Yuan Technology, USA, 1223 S. Dorsey Lane, Suite 203, Tempe, AZ 85281, 602-966-1557.

PortaShow and VIGA VGA+

PortaShow is an external box that converts your computer's VGA display signal to video. You plug the output of your VGA display card into the PortaShow, then connect your VGA computer monitor to the VGA output of the PortaShow.

At the same time you can connect a composite or S-Video device to another PortaShow port. Notice that the PortaShow uses your computer's existing VGA display adapter and resides outside your computer. This is an excellent choice when you need video output from more than one computer.

An alternative product from the same company is the VIGA VGA+, an internal PC card that supplies both VGA monitor and video output. The hookup is essentially the same as for the PortaShow except that the video and VGA circuitry both reside inside your computer on a single card. Visionetics also offers a Genlock version of the board for high-end video applications such as video overlaying and chromakeying.

Visionetics International, 21311 Hawthorne Boulevard, Suite 300, Torrance, CA 90503, 310-316-7940.

TelevEyes, TelevEyes/Plus and TelevEyes/Pro

This computer-to-TV converter group offers a variety of display conversion features through an external box. The standard model is appropriate for PowerPoint conversion or television monitor presentations. If you plan to move up to high-end desktop video applications, consider paying the premium for the Plus or Pro models (see Figure 7.30).

Figure 7.30 TelevEyes/Pro VGA-to-Video Adapter

You can display both VGA and television video at the same time. These converters include audio input and output support to add audio to your PowerPoint presentations on the computer or to mix audio with your images on video tape. The Pro model includes Genlock and overlay features. All models output composite and S-Video signals through standard connectors and cables.

Digital Vision, Inc., 270 Bridge Street, Dedham, MA 02026, 617-329-5400.

ViVA Basic and ViVA Basic/EX

The ViVA Basic/EX is an external converter box that translates computer VGA signals to S-Video, composite television, and RGB output simultaneously. Television and VGA outputs can be displayed at the same time. No software is required to make the conversion. However, utility software is included to control the positioning of the VGA data on the TV screen and to adjust such effects as overscan and underscan. The unit is supplied with the necessary cables.

The ViVA Basic provides essentially the same features as the ViVA Basic/EX model, but from an internal PC adapter card. The ViVA Basic card plugs into your PC's bus near the existing VGA adapter and connects to the VGA adapter through the feature connector on top of the card. Composite, S-Video, and RGB output are provided on the rear panel of the ViVA Basic card. As this book is written, the price for the two units is the same.

Omnicomp Graphics Corporation, 1734 W. Sam Houston Parkway North, Houston, TX 77043, 713-464-2900.

To Sum Up

It would be impossible to include information about all of the products and services available to support PowerPoint presentations. However, in this chapter I have shown you some of the major players in the service and hardware part of the marketplace to help you get more out of the presentations you prepare in PowerPoint.

In the next chapter we'll look at how you can integrate PowerPoint with other components of the Microsoft Office suite and other applications.

PowerPoint and the Microsoft Office Suite

Microsoft's PowerPoint is at the forefront of today's computer software development. It has an unusual marketing position brought about by its partnership with other members of the *Microsoft Office* suite. I think the new PowerPoint is a great program, and it is gaining popularity both among people who know up front they need it and among users who stumble across it in their Office package. But I have to say that by far the majority of users I polled as research for this book said something like, "Well, I know I have it on my system, but I haven't tried it."

That attitude is going to change, I predict, not only because version 4.0 is much easier to use and has more features than the previous release that most people have tried, but also as users learn that "presentation" software is good for much more than just presentations. With the close link among the members of the Microsoft Office suite, more users are likely to begin experimenting with PowerPoint and other packages they just happen to have because they wanted Word or Excel and found they could get the whole package for just a little more.

In this chapter I'll introduce you to some of the ways you can use PowerPoint with other software and other software with PowerPoint. (There is a slight difference!)

Microsoft Office Overview

Microsoft Office is among the leaders in a new software trend that bundles all of the major software applications most users are likely to need into a single package.

Why Microsoft Office?

WordPerfect Corporation is doing it, Lotus and Borland are doing it, and there likely will be others. The idea of such a bundle is threefold:

- Give the user all major applications at one time
- Lock the user into the products of a single vendor
- Make the marketing of some products easier

Another possible benefit of this type of marketing is price maintenance. Software retail prices have fallen rapidly over the past few years. You can buy applications for $100 or less today that would have cost thousands of dollars not too long ago. While the mainstream products—word processors, spreadsheets, and databases from major manufacturers—still are offered for $300 to $500 each, even that price plateau is being eroded. By packaging a popular product such as Microsoft Word with one that many users may not immediately perceive as important, the manufacturer can maintain a higher price for the popular program while promoting the use of the less popular one.

Whatever the actual motivation for current marketing posture, product groupings such as Microsoft Office can only benefit the user. You, as a user or potential user of PowerPoint, reap the benefits of full-featured software, a variety of software, and low prices. In addition, by installing and using multiple software packages from a single vendor, you benefit from a common user interface. When you load Microsoft Word and Microsoft PowerPoint you will be struck immediately at the similarity of the opening screens. The colors, the menus, and the screen design are all very similar.

Besides, you have a single company from which to seek technical support. You become familiar with the procedure for getting technical support, and you learn what to expect and how to get it. (See Chapter 9 for more information on technical support for PowerPoint.)

What is Microsoft Office?

Soon after the IBM PC was introduced and software developers began filling the applications gap, among the popular trends were integrated packages. There were a number of popular offerings early on, but they soon fell by the wayside as strong dedicated applications replaced them. The theory behind integrated applications was to provide users with all the software they were likely to need with a common user interface and from a single vendor. However, as vendors quickly found, users were more interested in features available within individual applications than they were in the integrated concept. Even users who bought integrated products frequently used only one or two of the integrated applications and bought additional third-party software to fill in the gaps.

The rule still holds. While a few integrated packages exist today, they are poor seconds, from a business standpoint, relative to single-application software. The suite movement in today's software business promises the benefits of both integrated and stand-alone packages. The concept is the same today as it was in the beginning: provide users with the major applications they need— word processing, spreadsheet, and database—within a common user interface and from the same vendor. However, today, instead of integrating all of these applications into one package, the trend is to provide separate applications that are closely linked. This allows vendors more freedom in designing applications. With today's Windows environment that supports Object Linking and Embedding (OLE), these separate applications can operate together rather closely. Besides the "big three" applications, most vendors are offering additional applications such as presentation software (which wasn't available when the early integrated software was around), electronic mail, programming languages, and so on.

Microsoft Office includes Microsoft Word 6.0, Excel 5.0, PowerPoint, and Mail. The professional version of the package includes Access 1.1 as an additional database component. The Suite conglomerations offer other incentives as well. For example, the Microsoft offering includes support for Visual Basic for Applications and OLE 2.0. The Visual Basic component is part of a Microsoft strategy to unify applications through a common macro and development language designed for end user as well as developer use. OLE 2.0, the follow-on to Microsoft's earlier Object Linking and Embedding technology, offers a sophisticated and capable way to link applications. With OLE 2.0, in-place editing across applications is possible. This provides users the ability to access external features from inside one application without actually launching the remote application in the conventional way.

The Microsoft Office concept lets you purchase the main application you need, learn to use it, become familiar with the user interface, and be able to access the power of other applications easily. A software scheme is evolving that lets you have a single interface into your computer system. This interface enables you to work with a number of computer features without having to learn a lot of different tools and screens. This single interface concept isn't flawless, but it does go beyond the common interface afforded by Windows alone.

In addition, even if you don't want to access a remote application from inside a current program, you can still launch and use other Office products easily with the Microsoft toolbar. Place the mouse pointer on any displayed toolbar and click the right mouse button. Choose Microsoft from the pop-up toolbar menu and you'll see the toolbar shown in Figure 8.1.

Each of the Office applications supports this toolbar, so you can launch any of the Office programs by simply clicking on the appropriate button.

Figure 8.1 Microsoft Toolbar in PowerPoint

Using Linked Objects

Whether you are using Microsoft Office products or other Windows-based applications, you can insert a class of objects in your PowerPoint presentations called *linked* objects. I have talked previously about inserting objects into PowerPoint using the Insert Object dialog. These are embedded objects because you import an object from a foreign application into PowerPoint, where it becomes static.

When you link an object, you create a soft or live link with the external data. That means that if the data to which PowerPoint is linked changes—as when someone updates the spreadsheet or Word document, for example—then these changes show up in PowerPoint. A live link is an excellent tool when multiple users are working on a presentation or on the data that supports a presentation. It is a good choice when you want to get on with the process of creating a presentation in PowerPoint but you know the facts will change. When you create a live link to data outside PowerPoint, you can specify that you want the information to change automatically each time you load PowerPoint and the presentation that includes links. Or, you can set up the presentation to let you check the new data before updating it manually with a keystroke. You may not want to use live links, on the other hand, if you are not on a network, or if the presentation you are creating will be moved from your system or network to another system or network.

If your system and presentation configuration seem to support live links, there are a couple of ways to create them. If you've read my description earlier about using the Insert Object dialog, you are 90 percent familiar with the linking process.

Make the slide on which you wish to place a linked object the current slide, then use Insert **Object...** to display the Insert Object dialog, shown in Figure 8.2.

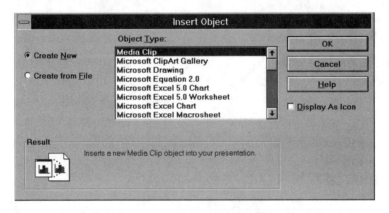

Figure 8.2 Insert Object Dialog

Click on **Create from File** to open the File window. Either type the path and file name in this field or use **Browse...** to locate the file you want to insert. Once the proper file name is in the File window of this dialog, click on **Link** to establish a link with the specified file. Notice that the Result window at the bottom of this dialog changes to show the nature of the object relationship with PowerPoint. Click on **OK** to complete the process.

PowerPoint places the selected file or object into the current slide and establishes a link with that object. Now when you load this presentation, PowerPoint automatically checks the status of the selected object. If it has changed since you established the link, the new version of the object will be placed into the presentation.

You can check the status of the link at any time by using Edit **Links...** to display the Links dialog shown in Figure 8.3.

Notice that this dialog lists any current links, and it shows you the update setting (Automatic is the default). This dialog provides facilities for updating the information, for launching the source application, or for breaking the link. You may want to use the **Update Now** button even though Automatic Update is selected, because unless you close the presentation and re-open it, PowerPoint won't update the object even if it has changed. If you know it has changed (or you suspect it has), you can use the Links dialog at any time to refresh the linked object or objects in your presentation. Simply select the object link as shown in the Links window of this dialog, then click on **Update Now** to have the latest version inserted into your PowerPoint presentation.

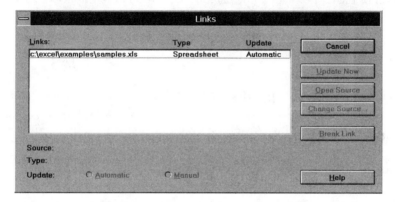

Figure 8.3 Links Dialog in PowerPoint

There's another way to create a link in PowerPoint. You can shrink PowerPoint to an icon and launch the source application. Load the text or object you want to link and then use Edit **Copy** to place a copy of it on the Clipboard. Return to PowerPoint and make current the slide on which you want this object to appear. Now use Edit **Paste Special...** to display the Paste Special dialog shown in Figure 8.4.

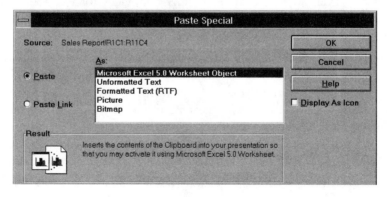

Figure 8.4 Paste Special Dialog

The information displayed in the As window of this dialog changes with the type of object you have copied to the Clipboard. If PowerPoint knows about the source application, then you have the option of choosing either a straight **Paste** or a **Paste Link** by clicking on the appropriate button at the left of the dialog. If you are using older Windows software or a DOS application as the source, PowerPoint may not recognize the source. In this case, you will be given only the option of **Paste**; no link can be established through the Clipboard route.

If PowerPoint recognizes the source application (as with the sample in Figure 8.4), then you can choose **Paste Link** on this dialog. When you do, the description in the Result area of the dialog describes what happens when you insert an object in this way.

Whether you use Insert **Object...** from the PowerPoint menu or use the **Copy** and **Paste Special...** technique, if the source application supports live links through OLE, then your PowerPoint presentation will be updated when the source object is modified.

I would like to discuss one more concept about PowerPoint objects, then we'll go on to some specifics about using Microsoft Office products with PowerPoint. Suppose you have information on a slide that is embedded from another application. For example, you may have a WordPerfect document fragment that you want to edit. However, you don't have WordPerfect on your system—you only have Word.

You can use PowerPoint's conversion facility to convert the WordPerfect document to a Word document so that you can use Word to edit it. This same technique works with spreadsheet data and other embedded information, as long as the converter knows about both applications involved. If the embedded object comes from another user or another computer, for example, you may lack the facilities to edit it directly. PowerPoint may be able to convert it so that you can.

Select the object and use Edit **Package Object** (or whatever the last entry on the Edit menu is—the wording of this option changes with the type of object). PowerPoint displays another menu level with a Convert... entry (the other entries on this menu will vary with the type of object you have selected). Click on **Convert...** to display the Convert dialog shown in Figure 8.5.

You will be given one or more options in the Object Type window of this dialog. The exact choices you see depend on the source application for the selected object. Click on the application type which you want to convert the selected object to and click on **OK** to make the change. If the dialog offers you the option of Activate as, then you can temporarily work with an object in the new format without changing it permanently.

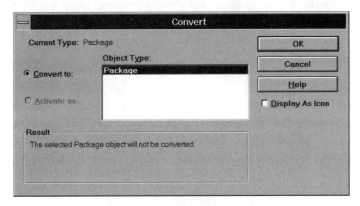

Figure 8.5 Convert Dialog in PowerPoint

You can use another technique to convert graphics objects into PowerPoint format so that you can use PowerPoint editing tools to manipulate the object. Select the object you want to convert, and then use Draw **Ungroup** to break the link with the source application and to separate the object into component parts. You will see the somewhat ominous message in Figure 8.6.

Figure 8.6 Imported Object Warning from Draw Ungroup

Click on **OK** to continue with the ungroup process. The display will change, showing many objects selected as individual components of the main image. If you want to work with individual components, you can click anywhere on the slide to deselect the individual objects. If, on the other hand, you want to work with the complete object in PowerPoint as a group, then use Draw **Group** to regroup the object components as a PowerPoint group. The link with the source application is not re-established. You only gather the object components together as a single object inside PowerPoint.

NOTE

If a complex object becomes ungrouped and you want to put it back together, don't try selecting each object sequentially. Use the mouse pointer to draw a box around the entire object. When you release the left mouse button all of the components of the object are selected. To select only some of the objects to assemble them as a group, hold the **Shift** key and click on the objects you want to select.

If you want to edit the object, use standard PowerPoint editing procedures by selecting the object or one of its components and then making the changes you wish. If the object includes text, you can add or change text from the keyboard. Graphics objects can be moved, rotated, and so on by grabbing them with the mouse and by using the features of the Draw menu and Drawing toolbars.

Using PowerPoint with Excel

Microsoft Excel has been a popular spreadsheet for some time. It has been a strong contender against Lotus 1-2-3 and other competitors. In this chapter, when I talk about Excel, I mean Microsoft Excel version 5.0. It is the latest version of this venerable spreadsheet package and the one that is shipping with the latest version of the Office package. With the new features of version 5 and its inclusion in the Office package, look for Excel to gain even more user support.

If you aren't using a spreadsheet, then you likely won't see any immediate use for this part of your Office suite. However, in this section I'd like to introduce the concept of spreadsheets, show you about Excel specifically, and discuss how you might use the Excel/PowerPoint combination.

Why Spreadsheets?

As I showed you earlier in this book, PowerPoint includes a fairly competent charting facility that is based on the Excel spreadsheet model. A full-fledged spreadsheet program, however, goes far beyond this simple charting facility.

A spreadsheet program is based on a ledger concept where there are multiple rows and columns separated by thin lines. You can write text or numbers into any of the resulting cells defined by the crossing horizontal and vertical lines. On a paper ledger you establish your own headings, enter the numbers, then use a calculator to add up the rows and columns.

With a spreadsheet program such as Excel, you establish your own headings and enter numbers. Then you use the built-in features of the software to add rows and columns, compute interest or payments, figure depreciation, predict income, and more. An electronic spreadsheet can serve the same functions as your familiar hand-kept ledger, except that it also has built-in intelligence to help with the math. A spreadsheet package is an excellent "what if" calculator, because once you set up the cell relationships, you can change one or more data entries and have all of the cells that depend on this data change automatically.

You can have Excel draw graphs and charts based on the data in your cells, and you can use Excel's fonts and other spreadsheet formatting features to make the most of the data you present. And, once you have an Excel spreadsheet designed the way you want it, you can import all or part of it into PowerPoint to illustrate a concept or make a point.

Why would you want to use Excel instead of PowerPoint's built-in graphing feature? You may already have the data and graphs you need in Excel, for one thing. Whenever you retype data you run the risk of introducing errors, and, if the data is complicated, it can take a long time to re-enter it. There may be spreadsheet features you want to use in Excel that PowerPoint simply doesn't offer. That's the main reason for having multiple applications in the first place. Whatever the reason, there will likely be times when you will want to incorporate Excel information into a PowerPoint spreadsheet. I'll show you how to do that in this chapter.

Why Excel?

You can use spreadsheet information from any Windows-compliant spreadsheet. You can even copy and paste or export and import spreadsheet information from a product that doesn't support object linking. So why use Excel with PowerPoint? For one thing, Excel and PowerPoint are both Microsoft products. As such they have a very similar appearance. The user interface for each will be familiar to you if you learn only one of the products well. This similar user interface lets you easily do in-place editing of Excel data while you are actually inside PowerPoint.

In addition, these two products work well together. Microsoft has implemented OLE 2.0 in Excel and PowerPoint, making the sharing of data between them particularly easy and reliable. Excel is relatively easy to learn and to use, but remember that when you launch an Excel editing window, you are working inside a full-featured, powerful application that is integrated with but separate from PowerPoint. Showing you how to use all the features of Excel is beyond the scope of this book, but I'll show you some of the more salient features in the next section of this chapter. As you gain experience and confidence with Excel, you will tap into more and more of its features.

Embedding an Excel Object

You can link or embed an Excel spreadsheet (or a portion of a spreadsheet) with a PowerPoint slide right from the PowerPoint Standard toolbar. (See the discussions on linking objects in PowerPoint earlier in this chapter and on how to link Excel objects in the next section.)

To embed an Excel spreadsheet, make the slide on which you want Excel data to appear the current slide. Then click on the **Insert Microsoft Excel Worksheet** icon on the Standard toolbar. PowerPoint pulls down a grid similar to a Microsoft Word table. (In fact, a Word table and an imported Excel spreadsheet can be very similar.) Specify the shape of the spreadsheet you want to insert by holding down the left mouse button and selecting as many cells (rows and columns) as you want to insert. This provides PowerPoint with the basic format you want to use. This is only a guide to help size the initial spreadsheet. You can change the number of rows and cells later if you wish.

When you release the mouse button, PowerPoint locates Excel and launches an editing window that lets you interact with Excel from inside PowerPoint. As you can see from Figure 8.7, the menu bars and toolbars also change. Although the main title bar still says Microsoft PowerPoint and your presentation slide is still on the screen, you are actually working in Excel at this moment.

In addition, you can use the Insert **Object...** menu sequence and specify a Microsoft Excel 5 object from the Insert Object dialog. In this case PowerPoint picks a default size for the spreadsheet and places it on the current slide for you. Again, you can grab a sizing handle and adjust the size of the grid to fit your current application. These two procedures—the toolbar icon and the Insert Object dialog—produce the same results. In both cases you are embedding an Excel spreadsheet into the current slide.

Note that even though you may have specified the shape of the spreadsheet segment to insert into your slide, you can grab one of the sizing handles on a spreadsheet border and drag the spreadsheet to any size and shape you want. Because you are working with Excel, this small window is actually a pane into a massive grid of cells, formulas, and other features that you have at your disposal.

Figure 8.7 Excel Editing Window, Menu, and Toolbars in PowerPoint with Labels

However, there are some limitations inherent in this application link. Although the full Excel menu and toolbar are presented with the spreadsheet, some of these items don't function and some of the menu items actually belong to PowerPoint. For example, you can't load an existing spreadsheet into the spreadsheet form on your PowerPoint slide, nor can you save the spreadsheet you create on your PowerPoint slide as a separate Excel file. These are potentially confusing aspects of working through OLE 2.0 with embedded objects. Once you get the hang of how this works, however, it seems fairly natural.

Once you have the spreadsheet form inserted onto your slide, you can begin to enter data, create formulas, format the cells, and so on. Suppose you want to create a spreadsheet that shows regional sales information. In this case you want to show the actual numbers in a spreadsheet grid rather than a graphical representation such as a chart.

A finished spreadsheet on a PowerPoint slide is shown in Figure 8.8.

To create this sample sales spreadsheet, use the **Excel** icon on the Standard toolbar or the Insert Object dialog to place a blank Excel spreadsheet on the current slide.

		United States Internet – Regional Sales			
		Fiscal 2001 – Monthly Averages			
Region	Prime Time	Other Time	Training	Materials	Total
Local	1023	990	900	555	3068
North	922	632	450	334	2338
South	1284	1120	400	123	2907
East	844	716	900	355	2815
West	990	432	300	557	2279
New England	322	145	800	765	2032
South West	678	321	324	456	1779
Canada	997	654	654	123	2424
Other Foreign	234	122	880	95	1341
		GRAND TOTAL:		$	20,983.00

Figure 8.8 Finished Regional Sales Spreadsheet

Click in cell D3 (or anywhere near the center of the grid you have defined) to place the insertion point, then type the title of the spreadsheet:

United States Internet—Regional Sales

NOTE

Depending on your screen configuration, the information you type can be quite small. However, the data you enter in a cell is duplicated at the top of the screen just under the Format bar. This lets you see what you type easily.

Press the down arrow or use the mouse to click in cell D4 to reset the insertion point, then enter the subtitle:

Fiscal 2001—Monthly Averages

Now enter the column titles. Start by moving the insertion point to cell B6, then enter the column titles in adjacent cells:

Region | Prime Time | Other Time | Training | Materials | Total

These titles will occupy cells B6 through G6 if you follow the guidelines I have suggested. Of course you can enter these column titles over any other set of columns you choose, in which case the cell addresses might be different.

You can either press the right arrow after entering data in each cell to move to the next column, or you can use the mouse to position the insertion point each time.

N O T E

Notice that some of the titles seem not to fit the cells because the default cell width is too narrow to hold all of the text. You can use the mouse pointer to grab the vertical lines between columns and drag them to the width you want. Simply move the insertion point into the area of the spreadsheet that holds the alphabetic letter column titles. As you move the cursor over the line it changes from a broad cross to a narrow cross with double-ended arrows. Hold the left mouse button and drag any lines you want to widen the columns.

Some screen configurations (such as 640 x 480) make the spreadsheet extremely small. If you find you can't work with the small display, you could create the chart in Excel, then insert the finished sheet into a PowerPoint slide.

N O T E

Next, you want to center the text in the columns for a more pleasing appearance. To do this, select all of the cells that hold column titles by placing the mouse pointer over the first cell, holding down the left mouse button, and dragging the highlight over the range of title cells. Now use Format **Cells** to display the Format Cells dialog shown in Figure 8.9.

Figure 8.9 Format Cells Dialog

Click on the **Alignment** tab to make the Alignment choices accessible. Click on **Center** under Horizontal alignment and then click on **OK**. This centers the text within each of the cells.

N O T E

You can also use the **Format Bar Center** button (similar to the center button on the PowerPoint Format Bar) to center the selected text.

While the text on the header line is still highlighted, let's enlarge the text and change its attributes. As you can see from the Format Bar at the top of the screen, the default is Arial font at a 10 point size. Click on the down arrow beside the point size field and choose 14 points. You may have to enlarge some cells once more to make the text fit.

Click on the **Bold** button on the Format Bar to set the selected text in bold-face. Now, while this text is still selected, let's color the background behind it. Click on the down arrow beside the fill color icon on the toolbar (the tipping bucket) to display the Color Selection dialog shown in Figure 8.10.

Figure 8.10 Color Selection Dialog

Choose the light blue color on the top row of this dialog (or any other color you like).

Next, pull down the Text Color Selection dialog by clicking on the down arrow beside the text color button (the large T with a color block beside it). Choose white for the text. Now you have a light blue background with white text for the header bar on this spreadsheet segment. Select the text in the title at the top of the spreadsheet and make it 18-point bold. This will make the title stand out from the rest of the spreadsheet.

Now, we'll add grids to the body of the spreadsheet and also enter sample data to match the figure. Use the mouse to select the section of the spreadsheet defined by the range B7..G25. To do this, place the insertion point in cell B7, hold down the left button, and drag the highlight across the grid to cell G25.

Use Format **Cells** (**Ctrl+1**) to display the Format Cells dialog shown in Figure 8.11.

Figure 8.11 Format Cells Dialog

Click on the **Border** tab to bring it to the front of the dialog. Click on **Left**, **Right**, **Top**, and **Bottom** to place a border around every cell in the selected range. Click on **OK** to close the Format Cells dialog.

Click in cell B7 to place the insertion point in that cell. Now let's enter data for the Region column of the spreadsheet. In cell B7, type **Local**. Press the down arrow to move the cell pointer to B8. In this cell type **North**. Continue in this way, adding region names in this column as follows:

B7	Local
B8	North
B9	South
B10	East
B11	West

B12	New England
B13	South West
B14	Canada
B15	Other Foreign

Now select the cell range B7..B17 and use the pull-down font size list on the Format Bar to enlarge the text to 12 points. Use the mouse pointer to enlarge the B column, if necessary, so that all the text fits within the column.

Next, enter numerical data to represent dollar sales from each of these regions for each of the sales types listed at the head of the columns. You can enter the numbers I used, or make up your own. Of course, you can also use different column headings if you want to make this sample spreadsheet match a business or other application that is closer to something you might actually use. One of my businesses is indeed US Internet, and we sell on-line time to Internet users. (The figures you see are strictly made up, however.)

When you have numbers in every cell of the range C7..F15, add a formula to add up totals by region in the Total column. Click in cell G7 to place the insertion point in that cell. Now type the following:

+SUM(C7..F7)

Press **Enter**. The sum of all the numbers in row 7 should appear in cell G7 (3068 in my example). The next step is to copy this formula down the G column so that all the rows will be added into totals. To do this, use Edit **Copy** to place a copy of the formula in cell G7 onto the Clipboard.

Next, use the mouse to select the range of cells G8..G15. Use Edit **Paste** to copy the formula to that range. Notice that Excel automatically adjusts the cell references so that the formula in each cell in column G refers to the cells in the row just to the left of the formula. The row totals should appear in the cells in column G, as shown in Figure 8.12.

Finally, we want to compute a grand total by adding up the totals for each row into a cell at the bottom of the G column. Click in cell E17 to place the insertion point in that cell, then type **GRAND TOTAL:** and press **Enter**. Click in cell G17, then click on the **SUM** button on the Excel toolbar. Excel suggests a formula in cell G17. Press **Enter** to accept the formula. The sum of the subtotals in column G is displayed in cell G17.

Figure 8.12 Spreadsheet with G Column Totals

Format the Grand Total value for currency by clicking on the dollar sign on the Format Bar. When the formatting changes, you may see a series of pound signs (#) in cell G17. This is because the resulting number, with its dollar sign and decimal places, is too long to fit inside the cell width. To correct the problem, simply grab the right column divider at the top of the column and drag the column width so it will accommodate the large number. Select cells E17..G17 and click on the **Bold** button on the Format Bar to make the Grand Total title and numerical value bold.

Now you have the completed spreadsheet on a PowerPoint slide that I first showed you earlier in this section. Click anywhere outside the spreadsheet area of your slide to close Excel and leave the spreadsheet embedded in the current slide. You can double-click on the slide to reopen the Excel editor and make changes to the spreadsheet at any time, but this spreadsheet exists only inside your PowerPoint slide. You can't load it as a separate file in Excel. If you want to link an Excel spreadsheet to a PowerPoint slide, read the next section.

Linking an Excel Spreadsheet to PowerPoint

You can link an Excel spreadsheet to a PowerPoint slide in the same way you can link other external objects to PowerPoint. Make the slide you want to hold the Excel data the current slide, then use Insert **Object...** and click on **Create from File** on the Insert Object dialog. PowerPoint displays a File Name window. You can enter a path and Excel spreadsheet file name, or use **Browse...** to locate the spreadsheet you want to link to PowerPoint. For this example, let's use one of the sample files that came with Excel. Use **Browse...** or type the path and file name:

```
C:.\Excel\examples\samples.xls
```

Now, click on the **Link** button to establish a link as opposed to an embedded relationship between PowerPoint and the Excel spreadsheet. Then click on **OK** to close this dialog and insert the specified spreadsheet onto the PowerPoint slide.

 This operation requires ample RAM memory and plenty of hard disk storage. A link with a large spreadsheet can still be a slow process.

N O T E

The spreadsheet specified is an interactive application that includes Excel macros that can respond to user input. The link to Excel is a live one, so if you or someone else changes the spreadsheet in Excel, these changes appear in PowerPoint. And, you can launch Excel and use the interactive aspects of the spreadsheet inside Excel. This technique adds another interactive level to your PowerPoint presentations. You can either display the Excel data as it is on the PowerPoint slide, or you can click on one of the interactive buttons to launch Excel and step through that program if you wish.

When you are through with Excel, use File **Exit** to close Excel and return to the PowerPoint slide. You can also edit a spreadsheet at any time by double-clicking anywhere inside the linked spreadsheet on your PowerPoint slide. PowerPoint launches Excel with all of its features. Make the edits, be sure to use File **Save** to store the changed version of the spreadsheet, then use File **Exit** to return to PowerPoint.

You can do a lot more with Excel in PowerPoint, but you'll have to read your Excel user's guide to learn more about how to use Excel.

Using PowerPoint with Word 6

If Microsoft Word is your window into your computer, the transition to PowerPoint should be easy because the screens of the two applications are very similar. You can't use PowerPoint directly from inside Word, but the similarity of the two packages and the close integration between them will help you get the most from both of these members of your Office package. There are several ways to use Word directly with PowerPoint right from the PowerPoint toolbar.

Using PowerPoint Report It

Suppose you have prepared all or most of a presentation within PowerPoint, but you'd like to develop a more complete outline using the features of Microsoft Word. Simply click on the **Report It** button on the PowerPoint toolbar. (See Figure 8.13. The location of this and all toolbar buttons may be different depending on whether you have customized your copy of PowerPoint.)

Figure 8.13 Report It Button on PowerPoint Toolbar

PowerPoint automatically launches Word and opens the current presentation outline. You can do this from within any view (except Slide Show) in PowerPoint. The current PowerPoint outline view of your presentation is inserted as a Word 6 document. (See Figure 8.14.)

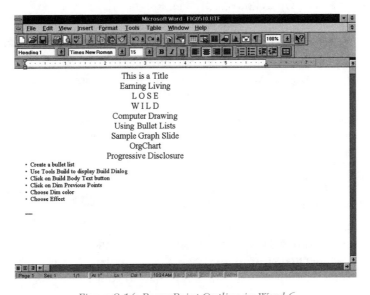

Figure 8.14 PowerPoint Outline in Word 6

The PowerPoint outline view has one limitation: only text that is inserted on a slide in a preformatted title or as a bullet list will appear in the outline. When you get to Word 6 you can create more outline text and levels. Word 6 supports up to nine outline levels, whereas PowerPoint supports only five. Any outline entries beyond level five in Word are imported into PowerPoint as level five.

If a particular slide doesn't have any title text or bullet text, you can still have something from the slide appear on a PowerPoint outline. Use Format **Slide Layout** to display the Slide Layout dialog. Choose a layout that includes a title by selecting the layout and clicking on **Apply** or by double-clicking on the layout. (The next-to-last layout has a title only and won't interfere with anything else on the current slide.) Click to add a title, then select the text and use Format **Font** to specify a color that is the same as the slide background. The title won't appear on the slide but it will show up in the outline.

When you have finished editing the PowerPoint outline in Word, you can export it to PowerPoint by using File **Save As...** and choosing a Rich Text Format. This is the format PowerPoint uses to import Word 6 outlines. When you restart PowerPoint, use File **Open** and specify the .RTF file you just saved.

Your PowerPoint documentation tells you to click on the PresentIt icon to export the outline directly to PowerPoint. Unfortunately, the PowerPoint documentation was written before Word 6 implemented this feature. If you are using an early version of Word 6, there is no PresentIt icon and no easy way to create it.

If you have upgraded your Word 6 installation to Word 6.0a, you may or may not have access to the PresentIt feature. I found that even after upgrading to version 6.0a of Word I didn't have PresentIt. A little investigation turned up the feature, still on the upgrade disk but not installed. In this section I'll show you how to install this feature with your version of Word. If you install a later version of Word, this procedure may not be necessary.

Locate the Word 6 upgrade disk. Use the Windows File Manager or DOS to copy the file **Present.DOT** from the upgrade disk to the Word Template subdirectory (**C:\WINWORD\Template**, if yours is a standard installation). In Word, use Tools **Macro...** to display the Macro dialog shown in Figure 8.15.

Figure 8.15 Macro Dialog

Click on **Organizer...** on the Macro dialog to display the Organizer dialog, shown in Figure 8.16.

Figure 8.16 Organizer Dialog

Under the In NORMAL.DOT window of the Organizer dialog, click on **Close File** to close out NORMAL.DOT. The Close File button should change to Open File. Click on **Open File** and choose (double-click) the **PRESENT.DOT** file from the Template subdirectory in the Open dialog.

If the Macros tab is not already at the front of the Organizer dialog, click on **Macros** to make it the current tab. The PresentIt macro should appear in the To PRESENT.DOT window of this dialog. Click on **PresentIt** to select this macro. Notice that the Copy button in the middle of this dialog changes direction and To PRESENT.DOT changes to In PRESENT.DOT. Click on **Copy>>** to copy the new macro to the NORMAL.DOT template. Click on **Close** to close the Organizer dialog and return to the Word edit screen.

Now the PresentIt macro is available in the NORMAL template. You have this macro available to you from inside Word. If you wish, you can create an icon for it to place on the Standard toolbar so that the instructions in your PowerPoint manual will be correct. To do this, use Tools **Customize...** to display the Customize dialog shown in Figure 8.17.

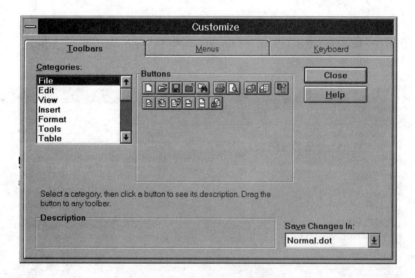

Figure 8.17 Customize Dialog

If the Toolbars tab is not current, click on it to bring it to the front of this dialog.

Use the scroll bar to the right of the Categories window of the Customize dialog to locate Macros. Click on **Macros** to select this category. Choose **PresentIt** from the Macros window that opens after you select the Macros category.

Hold down the left mouse button with PresentIt selected and drag the open box up to the Standard toolbar. When you release the mouse button, Word creates a blank button on the toolbar to represent the PresentIt macro. The Custom Button dialog shown in Figure 8.18 is opened automatically.

Figure 8.18 Custom Button Dialog

Double-click on one of the displayed icons to assign it to the new button you just inserted on the Standard toolbar. Click on **Close** to close the Customize dialog. This new icon becomes the PresentIt button described in your PowerPoint documentation.

Creating Outlines in Word 6

If outlining is a familiar tool for you and you are accustomed to working in Word 6, you may find it easier to start your outline and begin slide show creation in Word 6. Launch Word and use View **Outline** to turn on the outline view. Now use standard Word features to create an outline of a presentation. Figure 8.19 shows a sample Word slide show outline.

Figure 8.19 Word 6 Sample Slide Show Outline

For the outline to translate properly into PowerPoint, you should use Heading 1 style for the top level of the outline, Heading 2 style for the second level, and so on. Once you have the outline arranged the way you want it, you can export it to PowerPoint to serve as the basis of a new slide show by saving the Word outline in a Rich Text Format (RTF), then opening the file in PowerPoint. You will have a basic set of slides with titles and bullet lists.

N O T E If you installed the PresentIt macro on your Word toolbar as I described above, you need only click on the PresentIt icon to have Word save the current outline, close Word, and launch PowerPoint with the outline inserted in a new PowerPoint presentation. You'll be in the Outline view of PowerPoint. You can switch to Slide view to see how the outline translates to slides.

Once you have the basic slide show created, you can add templates, backgrounds, clip art, and more to enhance the basic presentation. To do this, first create the outline in Word. Use File **Save As...** and choose **Rich Text Format** from the Save File as Type field. You can save this file in any directory you wish. It is a temporary file that you won't need once you get your presentation started in PowerPoint.

 NOTE If you use the PowerPoint Report It tool to edit an outline in Word, the default directory for the exchange is the Temp directory used by Windows. This may be \Windows\Temp or \Temp or another directory, depending on how your version of Windows was installed.

Close Word and open PowerPoint. Use File **Open... (Ctrl+O)** in PowerPoint to display the Open dialog (see Figure 8.20).

Figure 8.20 PowerPoint Open Dialog

Pull down the List Files of Type list and choose **Outlines**. Select the directory where you saved the Word outline in the Directories section of this dialog. Choose the file you used to store your Word 6 outline and click on **OK**. PowerPoint opens the file in Outline view, as shown in Figure 8.21.

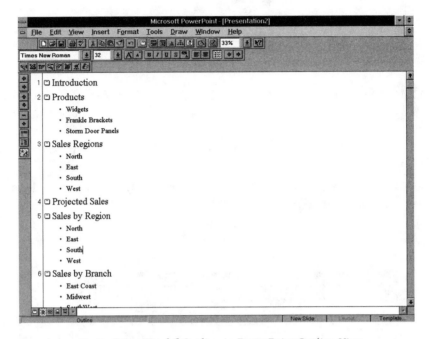

Figure 8.21 Word 6 Outline in PowerPoint Outline View

Now use View **Slides** to see how the Word 6 outline is converted to a PowerPoint slide show. Figure 8.22 shows the outline in Slide view. As you can see, there is no special formatting, but the basic outline information is there and the beginnings of a slide show are complete.

Notice that the top level entries in the Word outline are used for the titles of the slides and the subordinate items are used as bullet lists. The basic slide format chosen automatically by PowerPoint is the one on top of the second column of the Slide Layout dialog (title over a bullet list).

You can change this basic layout easily by using Format **Slide Layout...** to display the Slide Layout dialog. Choose a layout that includes a title and a bullet list, plus any other objects you want to include. PowerPoint places the title and bullet list from the outline into their proper position, and places other objects—such as room for clip art—on the slide as well.

Add the new objects, choose a template or background, and otherwise enhance the basic slide design you created with the Word outline. Be sure to save the slide presentation as a PowerPoint file. Otherwise you lose the additional formatting.

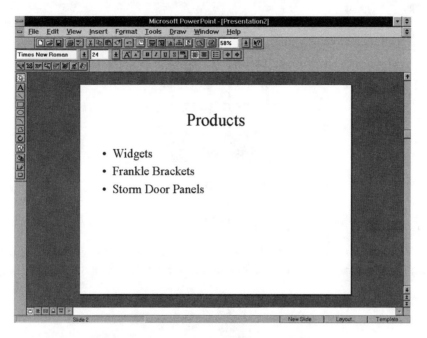

Figure 8.22 Word 6 Outline in PowerPoint Slide View

Creating a Word Table

Microsoft Word has a strong table creating utility. PowerPoint can use this Word feature to insert a table on a slide. To insert a Word table on the current slide, click on the **Insert Word Table** icon (see Figure 8.23).

Figure 8.23 Insert Word Table Icon

PowerPoint pulls down a dummy table form, just like in Word, to let you select the number of rows and columns. Figure 8.24 shows this basic table form.

Figure 8.24 Pull-down Table Form in PowerPoint

Place the mouse pointer inside the pull-down table, and drag the shape of the table to define the type of table you want. When you have the number of rows and columns you want specified, release the mouse button. PowerPoint opens a Table Editing window on the current slide, as shown in Figure 8.25.

Figure 8.25 Table Editing Window on a PowerPoint Slide

Although you are working inside PowerPoint, you actually are accessing the table features of Word through an OLE 2.0 link and a feature called in-place editing. Notice that the Format Bar at the top of the slide screen changes to the

Word toolbar. In addition, if Word is already open in Windows, you will see other toolbars and formatting that are current in the open version of Word. Some Word features may not function as you expect in this situation. If you are working with an outline in Word when you insert a table in PowerPoint, for example, the outlining toolbar would be displayed. However, if you tried to use the outline toolbar features, you would get an error message such as "This command is not available because the document is being edited in another application." This is a potentially frustrating anomaly that comes with working with in-place editing through OLE 2.0.

Also, while you are working with Word through PowerPoint, the toolbar choices (when you click the right mouse button while pointing to any currently-displayed toolbar) are different from what you find in PowerPoint. If the action you want to conduct is compatible with the PowerPoint environment, then the tools function just as they would in Word. When working with tables in PowerPoint, for example, you can insert borders or shading into a table cell with the Borders toolbar from Word. Just point to the Format Bar, click the right mouse button, and click on Borders on the pull-down menu.

Also, you can achieve the same effect with the Insert **Microsoft Word Table...** command from the main PowerPoint menu. When you use this method, PowerPoint displays the Insert Word Table dialog shown in Figure 8.26.

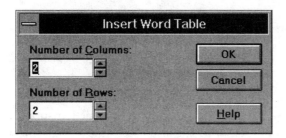

Figure 8.26 Insert Word Table Dialog

Specify the number of columns and the number of rows you want for the table in this dialog. This creates a table in the same way as using the pull-down table form from the PowerPoint Standard toolbar. When the table is specified as you want it, click on **OK** to close the dialog and display the Table Editing window on the current slide.

In addition, you can choose a slide with a table placeholder from the Slide Layout dialog. Click on the icon when PowerPoint prompts you to "Double-click to add table. The Insert Word Table dialog shown in Figure 8.26 is displayed. Proceed as described above".

Enter the text you want for each cell of the table. You can use standard text formatting procedures for the table elements. This includes selecting the font, specifying font attributes (bold, underline, etc.), and choosing positioning (left, center, right). Figure 8.27 shows a sample table after the data has been entered.

Region	Widgets	Frankle Brackets	Storm Doors
North	9,600	19,200	56,000
East	1,200	2,400	4,800
South	300	600	1,200

Figure 8.27 Completed PowerPoint Table

You can also insert clip art images from the collection supplied with Microsoft Word. Position the insertion point in the cell into which you want to insert an image. Then use Insert **Picture** to display the list of clip art files shown in Figure 8.28.

Choose the file name you want and click on **OK** (or double-click on the file name) to close the dialog and insert the image into the current cell in the PowerPoint table editor. Figure 8.29 shows the result of this process with one picture file.

Figure 8.28 Microsoft Word Clip Art Files Dialog

Region	Widgets	Frankle Brackets	Storm Doors
North	9,600	19,200	56,000
East	1,200	2,400	4,800
South	300	600	1,200

Figure 8.29 PowerPoint Table with Picture Inserted

N O T E

Once you have inserted a picture into a PowerPoint table, you can drag it to another cell if you wish. You can even drag it outside the table and place it onto the main body of the slide.

PowerPoint automatically selects a cell size for a new table, but you can change that if you wish. Simply move the mouse pointer into the leftmost column of the Table Editing window. Notice that as you move the pointer up and down this column, the pointer changes to a double-ended arrow as it moves across the boundaries between rows. Hold down the left mouse button when the pointer changes to an arrow, and drag the line that separates rows to change the height of any row. You can't make the row any narrower than the height of the current font, and in no case any narrower than about a 32-point font. But you can make the row much wider, if you wish. You can also change the width of any table cell by dragging the line that separates columns to the width you want. You can't make the column any narrower than one character wide.

Although the Table Editing window shows a grid of lines around table cells, when you exit the editing window (and leave Word), PowerPoint inserts the edited table into the current slide without the grid lines. If you want the table to appear on your slide with the grid lines, select the cell or cells that you want to have a border, and then click on the Borders tool on the Format Bar.

From the Format Bar, choose the type of table border you want. This is the same process as choosing a paragraph border within Microsoft Word. You can also add shading with this same toolbar. The default is clear, but you can choose from a range all the way from solid (100 percent) shading to a light 5 percent shading. Figure 8.30 shows the pull-down shading menu from the Borders toolbar. Notice that the type and pattern of shading is displayed in the small box to the left of the shading name on this pull-down list.

Figure 8.30 Shading Pull-down List from Borders Toolbar

In addition, you can specify some unusual shading formats such as dark vertical or dark trellis. These choices add another level of pattern to the shading.

Because you are really working with features of Microsoft Word, the main menu changes to reflect Word features. So, to make additional changes to the table format, pull down the Table menu from the main menu bar, shown in Figure 8.31.

Figure 8.31 Pull-down Table Menu from Menu Bar

To design a custom table with shading, grid lines, and more, click on **Table AutoFormat...** to display the AutoFormat dialog shown in Figure 8.32.

Figure 8.32 Word AutoFormat Dialog

When you have the format of the table as you want it, click on **OK**, then click anywhere outside the Table Editing window to close the table editor and insert the finished table onto the current slide. When you close the Table Editing window, the Word menus and toolbars are removed and the standard PowerPoint screen appears.

You can size the resulting table by selecting it and dragging a sizing handle. You can reposition the table by selecting it and dragging it to a new location on the current slide. If you change your mind and want to remove a table, select it by clicking once anywhere in the table area, then press the **Del** key.

Once a table is inserted onto a PowerPoint slide, you can edit it at any time by double-clicking on the table. PowerPoint automatically launches the Word table facility and opens a Table Editing window. Proceed as described above to make any changes or additions you wish to the selected table.

Creating Drill Down Documents

With linked applications such as those in the Microsoft Office group, you can use one program as the main interface into your computer, yet access the features and files from one or more other applications. A Drill Down document is one that lets you access additional layers of information from external applications. To create a Drill Down document in PowerPoint with Microsoft Word, make the slide on which you want to show additional information current.

Next, use the Insert **Object...** menu sequence to display the Insert Object dialog, shown in Figure 8.33.

Figure 8.33 Insert Object Dialog

Click on the **Create from File** button to open the File Selection window on this dialog. Select the Word document you want to use as a Drill Down document on this slide.

If you're not sure where the file you want is located, click on **Browse...** to open the Browse dialog. This will make it easier to locate the directory and file you want to use.

Click on the **Display As Icon** button, then click on **OK** to return to the slide. PowerPoint inserts an icon onto your slide that represents the specified Word file. Figure 8.34 shows a slide that holds a Word document icon for use as a Drill Down document.

Figure 8.34 PowerPoint Slide with Drill Down Document Icon

You can drag the document icon anywhere on the slide you wish. When you click on the slide outside the document icon, PowerPoint deselects the icon and makes it appear as an integral part of the slide.

During a presentation, the icon appears on the slide. When you want to display the additional information contained in the Word document represented by the icon, simply double-click on the icon to open the document, as shown in Figure 8.35.

NOTE With some screen configurations, Word may launch in full screen mode, covering up PowerPoint. Your presentation is still there. Grab the top of the Word window and drag it downward to reveal PowerPoint.

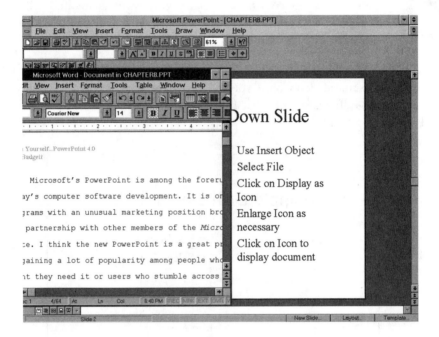

Figure 8.35 PowerPoint Slide with Open Word Document

Notice that when you click on the icon, PowerPoint actually launches Word and opens a separate editing window on the slide. You have standard Word editing and menu features at your disposal while this window is open. To return to the slide, simply click outside the Word window to close it. If Word covers your PowerPoint application, see the Note above.

NOTE If you launch Microsoft Word and shrink it to an icon by clicking on the **Minimize** button at the upper right of the screen before starting your presentation, the Word document will appear on your slides more quickly. This is because you bypass the step of loading and opening Word before the specified document is displayed.

Word is opened in a window smaller than your slide display. You can enlarge the Word window by dragging one or more of its edges. When you close a Word window by clicking outside the window, PowerPoint doesn't actually close Word; it simply moves the Word window to the background. Word remains open and ready for rapid access as required.

N O T E Although you can display any Word document in this window, it doesn't make sense to try to display a very long or complex document during a slide show. Keep the Word display as simple as possible, and it will serve as an excellent enhancement or a way to provide additional information on demand during a slide presentation.

If you have more than one Word document inserted into a slide show, each new document is inserted into Word as you call for it. As you move on to the next slide, Word is moved to the background with each new document kept in memory. You can check this by pulling down the Window menu inside Word to view the various documents you have opened. You can access these directly during a presentation by using the Window menu to select previous documents.

Using PowerPoint with Access

Microsoft Access is a database product that may or may not be part of your Office suite. There are two versions of the Office package. The professional version includes Access, but the regular package does not. Access is a useful tool for maintaining data records for sales contacts, inventory, accounting, customer lists, and more.

As a member of the Office group, Access also contains some of the features of Word 6 and Excel 5. It is not as closely tied to the rest of the Office suite as these other applications, but you can still use information from your databases inside PowerPoint. You may want to use Access information as part of a PowerPoint presentation for the same reasons you would want to use Excel data.

You may have spent many hours compiling and editing database information in Access, so why spend time re-entering this information for a PowerPoint slide? In addition, if more than one user can modify the Access data, you may want to use information directly from Access to ensure that you have the latest information on your PowerPoint slide at all times.

Inserting an Access Package Object

You can insert an Access package onto a PowerPoint slide. This acts as a place-holder that represents database information that you can view or edit by launching Access. To do this, make current the PowerPoint slide on which you want to include an Access package. Use Insert **Object...** to display the Insert Object dialog, then click on **Create from File** to display the File Selection window.

Use **Browse...** to locate the Access directory and the **sampapps** subdirectory under the main Access directory. Now click on the **NWIND.MDB** file within this subdirectory. This is one of the sample applications that comes with Access. You can use any *.MDB* file as the basis for the database package. Click on **OK** to return to Insert Object dialog.

Click on **OK** on the Insert Object dialog to close this dialog and return to the PowerPoint slide. An icon with the Access symbol and the name of the inserted file is placed on the PowerPoint slide, as shown in Figure 8.36.

Sample Access Slide

nwind.mdb

- Use Insert Object or choose object slide layout
- Choose Create from File
- Accept the Access Icon
- Double-click on icon to launch Access

Figure 8.36 Access Package with NWIND.MDB File

N O T E

If you use a large access file, this display step could take a long time. A lot of memory (16MB or more) and a large swap file help. You can also run Access then shrink it to an icon to bypass the loading step during your presentation.

Usually these package icons are small when inserted. You can grab any sizing handle on the object to enlarge the package icon if you wish. You can insert additional clip art, text, and other PowerPoint objects to make a completed slide. The Access object becomes an interactive button that you can use during a presentation to open Access with the selected data file loaded. You can step through the database, viewing data as desired, then use File **Exit** from the Access menu to return to PowerPoint and continue your presentation.

To open Access from inside PowerPoint, double-click on the package to display the screen shown in Figure 8.37.

Figure 8.37 Access Screen with NWIND Database Loaded

This approach to using an external application with PowerPoint is more like linking an object than embedding one, in that you must use Access in its native form to view or edit information. You can display an Access database directly on a PowerPoint slide. However, you can also use the full features of Access to view or change database information from inside Access, then exit Access to return to your PowerPoint presentation.

Copying Access Information to PowerPoint

If you want to display Access information directly on a PowerPoint slide, you can copy database information from an Access screen to a PowerPoint slide. To do this, launch Access and display the database information you want to include in a PowerPoint slide. (Consult your Access user's guide if you need help in displaying database information from Access.)

Figure 8.38 shows a sample Access data file (NWIND) on the screen.

Figure 8.38 Sample Data from NWIND Database

NOTE You can make it easier to switch between PowerPoint and other Microsoft applications by displaying the Microsoft toolbar. Move the mouse pointer to the main PowerPoint toolbar and press the right mouse button. Choose Microsoft from the list to display the Microsoft toolbar. Now you can launch Access by clicking on the Access icon (the icon with the key) on the toolbar.

Use the mouse to select the rows and columns on the database table that you want to include in a PowerPoint slide. Use Edit **Copy** to place a copy of this information onto the Clipboard. Now you can shrink Access to an icon by clicking on the **Minimize** button at the top right of the Access window. Then open PowerPoint. If you have the Microsoft toolbar displayed in Access, you can jump directly to PowerPoint by clicking on the PowerPoint icon.

In PowerPoint, use Edit **Paste** to place the information on the Clipboard onto the PowerPoint slide. This data will be inserted as text. You may find that you have to experiment with the amount of information you copy to make it fit the slide. You can also select this table, then the text, then use the Point Size pull-down list to shrink or enlarge the text to make it fit the area of the slide you want. PowerPoint inserts text from the clipboard as 24 point by default. If the amount of text you are inserting is relatively large, it may not fit onto the slide. Just make the point size of the text smaller to make it fit, or return to Access and select a smaller block of data to insert.

Using PowerPoint with Other Applications

Microsoft's Office products aren't the only applications that can offer you additional support when creating PowerPoint presentations. In fact, virtually any program you are using can supply data or graphics for a PowerPoint presentation.

PowerPoint and Screen Capture Utilities

One possible application for PowerPoint is as a training tool for computer users. If you need to demonstrate how a particular application screen looks and show your audience how to select various aspects of the software, it might be helpful to include actual images of the screen on a PowerPoint slide. For example, the image in Figure 8.39, shows a screen from Kodak's CD Access Software in a PowerPoint slide.

I used a utility called SnapPRO3 from Window Painters, Ltd. (9301 Bryant Avenue South, Suite 201C, Bloomington, MN 55420, 612-881-7576) to capture this screen. (This is the same utility used to capture all of the images for this book.) A utility such as this, or CaptureEze, a component of Pizazz Plus (Application Techniques, Inc., 10 Lomar Park Drive, Pepperell, MA 01463, 508-433-5201), can grab all or a portion of the computer display screen and save it into a graphics file. Most of these utilities support a wide range of file formats— TIF, PCX, BMP, GIF, and more. They grab the screen and save the graphics image to disk in the format you specify.

Figure 8.39 Kodak CD Access Software Screen. Photos by Tom DeMoss, Pictures & Words, Tucson, AZ

To use one of these images on a PowerPoint slide, use Insert **Picture...** to display the Insert Picture dialog shown in Figure 8.40.

Figure 8.40 Insert Picture Dialog

Select the directory where you stored the screen capture image from the Directories window, then choose the file you saved from the File Name window.

When you click on **OK** (or double-click on the file name), PowerPoint inserts the image into the center of the current slide. You can size the image or move it around on the slide just as you would any other PowerPoint object.

If you don't have a screen capture utility, you can still insert computer screen images into your PowerPoint presentations by using the Clipboard. First, shrink PowerPoint to an icon by clicking on the **Minimize** button at the upper right corner of the screen.

Launch the application you want to show in the PowerPoint presentation. Manipulate the application to present the screen you want to use. Press the **Print Screen** key on the keyboard. (It may be labeled Print Scrn, Prnt Scrn, or something similar.) Shrink the second application to an icon by clicking on the **Minimize** button at the upper right corner of the screen.

Maximize PowerPoint by double-clicking on its icon on the Program Manager desktop. Make the slide that will hold the screen image current. Use Edit **Paste** to copy the image from the Windows Clipboard onto the slide. Size or position the image as you would any other PowerPoint object.

The advantage to using a screen capture utility over the Clipboard is that screen capture utilities usually enable you to grab only a portion of the display screen if you wish. If you need only part of a screen on a PowerPoint slide and you don't have a screen capture utility, try using the Windows PaintBrush utility to crop the image. Open PaintBrush and use Edit **Paste** to place the image into PaintBrush. Now you can use the PaintBrush eraser to remove portions of the image, or you can use the other PaintBrush tools to color, crop, and otherwise edit the image.

Once you have the PaintBrush image edited as you want it, use File **Save As...** to store it as a graphics image. Then relaunch PowerPoint and import the file as described above as if it had been created by a screen capture utility.

PowerPoint and DOS Applications

DOS-based applications can't share data directly with a Windows-based application, but you can use information from a DOS program in PowerPoint in a number of ways. You can use the Clipboard in the same way I described earlier in this chapter, but you have to remember one simple trick to make this work with DOS.

First, shrink PowerPoint to an icon by clicking on the **Minimize** button at the top right of the screen. Now, launch the DOS-based program you want to incorporate into PowerPoint. Reduce the DOS application to a window by pressing **Alt+Enter**. Now you can use Windows facilities on the DOS program because the less-than-full-screen window is incorporated into the Windows desktop.

Press **Print Screen** to copy the current screen to the Clipboard. Use PaintBrush to edit the image, if you wish. Then launch PowerPoint and use Edit **Paste** to copy the screen from the Clipboard onto a PowerPoint slide.

Another way to use data from a DOS application in PowerPoint is to print the information to a disk file. Then either import it into Word for editing or import it directly into a PowerPoint slide.

PowerPoint and Microsoft Mail

If you are using PowerPoint with Windows for Workgroups or you have another system that uses Microsoft Mail, the Send... command appears on the File menu. (See Figure 8.41.)

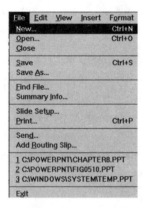

Figure 8.41 PowerPoint File Menu with Send... Command

This interface to Microsoft Mail lets you send your PowerPoint presentation to one or several other people who are also on your network and have access to Mail.

To send a presentation via Microsoft Mail, make the presentation you want to mail the current one. Then use File **Send...** to display the Mail Sign In dialog shown in Figure 8.42.

In most cases you probably will only have to press **Enter** or click on **OK** to close this dialog. If your Mail system is configured to require that you enter a password in this dialog, then enter the password in the Password field. If you have more than one mail server available, you can also enter a mailbox name in the Mailbox field of this dialog. If you aren't sure which mailbox to use or whether you need a password, contact your system administrator.

Figure 8.42 Mail Sign In Dialog

 If you have previously used the Mail system, you are already logged on and you will bypass the Mail Sign In dialog.

NOTE

When you close the Mail Sign In dialog, the Microsoft Mail system is launched and the Send Mail dialog shown in Figure 8.43 is displayed.

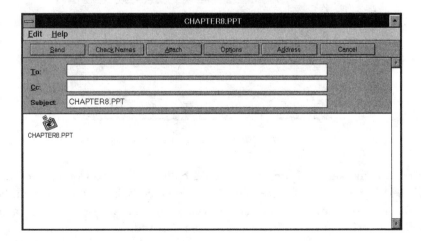

Figure 8.43 Send Mail Dialog

The name of the current presentation appears on the title bar of this dialog and in the Subject field of the Mail address.

Enter the address of the person to receive your presentation in the To field of this dialog. If you want to send a copy to another person, enter that address in the Cc field.

You can enter the first few characters of a user name in the To or Cc field, then press **Alt+K** to have the mailer fill in the rest of the name from the internal database of Mail users on your network.

N O T E

If you're not sure of the names or addresses of recipients, click on the **Address** button on the Mail toolbar. This displays the Address dialog shown in Figure 8.44.

Figure 8.44 Address Dialog from Microsoft Mail

Select a name and click on the **To** or **Cc** button at the Add prompt to add the selected name to one of these lines. You can enter multiple addresses on the To or Cc lines by separating the names with a comma. When you enter a name from the keyboard or specify a name from the Address dialog, the Mail system underlines names that are known. If you enter an address the Mail system doesn't recognize, then Mail displays the error message shown in Figure 8.45.

Figure 8.45 Mail Error Message: Addressee Unknown

Notice that an icon representing the current presentation appears in the message area of the Send Mail dialog. You can add text to go with the presentation, if you wish. Simply click in the message area beneath the presentation icon and type any message you want to mail along with the PowerPoint file (see Figure 8.46).

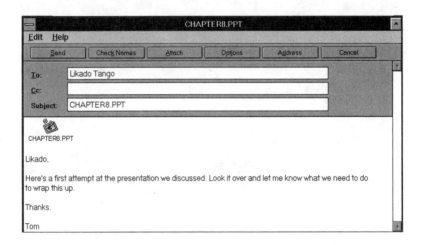

Figure 8.46 Send Mail Dialog with Typed Message

If you want to send another file along with the presentation and any typed message, click on the **Attach** button. Mail opens a directory and file name dialog to let you choose a file name to attach with the Mail message. You might want to do this if you have a separate word processor file of notes or ideas that go with the presentation, for example.

When you have the address and the message the way you want them, click on the **Send** button. Mail clears the screen and sends the message to the users you specified.

On the receiving end of a PowerPoint Mail message, you'll need to have PowerPoint or the PowerPoint viewer installed to look at a slide presentation sent to you over a network. If you receive a Mail message with a PowerPoint icon, like the message in Figure 8.47, you can double-click on the icon to open the presentation.

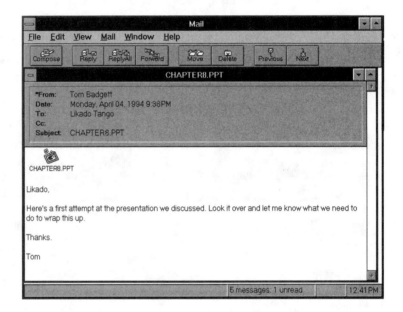

Figure 8.47 Mail Message with PowerPoint Icon

If you don't have PowerPoint or the viewer installed, you'll get an error message like the one in Figure 8.48.

Figure 8.48 Mail Error without PowerPoint Installed

If you do have the viewer or PowerPoint itself installed, when you double-click on the PowerPoint presentation icon on your Mail screen, the link is made automatically. You can view the slide show in full screen, Slide Show mode. In addition, you can forward the message to others if you wish. You can add more text, such as your comments or suggestions to the next recipient.

PowerPoint and Other Windows Applications

You can use PowerPoint with almost any Windows program using the techniques I've already described. With the spread in popularity of OLE links, you can use links to external applications in many cases. But even if the application you want to use doesn't support OLE, you can export data for use in PowerPoint.

In a word processor, database, spreadsheet, or other application, you frequently can select blocks of data and use an Edit **Copy** command sequence to place a copy of the selected data onto the Clipboard. Then you can make PowerPoint the current application and use Edit **Paste** to copy the Clipboard information onto a PowerPoint slide.

You can also print Windows application data to a file and import that information into Word, into another application, or directly into PowerPoint.

Using PowerPoint with Other Applications

I've talked a lot in this chapter about how to integrate files or data from external applications into PowerPoint presentations. There may be times when you want to include slides you have created in PowerPoint with other applications.

Suppose you want to use a slide you have designed in PowerPoint in a Word document, for example. You can capture the PowerPoint screen with the Clipboard or a screen capture utility, of course, and then use Edit **Paste** in Word. An alternative to that is to save a slide you want to use in an external application as a Windows Metafile. To do this, manipulate your PowerPoint presentation so that the slide you want to use is current. Then use the File **Save As...** command to display the Save As dialog. In the Save File As Type field of this dialog, choose **Windows Metafile**. Pick a directory and file name, then click on **OK** to save the file and exit the Save As dialog.

Now, open the application with which you want to use the slide you just saved. Use Insert **Picture** (or an equivalent command) and choose the file you saved. If the external application supports Windows Metafiles, you should be able to import the slide you saved directly into the other application. (This works well with Microsoft Word, for example.)

You can also print a PowerPoint presentation, or a portion of a PowerPoint presentation, to disk instead of to a printer. (See Chapter 6 if you need help in doing this.) Then import the print file into an external application. This won't work with all printer types, nor can all applications import printer files, but you may find that it works with the program that matters to you.

To Sum Up

Few software applications stand alone today. Thankfully, the newest designs enable applications to exchange data and to provide a common user interface. This makes the transition from one application to another much easier than it was a few years ago. Although PowerPoint, as part of the Microsoft Office package, is more closely related to Word, Access, and Excel than to other applications, you can use any product that supports OLE to share inserted or linked applications directly.

In addition, any product that generates graphics or text images that you might want to incorporate into a PowerPoint presentation can serve as a resource for you. This is because most applications have the ability to save their output in a format that PowerPoint can use. Sometimes this is a direct transfer, where PowerPoint can import another application's files directly. Sometimes it is an indirect transfer, where the foreign application exports its files into a format that PowerPoint can use. Either way, don't ignore the possibility of using the features of another software package with which you are familiar or that offers special features you want. This will help you produce imaginative presentations that have the maximum impact and effectiveness.

In the next chapter, I'll show you how to get the most out of the PowerPoint on-line Help system. Like a growing number of current software applications, PowerPoint depends heavily on its Help system to provide you with in-depth information about using the product.

Using PowerPoint Help

The trend in modern software is to make user interfaces as similar to each other as possible. This makes the transition from one program to another easier. In addition, because an increasing number of software packages follow the Microsoft Windows format, software suppliers tend to put more and more information into the on-line help facility and less information into the printed manual.

In general, if you are comfortable with the on-line help system of any other Windows-based product, you should have no problem finding your way around PowerPoint Help. However, because there is a lot of information in Help, and because it isn't always where you might expect to find it, I'll give you a brief tour of the PowerPoint Help system in this chapter.

Context Sensitive Help

The concept of *context sensitive help*—help that directly addresses the current task—has been around for some time, but only with the latest Windows products have we seen it applied consistently and effectively. You can get context sensitive help in PowerPoint with the toolbar Help button or by choosing Help on any PowerPoint dialog.

Using the Toolbar Help Button

Probably the quickest way to get direct help with something on the PowerPoint screen is to use the context sensitive Help button from the Standard toolbar (see Figure 9.1).

Figure 9.1 Context Sensitive Help Button

When you click on this button, the PowerPoint mouse cursor changes to a question mark beside an arrow, indicating that you have activated the Help pointer. Now move the pointer to the PowerPoint menu, button, dialog, or other object about which you'd like more information, then click the left mouse button. PowerPoint opens a Help file that describes that object.

For example, if you click on the Help button, then click on the check mark icon on the Standard toolbar, the Help window shown in Figure 9.2 is displayed.

Figure 9.2 Spell Check Help Window

Notice that this is a standard Help window with a menu bar, a toolbar, and hypertext links to other Help topics. These Help window components in Figure 9.2 are labeled in Figure 9.3.

Figure 9.3 Help Window with Labeled Components

To get more information on any topic listed under the **See also** title, simply move the mouse pointer over the green underlined text until the pointer changes to a hand, then click the left mouse button. The current Help window is closed and the window about the topic you just selected is displayed. Because this is a standard Help window, you can use other features of the Help system to display other Help topics, to search for topics, to review Help history, and so on. I'll show you more about these PowerPoint Help features later.

After you read the displayed Help window, you can return to PowerPoint and your work in progress by using File **Exit** from the Help window, or by clicking on the **Control Menu** button and choosing **Close** (**Alt+F4**).

 If you click anywhere outside the displayed Help window, PowerPoint removes the window and returns you to the PowerPoint slide screen. However, the Help window isn't actually closed. It **N O T E** remains open on the Windows desktop behind PowerPoint. If you select another Help topic, this hidden window is brought to the front and replaced by the new topic. If you don't choose another Help topic, this window stays open until you close it or until you exit PowerPoint.

Using Dialog Box Help

Another way to get context sensitive help is to choose a Help button on an open PowerPoint dialog. The Help window you get may contain very specific information about the task you are attempting, or it may be a more general Help window that also addresses the current task. This depends on the operation. For example, if you use Insert **Clip Art...** to display the Clip Art dialog and then click on the **Help** button, you'll get the very detailed Help window shown in Figure 9.4.

On the other hand, if you use Insert **Picture...** to display the Insert Picture dialog and then click on Help, you get the more general Help window shown in Figure 9.5.

Figure 9.4 Insert Clip Art... Help

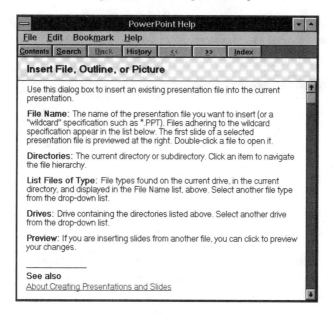

Figure 9.5 Insert Picture... Help

This is the same Help window you get from the **Insert Slides from File...** and the Insert **Slides from Outline...** dialogs. But as you can see, the quick answers to your questions are there, and you can use this window as a jumping off place for additional information from anywhere in the Help system.

Using Help Bookmarks

Sometimes one quick look at a Help topic isn't enough. When you want to have quick help available on a specific topic, you can create a Help *bookmark*. A bookmark is a way to mark a Help window so that you can call it up at any time without having to step through the Help menu or call up the dialog with which it is associated.

To create a bookmark, display the Help window you want to mark, then click on **Bookmark** from the Help menu bar. A single selection, **Define...**, is displayed. Click on **Define...** to display the Bookmark Define dialog shown in Figure 9.6.

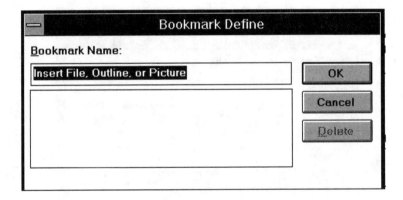

Figure 9.6 Bookmark Define Dialog

Notice that the default bookmark name is the title of the Help topic. You can accept that default, if you wish, or you can type any other name you want to use in the **Bookmark Name** field of this dialog. The default name is selected when this dialog opens, so you can just start typing a new name. The default name will be erased and replaced with what you type.

NOTE

The bookmark names you choose can be important, particularly if you are setting up the system for someone else. You could, for example, establish Help bookmarks that are named in a sequence so that new users can go through the bookmarks to learn the steps for creating a presentation or another PowerPoint task. You could label the bookmarks Task#1, Task#2 ... Task#N, for example, to provide a customized Help system for new users.

Click on **OK** to accept the new bookmark name and close the Bookmark Define dialog.

To use bookmarks, click on **Help** on the main PowerPoint menu bar, choose a Help topic, then choose **Bookmarks** from the Help window menu. All of the bookmarks you created will appear as part of a pull-down list. You can select the bookmark you want to use. You can see from this list that an obviously sequential naming convention can make it easy for users to step through Help windows for a particular task.

To get continuous help on a task, shrink PowerPoint so that it takes up less than a full screen by clicking on the **Shrink Document** button at the far right of the title bar. Now you can open a Help window and, by adjusting the size of the Help and PowerPoint windows, produce a side-by-side display like the one in Figure 9.7. This provides easy access to Help while you work with PowerPoint.

Figure 9.7 Side-By-Side Help with PowerPoint

Notice that I have shown the display with a rather narrow Help window and a wider PowerPoint window. You can adjust either of these as needed by grabbing any of the edges of a window and dragging the window to a new size. Obviously, in working with PowerPoint you need the PowerPoint window to be as large as possible and still let you see Help.

Another way to do this is to make the PowerPoint window almost fill the screen and leave just enough room to display a small segment of the Help window. Then, when you want Help, you can click anywhere in the Help window. PowerPoint will bring the Help window to the front of the display, covering PowerPoint. When you're ready to return to PowerPoint, just click anywhere inside the PowerPoint window to send Help to the background and bring PowerPoint to the foreground. Figure 9.8 shows a screen with PowerPoint on top of Help. Figure 9.9 shows a screen with Help on top. You can switch between Help and PowerPoint whenever you need.

Figure 9.8 PowerPoint/Help Screen with PowerPoint on Top

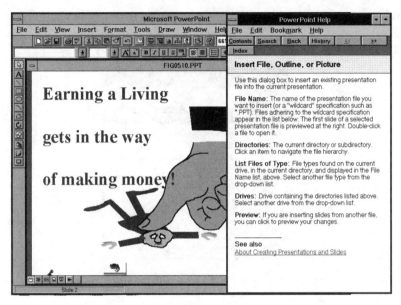

Figure 9.9 PowerPoint/Help Screen with Help on Top

If you want the Help window to stay on top of PowerPoint no matter what, click on **Help** on the Help menu (NOT the PowerPoint menu) and choose **Always on Top**. This forces the Help window to be always visible, but it causes the Help window to obscure part of the PowerPoint window. As you learn how to conduct certain tasks, however, having Help always visible may be useful.

Help from the Menu

I've already shown you a little bit about accessing Help from the main PowerPoint menu. In this section we'll look deeper into what's available from the Help menu. As with an increasing number of Windows-based software packages, PowerPoint keeps a complete user's manual on-line for quick access. Because the information is in electronic form, you can search for the specific information you need when you need it. When you don't have a context for Help in mind, you can start with the Help menu selection and work your way through the system to learn what you need to learn.

When you click on the Help selection on the main PowerPoint menu bar, you get the menu list shown in Figure 9.10.

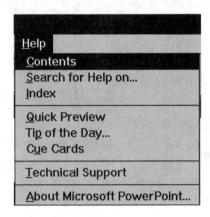

Figure 9.10 Main PowerPoint Help Pull-down Menu

The basic Help window is the Contents window, which is the first selection on the Main PowerPoint Help menu (see Figure 9.11).

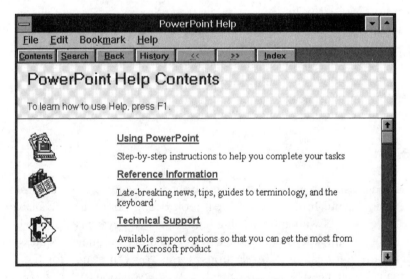

Figure 9.11 Help Contents Window

The Help Menu Bar

The Help menu bar looks very much like the main PowerPoint menu bar and, in fact, like the menu bars of most Windows-compliant products. Let's look at the menu bar items in reverse order.

Help on Help

The Help selection shows you how to use Help, and it also lets you choose whether to keep the Help window on top of PowerPoint when both PowerPoint and Help are open. When you click on **How to Use Help**, the window in Figure 9.12 is displayed.

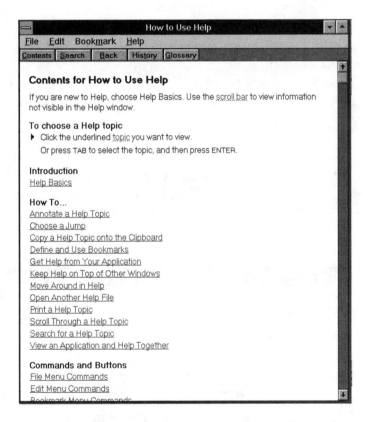

Figure 9.12 How to Use Help Window

Using the How to Use Help window will, in itself, show you how to use Help because this window works the same as the main Help window. If you click on **Contents**, you get a display of the topics covered in the Help on Help windows. You can also create bookmarks and conduct the other procedures available on the main Help window. I'll show you how each of these features works in the following sections.

NOTE

You can view a Help Glossary by clicking on the **Glossary** button on the How to Use Help window.

Bookmark

I've shown you already how to use the Bookmark selection to create quick reference Help windows. In short, all you need to do is display the Help topic for which you want to create a bookmark, then click on Bookmark **Define...** and give the bookmark a name. When you want to recall that Help window, click on **Bookmark** and select the name.

Edit

The Edit menu gives you two choices: **Copy...** and **Annotate...**. The Copy choice works like Copy on most Windows-compliant software menus. When you click on **Copy...**, PowerPoint displays the Copy dialog shown in Figure 9.13.

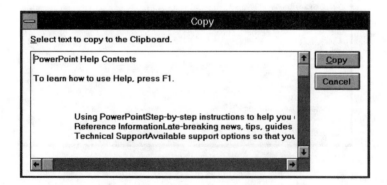

Figure 9.13 Edit Copy... Dialog

The Copy dialog contains the text from the current Help window, and it includes two buttons: Copy and Cancel. If you choose **Cancel**, the copy operation is stopped and you are returned to the current Help window.

If you click on **Copy**, the selected text form the current Help window is copied to the Windows Clipboard. Or, you can use the mouse or the keyboard to select a portion of the text in the Copy window, copying only a portion of the total help text to the clipboard. Now you can close Help and load a word processor or text editor and use Edit **Paste** to paste the Help text into the current document. You could use the same technique to paste the Help text onto a PowerPoint slide. You might want to do this if you are developing a presentation to explain PowerPoint to new users. For example, you may want some Help text on a slide so that you can project it, print it, or otherwise incorporate it into a PowerPoint presentation.

The **Annotate...** option is also useful in helping you or other new users learn about PowerPoint. You can display a Help window on which you would like to include additional information, then use Edit **Annotate...** to display the dialog shown in Figure 9.14.

Figure 9.14 PowerPoint Help Annotate Dialog

You can type any text you wish to add to the current Help window into the Annotation window of this dialog. In addition, you can use the **Paste** option on this dialog to incorporate text from the Clipboard into the annotation. You could copy text from Word or another text product, for example, or from other annotation dialogs.

When you have the annotation as you want it, click on **Save** to place the text and any included graphics onto the current Help window. Notice that this dialog also includes a **Copy** button. When you click on this button, PowerPoint copies the contents of the Annotation window to the Clipboard. This lets you incorporate this custom Help text into another document, or paste it into another annotation window if you want the same text to appear in more than one location within PowerPoint Help.

When you click on **Save** on the Help Annotate dialog, PowerPoint places a hypertext paper clip on the current Help window, indicating that an annotation exists for this window (see Figure 9.15). You can display the contents of this annotation by clicking on the paper clip.

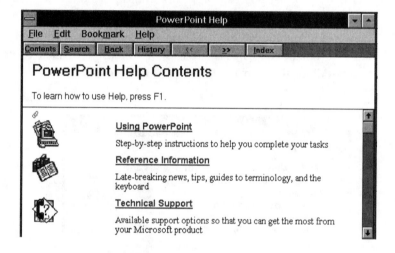

Figure 9.15 HyperText Paper Clip on Help Window

File

The PowerPoint Help File menu offers four choices: **Open...**, **Print Topic**, **Print Setup...**, and **Exit**. This menu points up the fact that Windows Help, including PowerPoint Help, is a standard application much like a word processor, a database, or a presentation package. The files of Help information are stored in a standard format that you can access directly.

Use File **Open...** to display the Open dialog shown in Figure 9.16. This is a standard file open dialog like you might find in any Windows application. It displays files that have an .HLP extension.

Figure 9.16 File Open Dialog from PowerPoint Help

The first file at the top of this list, **powerpnt.hlp**, is the Contents Help file that you can load from the PowerPoint Help menu as described earlier in this chapter. You can click on any of these file names and see a different aspect of PowerPoint Help. But you can also search your system and load Help files from any Windows application that conforms to the Windows Help file format.

For example, use the Directories window of this dialog to locate your main Windows directory (**C:\windows**, if yours is a standard installation). You can see in Figure 9.17 that there are many files that end in **.hlp** in the Windows directory. There is one for the Calculator program (**calc.hlp**), one for the Cardfile program (**cardfile.hlp**), one for the Clipboard (**clipbrd.hlp**), and so on.

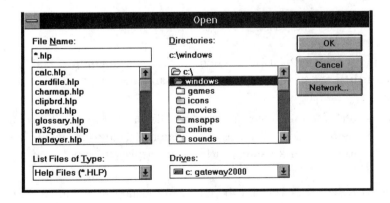

Figure 9.17 Windows Help File List Display

If you'd like to look at the Clipboard Help file, for example, double-click on **clipbrd.hlp** to call up the display in Figure 9.18. You can resize the window to show more or less of the help text.

Figure 9.18 Clipboard Help File

To return to the PowerPoint Help system, either use File **Open...** again and load **powerpnt.hlp**, or close Help (File **Exit**) and then click on **Help** on the PowerPoint menu bar.

Use the **Print Topic** selection from the File menu to print the contents of the current Help window. There is no additional dialog presented when you choose this topic, so make sure you have on display the portion of Help you want to print.

Use **Print Setup...** to display the Print Setup dialog shown in Figure 9.19.

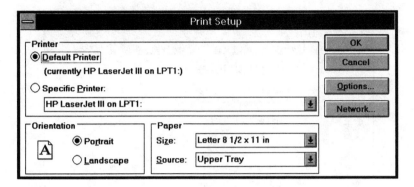

Figure 9.19 Print Setup Dialog from PowerPoint Help

Use this dialog to specify what printer definition you want to use to print Help information and what printer you want to use as the standard default. Notice that this setup dialog is slightly different from the one you get with PowerPoint's main menu File **Print... (Ctrl+P) Printer...**. It does not change the defaults you have previously set.

The **Exit** choice on the PowerPoint Help window does what you would expect. It exits Help and returns you to PowerPoint.

Toolbar

The Help window toolbar is located just below the Help menu bar. The buttons include Contents, Search, Back, History, <<, >>, and Index. As with other PowerPoint toolbar options, these buttons let you jump directly to some aspect of Help without going through the full menu procedure.

Contents Button

The Contents button lets you jump to the main Help Contents window. This is the window shown in Figure 9.20.

Search Button

The Search button lets you search throughout PowerPoint Help for a specific topic. When you click on **Search**, you get the Search dialog shown in Figure 9.21.

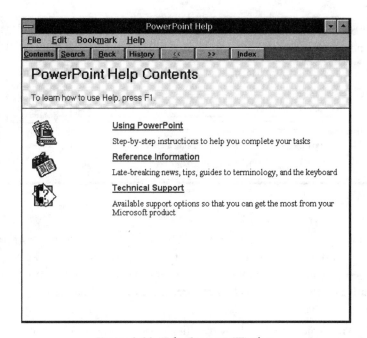

Figure 9.20 Help Contents Window

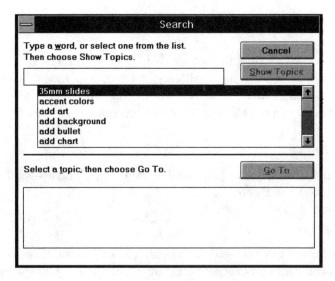

Figure 9.21 Help Search Dialog

The insertion point is placed in the search field of this dialog. You can start typing a word or phrase and watch the Help system try to match what you are entering. As you add each new letter, the search routine jumps to the next topic according to the letters you type.

For example, if you enter the letter **S**, the topic list jumps to **save**, which is highlighted automatically in the topics window. Add a **T** and the topic highlighted is **stack**. Add an **A** and the display doesn't change, because you already are on a word that begins with **STA**. Now add a **T** and the highlighted topic is **status bar**. You can step through any topic in this way, narrowing down the topic as you add new letters. Figure 9.22 shows the Search dialog after the status bar topic has been found.

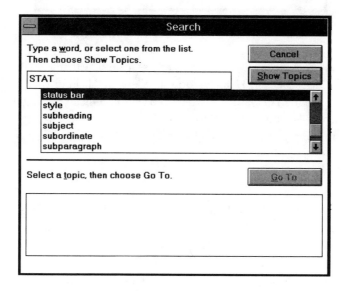

Figure 9.22 Search Dialog with Status Bar Topic Highlighted

There may be several subtopics associated with any word or topic highlighted in this window. You can double-click on any general topic or highlight a topic and then click on the **Show Topics** button to expand the basic topic. Figure 9.23 shows the Search dialog after the status bar topic has been expanded.

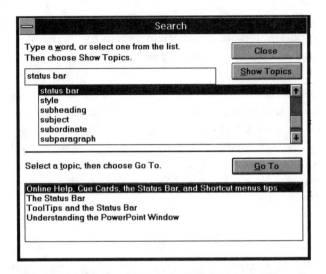

Figure 9.23 Search Dialog with Status Bar Topic List

Now you can scan the available subtopics associated with the main topic you have found. Choose which Help window to view by clicking on a topic in the Select a topic list, then clicking on the **Go To** button. Once you highlight a topic and click on **Go To**, the **Help** window associated with that topic is displayed. Then you can jump to hypertext topics shown on this window, or you can step up and back in the Help text (see below).

Back Button

When you first open a PowerPoint Help window the Back button is dimmed, which means that you can't use it. That's because **Back** is used to step back through the Help topics you have viewed during the current Help session. If you have not yet viewed a Help topic, there is nothing to recall. Once you have looked at one or more Help windows, you can use **Back** to review previous topics in reverse order.

History Button

The History button is another way to look at topics you have viewed during the current Help session. When you click on the **History** button, the names of topics you have seen are displayed in a pull-down list like the one shown in Figure 9.24.

You can jump back to any of these topics by double-clicking on one of them. Notice that the History list shows you the file used to store the topic.

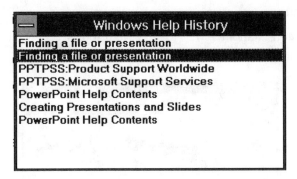

Figure 9.24 Pull-Down Topic List with History Button

Chevron Buttons (<< >>)

The chevron (left and right pointer) buttons let you step up and down through the current Help topic. For example, open the Using PowerPoint window from the Contents list, then choose **Creating Presentations and Slides** (Chapter 2) and pick one of those topics. You can move through the outline (see Figure 9.25) by clicking on the arrow buttons.

Figure 9.25 Creating Presentations and Slides Window

Index Button

The Index button is another way to find Help topics you want to review. The initial Index window is shown in Figure 9.26.

Figure 9.26 Help Index Window

Click on a letter to change the terms displayed on the screen. Then you can jump directly to one of the displayed topics by clicking on the topic you want to view.

To Sum Up

On-line PowerPoint Help is a useful and important part of your PowerPoint package. It is a standard, Windows-compliant Help system that gives you several ways to access the information it contains. Whether you use the main Help menu, search for Help, or use the context sensitive features of Help, you can view detailed information about all aspects of using PowerPoint. In addition, by creating bookmarks and adding annotations, you can create a custom Help system that can help you or other users become familiar with PowerPoint in general or learn how to conduct specific tasks within the system.

The remainder of this book details some of the hardware and software issues with which you should be familiar and provides you with a menu and command reference.

Hardware
and Software Issues

I n this appendix, I'll give specific hardware and software requirements and suggestions that can help you get the most out of PowerPoint 4.0.

Required Hardware and Software

If you are running Microsoft Windows 3.1 or later, you should be able to run PowerPoint 4.0. Microsoft recommends 4 MB of RAM for PowerPoint 4.0. However, you'll get along much better if you have 8 MB of RAM or more. In fact, I don't recommend that you try to run any Windows application with less than 8 MB of RAM. 16 MB is better, especially if you plan to run more than one program at once.

To take advantage of the features offered by Microsoft Windows and PowerPoint 4.0, you need a relatively high-end PC. A machine that uses the 80386 DX processor running at 33 MHz or higher should be considered the minimum power for any serious Windows-based application today. It is true that Windows will load and run on a less powerful machine, but you won't be happy with it for very long. Windows and the applications that use Windows offer many improvements in user interface, online help, graphics, and more, but these features require a lot of memory, a lot of storage (disk space), and a powerful processor (CPU). Anything less than a 386DX/33 with 4 to 8 MB of memory runs painfully slow.

In fact, if you are outfitting for PowerPoint and have to buy a new machine, look carefully at your budget and what is available from suppliers you can use. Then consider a machine that uses an 80486DX/33 or more powerful CPU. With Pentium and Power PC machines hitting the market, 486 machines should become even cheaper than they've been. You don't need a Pentium machine to run Windows and PowerPoint adequately, but you should search for the bargains and buy the most powerful hardware you can find and afford. Even though you will pay a little more in the beginning, you'll have a machine that will grow with your applications and you'll be happier in the long run.

You will need at least one floppy disk drive, of course, to copy the distribution disks to your hard drive. This should be a 1.44 MB high density, 3.5-inch drive. Your hard disk needs about 25 MB of free space. You can install PowerPoint for a laptop or minimal installation with less storage space than that. However, to get a full installation with all the templates, drivers, and help files, and still have room for presentations, you should free up at least 25 MB for PowerPoint 4.0.

Your display adapter should be SVGA compatible, and the monitor should be a high resolution color device. Part of the power of PowerPoint is in its handling of color and graphics. You'll be able to design better presentations and get more out of PowerPoint itself with a high quality monitor. I recommend setting up Windows for 1,024 x 768 resolution. This gives you a full screen of information that should be reasonably easy to read if your monitor is of good quality. When you use the standard VGA 640 x 480 display, the screen is crowded and you can't display as many Windows applications or objects as you might like.

You'll need a laser printer for PowerPoint. With a quality laser printer you can print directly to overhead projection foils, and you can produce high quality black and white pages for reports or audience handouts. Today's printer standard is 600 dots per inch resolution, compared to the 300 dots per inch of just a couple of years ago. If you're buying a new printer, don't settle for less than 600 dpi. The cost difference is slight, but the quality difference between 300 dpi and 600 dpi is very noticeable.

In fact, with prices the way they are today, you also should consider a color printer, especially if overhead projection is a large part of your presentation output. For anywhere from $600 to $2,000 you can have quality color output that can make a real difference in how the audience receives your presentation.

Microsoft says that you can run PowerPoint with DOS 3.1 or later, but it certainly is to your benefit to keep up with software developments and run the latest versions of system software. Therefore, you should be using DOS version 6.2 and Windows 3.11 (as this book is written). Each new version of DOS and Windows offers significant enhancements that can make your computer life easier and more productive.

Tuning for Top Performance

Even if you have the basic hardware and software I recommend to run PowerPoint, you may find that performance isn't what it should be. There are a few things you can do if you find PowerPoint—and Windows in general—running a little slow.

First, look at your memory. If you have only 4 MB of RAM, double it, at least. Again, I believe that an 8 MB system is the minimum for running modern Windows applications. If you can afford 16 MB, that's better still. More memory enables Windows to run more in RAM instead of swapping information to the hard drive, which is a much slower device than solid state RAM.

Next, check out your hard drive. If it is nearly full, that could slow things down. Use DOS, DOSSHELL (a DOS application), or the Windows File Manager to find out what is on your disk and whether there are any files you can eliminate. With additional free space, some applications become more efficient and may run faster. In addition, you should run SCANDISK (from DOS 6.2) or another optimizing utility to eliminate disk fragmenting. Files that are scattered across the surface of your hard disk load and save a lot slower than files that reside in contiguous disk space. SCANDISK or another utility will remove fragmentation and place files in side-by-side disk locations.

Check your Windows configuration to find out how much permanent swap disk space you have, if any. Even if you have a lot of RAM, Windows uses your hard disk to swap out applications or portions of applications as they run. If you haven't established a permanent swap file, chances are that Windows is using a temporary swap file, which may change size and may cause disk fragmentation problems.

To find out what permanent swap space you have or to change the configuration, open the Control Panel located in the Main applications window of the Program Manager and choose **Enhanced** from the Control Panel display. Your screen should look like the one in Figure A.1.

Figure A.1 Control Panel Enhanced Dialog

Click on the **Virtual Memory...** button on this dialog to change the display to the one shown in Figure A.2.

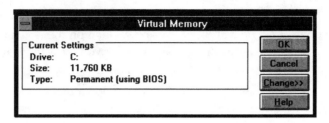

Figure A.2 Virtual Memory Dialog from Control Panel

If your display shows a permanent swap file in the Swapfile Settings area of this dialog, then you already have some permanent disk space set aside for swapping out data to the hard disk. The permanent swap file is important because it is contiguous memory of a specified size that is always in place. The next task is to check the size of this file to see if it is appropriate for the memory and storage available on your machine. Obviously, if the Type field of this dialog shows you are using a temporary swap file, you should establish a permanent file.

To set up a permanent swap file to replace a temporary file or to change the size of an existing permanent file, click on **Change>>** on the Virtual Memory dialog. This expands the Virtual memory display like the sample in Figure A.3.

Figure A.3 Expanded Virtual Memory Dialog

The New Swapfile Settings portion of this dialog lets you specify the disk drive to use for the swap file, the type of swap file you want to create, the size of the file, and the type of access you want to use for the disk and for memory.

If you want to use a drive other than the one Windows selects as the default, pull down a list of available drives by clicking on the down arrow to the right of the Drive field on this dialog. Select the drive you want to use by clicking on it.

Next, choose the type of swap file by pulling down the list in the Type field of this dialog. If Permanent isn't already the default, click on **Permanent** on the pull-down list to select it. Windows shows you the available space on disk, the maximum size for a swap drive, and the recommended size.

Windows will recommend a size based on the size of your hard drive, the amount of storage available, and the amount of RAM you have. In most cases, it is best to accept this recommended size. In any case, it doesn't make sense to specify a swap file larger than the recommended size. Anything larger than the recommended size simply wastes disk space. If you find that you need to use some of the disk space recommended for permanent swap file, then you can specify a smaller space. You may also specify a smaller than recommended swap file if you don't normally run multiple Windows-based applications simultaneously.

If you are using a newer computer, chances are you have a 32-bit disk controller. You can speed up disk access by specifying 32-bit access. Click on the **Use 32-bit Disk Access** box to turn on 32-bit disk reads and writes. If your computer doesn't have the hardware to support 32-bit access, Windows will return this setting to 16-bit access. Likewise, speed up memory access by clicking on **Use 32-bit File Access** to turn on this feature. This speeds up disk access and reduces the time required to read and write information to your disk cache.

The final setting on this dialog is the Cache Size window. Note the Windows default and increase it if you can spare the RAM and if you would like improved disk performance. Anytime you are experiencing slow access to your hard drive, you could consider enlarging the cache size. In most cases you'll do well to accept the Windows suggested size for the cache. If performance isn't what you expect it to be, experiment with larger cache size. Remember, however, that when you give up more memory to cache, you reduce the amount of memory available for running applications. Again, if you don't frequently run several applications at once, you can probably give up some additional RAM without hurting anything. Notice that cache size is given in kilobytes, so if you select

4,096 in the Cache Size window, you are really telling Windows to set aside a 4 MB cache.

When you have the permanent swap settings the way you want them, click on **OK** to close the Virtual Memory dialog. This displays the warning in Figure A.4.

Figure A.4 Confirmation Warning for Virtual Memory Changes

Click on **Yes** to accept the changes. Windows returns the display to the Enhanced dialog. Click on **OK** again to return to the main Control Panel display. From this display you can click on **Settings** to pull down the menu of Control Panel choices. Click on **Exit** to close the Control Panel.

Beyond the Basic PC

I've already mentioned in Chapter 7 how you can enhance your basic PC setup by including screen cameras and other tools for presentation. In this section I'll summarize some of this hardware that you can add to your PC for more creative presentations.

Screen Capture Cameras

If you need an occasional color slide, the best choice is to use a slide service such as Genigraphics, the company that designed the templates and slide views for PowerPoint. If you regularly produce slide-based presentations, on the other hand, you should consider investing in a screen capture camera. These devices generally attach to your PC's video display to present a parallel screen image. A 35mm camera body takes pictures from this display to produce a high resolution color slide of the computer screen.

Multimedia Hardware and Software

PowerPoint 4.0 supports many enhanced presentation features, including the ability to embed sound files and motion video. I showed you how to use these features in Chapter 7. However, to produce your own sound and video files, you'll need some additional hardware beyond the basic out-of-the-box PC.

Video Hardware

I showed you in Chapter 7 how you can connect a converter to change your computer's VGA output to standard television signals that you can display on a TV monitor or record on a video tape recorder. That's just one aspect of using video with your PowerPoint presentations. Because PowerPoint has the ability to link with the Windows Media Player, you can play motion video from inside PowerPoint.

You can purchase video clips from stock agencies, but these generally serve only as concept footage. When you want to convey something specific, you'll want to insert your own video within your PowerPoint presentation. To do this you'll need hardware to interface a standard video source to your computer. Some of the hardware I mentioned in Chapter 7 is two-way. It can be used to convert VGA video information to standard NTSC television video, and it can also take input from NTSC (television) sources and convert it to computer files.

Below, I've listed sources for hardware you can use for video conversion. Some of these devices aren't inexpensive. They can cost $2,000 to $3,000. However, prices are falling all the time and some inexpensive units are hitting the market as this book is written. Contact several of the vendors listed below to find out the current state of the art and pricing information.

Creative Labs, Inc.

1901 McCarthy Boulevard

Milpitas, CA 95035

408-428-6600

800-647-9933

Fast Electronics U.S., Inc.

5 Commonwealth Road

Natick, MA 01760

508-655-3278

IBM Corporation

4111 Northside Parkway

Atlanta, GA 30327

404-238-1282

800-426-9402

Jovian Logic Corporation

47929 Fremont Boulevard

Fremont, CA 94538

510-651-4823

New Media Graphics Corporation

780 Boston Road

Billerica, MA 01821-5925

508-663-0666

800-288-2207

TrueVision

7340 Shadeland Station

Indianapolis, IN 46256

317-841-0332

800-344-8783

With a board that lets you connect a video camera or recorder to your computer, you can capture live video, such as a short statement from a company owner, engineering director, or sales manager. This can give a personal and believable quality to your presentation. Or, you can dub portions of an existing company or personal video into the computer so you can attach them to a PowerPoint slide.

Audio Hardware

I showed you in Chapter 7 how to attach audio clips to a PowerPoint slide, and I listed some sources for prerecorded digital music and sounds. The audio information in PowerPoint is presented on the slide as an icon that you can click to play music, sound effects, or narration. Windows and other applications ship with some sound files, and you can purchase presentation audio. However, the key to successful sound integration with PowerPoint presentations is to have available the sounds or narration you need and to have the proper hardware to output sound. In most cases a single sound board is all that you need to accomplish both tasks.

A number of companies supply sound adapters that plug into your PC bus much like a video display adapter card or a hard disk controller. Connectors on the rear of the board let you attach the sound output to an external amplifier, directly to a set of low-power speakers, and to a microphone or other audio input device. Software that ships with your board lets you digitize sound presented to the input connector, usually in stereo. Sound you digitize in this way—or sounds you purchase or obtain from another source—can be sent out from the sound card. Most cards include internal amplifiers so that you can attach speakers directly to the card for low-level sound output. A sound level of one to four watts is usually provided with these cards. If this level of sound is not enough, you can plug the output of your sound card into the input connector of an external amplifier and a set of speakers that can handle the output. This lets you produce sound levels appropriate for a small room or an auditorium.

I can't possibly list all the suppliers of PC sound cards here, but the following list will get you started.

Ad Lib, Inc.
50 Staniford Street
Suite 800
Boston, MA 02144
800-463-2686

Advanced Strategies Corporation
60 Cutter Mill Road
Great Neck, NY 11021
516-482-0088

Alpha Systems Lab

2361 McGaw Avenue

Irvine, CA 92714

714-252-0117

Antex Electronics

16100 South Figueroa Street

Gardena, CA 90248

310-532-3092

ATI Technologies, Inc.

3761 Victoria Park Avenue

Scarborough, Ontario, Canada M1W 3S2

416-756-0718

Aztech Labs, Inc.

46707 Fremont Boulevard

Fremont, CA 94538

510-623-8988

Computer Peripherals

667 Rancho Conejo

Newberry Park, CA 91320

805-499-5751

800-854-7600

Covox, Inc.

675 Conger

Eugene, OR 97402

503-342-1271

Creative Labs, Inc.
1901 McCarthy Boulevard
Milpitas, CA 95035
408-428-6600
800-647-9933

Digispeech, Inc.
550 Main Street, Suite J
Placerville, CA 95667
916-621-1787

Kurzweil Music Systems
Young Chaing Research and Development Institute
1432 Main Street
Waltham, MA 02154
617-890-2929

Media Vision
3185 Laurel View Court
Fremont, CA 94538
510-770-8600

Microsoft Corporation
One Microsoft Way
Redmond, WA 98052-6322
206-882-8080

Roland Corporation, USA
7200 Dominion
Los Angeles, CA 90040
213-685-5141

Turtle Beach Systems

PO Box 5074

York, PA 17405

717-843-6916

Yamaha of America

6600 Orangethorpe

Buena Park, CA 90620

714-522-9240

Before you purchase a sound card, check with the manufacturer to make sure it will function properly with the other software and hardware you have or plan to use. Also, different products ship with different kinds of support and utility software.

As this book is written, the Sound Blaster series from Creative Labs, Inc., is probably the most popular of the sound card offerings. It is this standard to which most software is written. You can see that this is true as you read the specifications of the offerings of other companies. Most claim to be "Sound Blaster compatible." Some are, others are not. If Sound Blaster compatibility is important to you, the safest route is to buy Sound Blaster. The Sound Blaster card and any truly Sound Blaster compatible cards work fine with PowerPoint.

Menu and
Command Reference

I've shown you the majority of PowerPoint menu commands throughout this book, within the context of a particular task. This appendix is designed to provide a succinct reference to all the menu commands and to help you relate the main menu entries to the tasks performed under these main headings.

The File Menu

The PowerPoint File menu is similar to the File menus in all Windows-compliant products. This series of commands lets you start a new presentation, open an existing one, save the current presentation, print it, or send it. The main File menu is shown in Figure B.1. If your Windows installation does not include networking capability, your menu may not be exactly like this one.

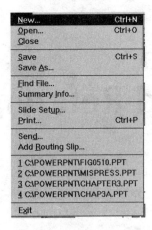

Figure B.1 PowerPoint File Menu

New...   Ctrl+N

Use **New...** to start designing a new presentation. PowerPoint lets you choose how you want to create a new presentation (from a Wizard, template, and so on), and then what slide layout to use for the initial slide.

You can use File **New** from a blank PowerPoint screen, or with other presentations displayed. Either way, PowerPoint opens a new screen, placing existing material in the background.

Open... Ctrl+O

Use **Open...** to load from disk an existing presentation. PowerPoint displays a typical Windows file and directory list, showing files that end in the *.ppt extension. Double-click on the file you want to open, or select the file name and click on **OK** to open the presentation.

Close

Close removes the current presentation from memory and from the PowerPoint screen. If you have saved the file since the last changes were made, no further message will appear. PowerPoint will simply close the file and switch to the previous open file or to the blank PowerPoint screen. If you have made changes to the presentation since saving it last, PowerPoint will ask you if you want to save the changed file prior to closing it.

You may want to say **No** at this prompt if you have made temporary changes that you don't want to save. Otherwise, answer **Yes** so PowerPoint will save the changed presentation to disk. If you have changed the presentation and say **No** at this prompt, any changes since the last save will be discarded.

Save Ctrl+S

As you work on presentations, you should save them every few minutes. The File **Save** command stores to disk the current presentation. If you have not previously saved the file, PowerPoint displays a typical Windows Save As dialog. Otherwise the version of your presentation that is in memory is copied to disk, replacing the previously saved version.

Save As...

Use **Save As...** the first time you store a presentation (or use **Save**, in which case PowerPoint displays the Save As dialog automatically). This gives the presentation a name, establishes the directory where you want to store it, and sets up the system so that the File Save command knows where to put the current file.

You can also use File **Save As...** to store a changed version of a presentation to a new location. Suppose you have a completed presentation that you want to modify or experiment with. Load the presentation from disk, then immediately use File **Save As...** to store it under a new name. Now as you work with the file, use File **Save** to store the new version, leaving the original unchanged.

Find File...

The Find File... command offers a powerful set of commands and features to help you find presentation files or any type of file on your disk or network. Built-in commands also let you manipulate these files in certain ways. In fact, the Find File... command serves as a fairly powerful file manager that you can access without leaving PowerPoint.

Use this command to locate a file on disk. The File Find File... command displays the dialog shown in Figure B.2. If you have conducted previous searches, you may get a Find File screen summary. Click on **Search** to display the dialog in Figure B.2.

Figure B.2 Search Dialog

PowerPoint automatically inserts *.ppt in the File Name field of this dialog so that you can search specifically for presentation files. You can pull down a file type list by clicking on the down arrow to the right of this field and choose **All Files**, or you can type any file filter specification you wish on this line.

The Location field is for the disk and path you want PowerPoint to search. You can pull down a list of available drives by clicking on the down arrow to the right of this field (see Figure B.3).

Figure B.3 Location Pull-down List in Search Dialog

Unless you click on the **Include Subdirectories** button at the right of the dialog, PowerPoint searches only the specified drive and directory. However, if you specify the root directory, then click on **Include Subdirectories** PowerPoint may not be able to search the entire drive. If the program runs out of room, you'll get a "Too many subdirectories" error message, and the list will be built based on the directories that were searched.

If you want PowerPoint to start over, removing any previously found files and directories from the list, click on the **Rebuild File List** button. Otherwise, the results of previous searches are retained. This is a way to search successive directories to build a complete list of all presentation files.

Using Advanced Search

You can set advanced search parameters by clicking on the **Advanced Search...** button on the Search dialog. This displays the Advanced Search dialog shown in Figure B.4.

Use this series of tabbed dialogs to further refine the search. For example, the Location tab (shown in Figure B.4) lets you build a list of disks and directories to search. The Search In window at the left of the dialog shows which disks and directories PowerPoint will search for the specified files. The Directories window at the right of the dialog displays the available directories. You can highlight a directory in this window and click on **<<Add** to add that directory to the list of directories you want PowerPoint to search.

Figure B.4 Advanced Search Dialog

Below the Directories window is a Drives list. Pull down a list of available drives by clicking on the down arrow to the right of this window. Choose a drive to display that drive's directories in the Directories window. Notice that you can click on the **Include Subdirectories** button to tell PowerPoint to search in directories subordinate to the ones shown in the Search In window.

If you are using a network and want to connect to network drives that aren't already displayed in the Drives window, click on the **Network...** button. This displays the Connect Network Drive dialog shown in Figure B.5. If your Windows installation does not include network support, then this facility is not available to you.

Click on a computer name in the Show Shared Directories on window to display the available directories on that machine. You can select a directory to assign a disk drive number by clicking on a name in the Shared Directories window. Then pull down a list of disk drive letters in the Drive window and choose one for the selected directory. When you have connected to all the new network drives you wish, click on **OK** to return to the Advanced Search dialog.

To remove a search directory from the list in the Advanced Search dialog Search In window, highlight it and click on the **Remove** button. To start a new search, click on **Remove All**. The Search In window will be cleared. Click on the **Summary** tab to show the dialog in Figure B.6. This dialog contains fields for a presentation file's summary information (see below). This lets you narrow the search to presentations by a specified author, for example, or to presentations that contain a specified keyword in the Keywords field of the Summary dialog.

Figure B.5 Connect Network Drive Dialog

Figure B.6 Summary Dialog from Advanced Search Dialog

If you have not completed the Summary Info dialog for a given presentation, then the search routine will not find a presentation if you enter information on the Summary dialog. Obviously, if the summary information in the file you are trying to find is blank and you tell PowerPoint to search for a certain keyword, it won't be found. As the number of presentations you have on disk grows, it is a good idea to fill out the Summary Info dialog for each one. This makes it easier to locate the file later. You can access the Summary Info dialog by choosing **Summary Info...** from the File menu.

The Summary dialog offers additional search options as well. Pull down the Options list to select from Create New List, Add Matches to List, or Search Only in List. Create New List is the default. You can specify whether PowerPoint should match the case of your search parameters. Ordinarily a file search is not sensitive to case. To make it so, click on **Match Case**.

If you know that certain text appears within the presentation you want to find, type that text into the Containing Text field of this dialog. You can specify patterns to look for by clicking on the **Use Pattern Matching** button. Then you can pull down the Special list (see Figure B.7) to select a pattern for searching.

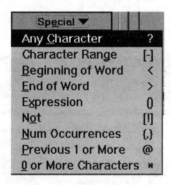

Figure B.7 Special List for Pattern Matching

Use these symbols to narrow your search for text in the Containing Text field of the Summary dialog. These are wild card characters and other specifiers that tell PowerPoint how to look for the text you enter in the Containing Text field.

For example, if you enter **Fig.04??** in the Containing Text field, PowerPoint will look for text that begins with **Fig.04** and ends with any two characters. A more general wild card character is the asterisk. To search for any number of characters in a position (or no characters), place an asterisk in the search string: **Fig.***. To look for the pattern **rec** only at the beginning of a word, enter **<rec**.

By using these special characters carefully, you can construct a very sophisticated search strategy that will find the precise file you seek from among a list of hundreds of files. Especially if you are working with several other users on a network and you aren't sure what naming conventions they may have used, such precise searching capabilities can be quite useful.

Click on the **Timestamp** tab to display the Timestamp dialog, shown in Figure B.8.

Figure B.8 Timestamp Dialog

This dialog lets you specify a range of dates for searching. You may want to look at only older files, for example, or only those that have been created since the first of the year, and so on. You can specify two types of date searching on this dialog: a Last Saved date range and a Created date range. You can also enter the name of the person who last saved or created the file in the By fields of this dialog.

Click on **OK** when you have completed all the data you wish on the Advanced Search dialog to return to the Search dialog. Click on **OK** once again to begin the search and to display the Find File dialog.

Using the Find File Dialog

If your search parameters located any files, PowerPoint will list the directories and file names in the Listed Files window of the Find File dialog. In addition, the first slide from the first file in the list will be displayed in the Preview of window of this dialog (see Figure B.9).

Figure B.9 Find File Dialog

Once you have used the Find File command and located a series of files, each time you use the command again during the current session, the results of the previous search will be displayed in the Find File dialog. You can conduct a new search to replace or add to the current list by clicking on **Search...** on this dialog.

Select different views of the found file information by pulling down the View list at the bottom left of this dialog. Figures B.10 and B.11 show two more views of this same found list. The Preview view, shown in Figure B.9, is the PowerPoint default.

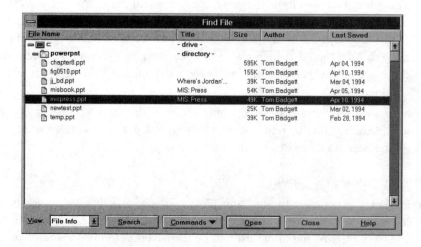

Figure B.10 File Info View

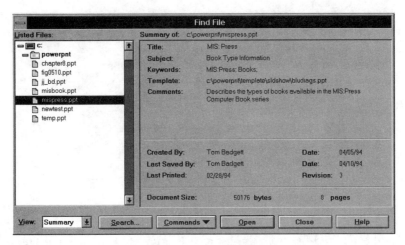

Figure B.11 Summary View

You can also use the Find File dialog to conduct a number of other operations on the files you find. Click on the **Commands** button to pull down the Commands list shown in Figure B.12, which shows you what you can do with the files on this dialog.

Figure B.12 Commands List from Find File Dialog

This set of commands offers another level of file management. It lets you open the file as read only, print the file, edit the summary information for it, delete the file, copy it, or sort the file list in the Find File dialog.

If you choose **Summary...**, the Summary Info dialog for the selected file will be displayed and you can edit it. If you choose **Sorting...**, the Options dialog shown in Figure B.13 will be displayed. Click on the options you wish to enable and choose **OK** to begin the sort.

Figure B.13 Sorting Options Dialog

To open the selected file from the list as a Read/Write file, click the **Open** button at the bottom of the Find File dialog. To close the Find File dialog, click on **Close**.

Summary Info...

Use the **Summary Info...** command on the File menu to enter details about the current file before you save it. The Summary Info dialog is shown in Figure B.14.

Figure B.14 Summary Info Dialog

Notice that PowerPoint fills out some information about the file: the file name, the directory, the template, the number of slides, and the author name. The author name is based on the name of the registered user of the PowerPoint software. You can change this field if you wish.

You can enter information about the title of the presentation and the subject. In addition, you can type in keywords or make any comments you wish. As you saw from the previous section, the information on the Summary Info dialog can make it easier to locate a specific file later, especially when several people are involved in designing PowerPoint presentations. The summary information also helps you remember details about a presentation later. Sometimes you will design a presentation, present it, and then not use those slides for a long time. Later, when designing another presentation, you may want to use all or part of an existing presentation. Reviewing the summary information can help you recall what's in the file.

Slide Setup...

The Slide Setup... command displays the dialog shown in Figure B.15.

Figure B.15 Slide Setup Dialog

Use the Slides Sized for list to tell PowerPoint how to size the slides in your presentation (see Figure B.16).

Figure B.16 Slides Sized for Pull-down List

For most applications you probably will use either **On-screen Show** or **Letter Paper**. The On-screen Show sizing is for times when you will present the show from your computer, whether you actually show it on the computer screen or project it for a larger audience. The Letter Paper sizing will probably produce overhead projection foils of the proper size and orientation.

When you select one of these preformatted sizes, PowerPoint automatically sets the Width and Height values. When you choose **Custom** from the size list, you can change these values. If you attempt to change the Width or Height values with anything other than Custom selected in the Slides Sized for window, PowerPoint automatically selects Custom sizing.

You can also choose orientation for the slides and for the notes and hand-out material from this dialog.

Print...   Ctrl+P

The Print dialog, shown in Figure B.17, lets you specify what you will print and how it will be printed.

I provided details on printing PowerPoint presentations in Chapter 6. Refer to this material for more information on using the File Print... command.

Send...

Use the File **Send...** command to access Microsoft Mail and send the current presentation file to one or more users across your network. If your computer is not part of a network, then this option is not available. When you use the

Send... command for the first time during the current session, and if you haven't used Mail from another application previously, then you must sign in to the mail system. Then the standard Mail dialog shown in Figure B.18 is displayed.

Figure B.17 Print Dialog

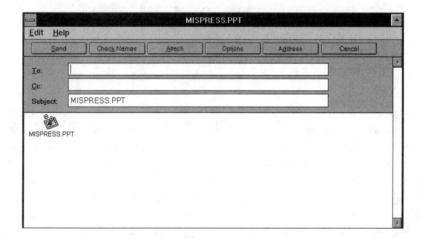

Figure B.18 Microsoft Mail Dialog

Refer to Chapter 8 for details on how to send a PowerPoint presentation file via network mail.

Add Routing Slip...

If you are sending the current presentation to a single recipient via Microsoft Mail, you probably don't need the Routing Slip option. However, if you want to send the presentation to several other people and you want to control the sequence in which they receive it, use the **Add Routing Slip...** command to display the Add Routing Slip dialog shown in Figure B.19.

Figure B.19 Add Routing Slip Dialog

The To window of this dialog lists the recipients you want to receive the file. Use the **Address...** button to access Mail's Address dialog to choose recipients. Once you have built a list of recipients, you can select individual names and move them up or down in the list by clicking on the up or down Move arrows. The position of the names in this list determines the order of receipt when you specify a serial routing by clicking on **One After Another** in the Route to Recipients area of this dialog. Specify serial routing (the PowerPoint default) if you want each person on the list to see the comments offered by everyone before them on the list. If you choose parallel routing (**All at Once** from the Route to Recipients area), then the order of the To list doesn't matter. Choose parallel routing when you simply want everyone on the list to get the message and perhaps make individual comments.

Once you have built a To list, you can remove a selected addressee by clicking on the **Remove** button beneath the To list. Add new recipients to the list at any time by displaying the Address list again and choosing new names.

PowerPoint automatically adds text to the Subject field of this dialog, but you can type anything you want there. The text in this field appears on the Subject line of the received mail at the other end of the connection. You can also type a message in the Message Text box. This text will appear with the icon that represents the presentation file at the receiving end of the mail message.

If you enable **Return When Done** (the default), the message will be routed back to you when everyone on the list has seen it. The **Track Status** option (also a default) keeps track of where the message is along a serial route. If you specify **All at Once**, this option is not available.

You have two final options for completing the routing information. If you click on **Add Slip** at the top of the dialog, then the routing information you have just specified is attached to the file and the dialog is closed, but the mail isn't actually sent. Note that the routing option on the File menu changes when a routing slip has been added. The new command is Edit Routing Slip instead of Add Routing Slip. Also, you must save the file (File Save or File Save As...) to retain the routing slip information.

If you want to add the routing slip to the file and also send the mail, click on **Route**. In this case, the routing slip is added to the file and the mail system is launched to send the message according to the routing information you have just specified. Again, if you want to retain the routing information, you must save the file after specifying Route.

The Edit Menu

Like the File menu, the PowerPoint Edit menu shares many characteristics common to all Windows-compliant applications. It also has a few commands of its own. When you click on **Edit** from the main PowerPoint menu, the pull-down list shown in Figure B.20 is displayed. Note that many Edit menu choices are frequently grayed-out, meaning they are unavailable. The available options change depending on what previous commands you have executed, what portions of a presentation are selected, and so on.

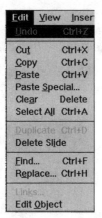

Figure B.20 PowerPoint Edit Menu

Undo   Ctrl+Z

The Undo command lets you change your mind about the most recent PowerPoint operation. Suppose you delete a slide, then decide you'd like it back, or you remove some text and want to replace it. Just use Edit **Undo** (**Ctrl+Z**) or click on the **Undo** button on the Standard toolbar. You can also remove new text or a new slide you've added with the Undo command.

After you use Undo, and before you do anything else, the Undo command functions like Undo Undo. Suppose you remove a slide, then click on Undo to replace it. If you use Undo again, the slide is removed. If you type any characters, remove objects, or do anything else after using Undo, then Undo reverses that most recent operation.

Cut   Ctrl+X

The Cut (**Ctrl+X**) command is a standard Windows command. It removes a selected object or text and places it on the Clipboard. You can copy it from the Clipboard back to PowerPoint or another Windows application with Edit Paste.

Copy   Ctrl+C

Copy (**Ctrl+C**) works like Cut except that it leaves the original text or object and places a copy of it on the Clipboard.

Paste   Ctrl+V

Use **Paste** (**Ctrl+V**) to copy information stored on the Clipboard to the current slide.

Paste Special...

The Paste Special... command lets you control how information from the Clipboard is stored in your PowerPoint presentation. The command presents the Paste Special dialog shown in Figure B.21.

Figure B.21 Paste Special Dialog

What you see on this dialog varies slightly, depending on the type of information you have stored on the Clipboard. If PowerPoint recognizes the type of information, then a source is listed. You may be able to specify a Paste Link, which creates a live relationship between PowerPoint and the source application. This lets you update your PowerPoint slide automatically when the source data changes. (See Chapter 8 for more information on using Paste Special.)

Clear   Del

Clear is the equivalent of Delete. When you use Clear, any selected text or objects are removed from the slide. The difference between Cut and Clear is that Cut places the removed object or text on the Clipboard, whereas Clear simply removes it without storing it on the Clipboard. You can, however, restore deleted objects with the Undo command if you haven't done anything else in between.

Select All   Ctrl+A

The precise operation of Select All (**Ctrl+A**) varies depending on what you have displayed on the screen and what portion of that displayed data is selected already. If you have a text window on a slide with other text windows and graphics, for example, and one of those text windows is selected, the Select All command selects all of the text inside the current text box. If nothing on the slide is selected, however, then Select All selects all the individual graphics objects on the slide. You may want to use this command to delete all of the text within a text box, or to group a collection of graphics objects so you can manipulate them together.

Duplicate   Ctrl+D

Use **Duplicate** (**Ctrl+D**) to make a copy of a selected object and place it on the same slide slightly offset from the original position. This feature is useful in creating special effects, shadowing, and so on.

When you use Duplicate, PowerPoint chooses the amount of offset. You can also create your own offset by selecting an object, then pressing the **Ctrl** key while you drag the object with the mouse. Use **Duplicate** when you want to show several objects stacked on top of each other, for example, or to create the illusion of depth.

Delete Slide

Delete Slide removes the current slide. Unlike Cut, Delete Slide does not place a copy of the slide on the Clipboard. You can restore a deleted slide with the Undo command if you have not conducted additional PowerPoint operations in the meantime.

Find   Ctrl+F

The Find (**Ctrl+F**) command displays the Find dialog shown in Figure B.22.

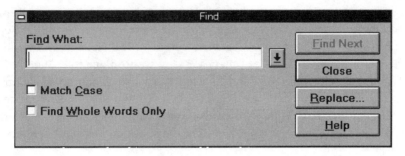

Figure B.22 Find Dialog

Enter any text you want to locate within the current presentation into the Find What field of this dialog. You can refine the search by specifying **Match Case** or **Find Whole Words Only**. Click on **Find Next** to locate the next occurrence of the text you specified.

The Find command locates only text on the body of PowerPoint slides. If the text you seek is part of a graphic—such as text on an organizational chart, for example—the Find command won't locate it.

You can use this same dialog to change a string of text throughout a presentation by specifying the text you want to find, then clicking on **Replace...** to add the Replace With field shown in Figure B.23.

Figure B.23 Replace Dialog

Enter the new text into the Replace With field. If you click again on **Replace**, PowerPoint replaces the next occurrence of the Find What text with the Replace With text. If the Replace button is grayed out, use **Find Next** to locate the next occurrence of the Find What text; then you can use **Replace** to change it. If you want to replace all occurrences of the Find What text in the presentation with the Replace With text, click on **Replace All**. Unlike some word processors which display the last occurrence of the found and replaced text, PowerPoint keeps the current slide on the screen (all of the specified text has been replaced, however).

Replace... Ctrl+H

The Replace command (**Ctrl+H**) is a variation of the Find command. Instead of displaying the Find dialog shown in Figure B.22 as the initial dialog, the Replace command displays the Replace dialog shown in Figure B.23. Simply enter the Find What and Replace With text and use the **Find Next**, **Replace**, and **Replace All** buttons as described in the Find section.

Links...

The Links... command may not be available. If it is grayed out, that simply means that you do not have any active links as part of the current presentation. If the Links... command is available, you can use it to display the Links dialog shown in Figure B.24.

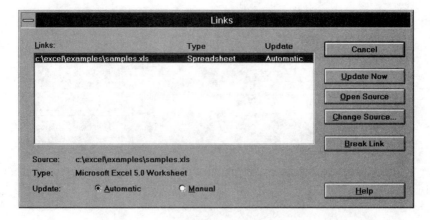

Figure B.24 Links Dialog

You can use this dialog to manipulate any links between the current presentation and external files. Refer to Chapter 8 for more information on using the Links dialog.

Object

The Object command (or the Edit Object command if you have selected an object prior to using this menu) is a variable menu item. It changes according to the type of objects you have within the current presentation or on the current slide. When you select an object inserted from an external application, the Object menu entry changes to reflect the type of object. If you select a Media Clip object, for example, the menu entry becomes Media Clip Object. If you select a linked spreadsheet object, this menu item becomes Linked Spreadsheet Object, and so on.

When you click on this menu item, another menu is displayed, such as the one in Figure B.25.

Figure B.25 Object Pull-down Menu

The selections available on this menu also vary depending on the type of object you have selected. In Figure B.25, for example, one of the choices is Play. If this were a spreadsheet object, Play would not be an appropriate choice.

Regardless of the type of object selected, the final selection on this pull-down menu is Convert.... If you choose this entry, the dialog shown in Figure B.26 is displayed.

Some objects can not be converted. Others can be changed from one file format to another. For more information about using the conversion feature of this dialog, refer to Chapter 8.

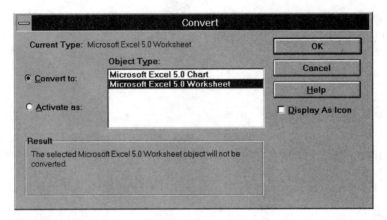

Figure B.26 Object Convert Dialog

The View Menu

The View menu changes how you see the components of your presentation. The default view is Slides, with one slide per screen. You can choose other views as required to work with or print different components of the presentation. Figure B.27 shows the View Menu.

Figure B.27 View Menu

Slides

Slides is the default view, with one PowerPoint slide on each screen. You can have multiple presentations in memory at once and display multiple slides on the screen, but you will see only one slide per presentation at a time.

Outline

The Outline view shows the text outline of your presentation. PowerPoint automatically builds the outline based on the major text components of your slides. If you have created a presentation from blank slides (which do not have title or bullet list templates from the layout dialog), then the outline will be blank. You can create an outline without displaying unwanted title or bullet list information on the screen by editing the outline in the Outline view to add the topics you want. These topics will appear on your slides, but you can use the **Text Color** button to make the text the same color as the background so that unwanted text won't be visible.

Slide Sorter

The Slide Sorter view lets you look at a screen full of slides at once. This is an excellent way to get an overview of your presentation or to move individual slides to new locations if you need to. Figure B.28 shows a typical Slide Sorter view.

Figure B.28 Slide Sorter View

Notes Pages

Choose **Notes Pages** to view your slides with a notes area beneath them. You can type whatever text you want to accompany this notes version of each slide. Use these slides as speaker's notes, as an aid to presentation planning, or as part of your handout package. Figure B.29 shows a Notes Pages view of a slide shown in Figure B.28.

Figure B.29 Notes Pages View

Slide Show...

The Slide Show view is the view you use to actually present the slide show. It is a full-screen view that is advanced by clicking the mouse or by pressing keys on the keyboard. For more information on presenting PowerPoint shows, see Chapter 5.

Master

The Master menu choice presents an additional list of menu items, shown in Figure B.30. A dot appears in front of the selected view on the screen.

Figure B.30 Master Pull-down Menu

The master sheets for Slide, Outline, Handout, and Notes let you set parameters for the display of each of these slide show components. Figure B.31 shows the Notes Master page. Other Masters are similar.

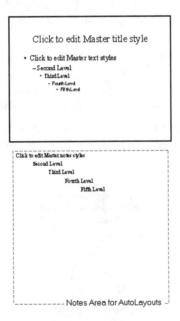

Figure B.31 Notes Master View

See Chapter 5 for additional information about using master sheets.

Toolbars...

The Toolbars menu choice displays the Toolbars dialog shown in Figure B.32.

Figure B.32 Toolbars Dialog

The choices on this toolbar are toggles. If there is an **X** inside the box beside one of these entries, that toolbar is displayed. If you click on this box, the **X** is removed and the toolbar is removed from the display. If you click on a blank box, an **X** is added and the selected toolbar is added to your screen display.

You can conduct the same tasks by pointing to one of the active toolbars and pressing the right mouse button to display the pop-up Toolbars menu shown in Figure B.33.

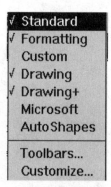

Figure B.33 Pop-up Toolbars Menu

Ruler

Use the Ruler display to show precise screen positioning as you place objects or text on a PowerPoint slide. With the Rulers enabled, you will see a vertical and a horizontal grid beside your slides, as shown in Figure B.34.

Figure B.34 Ruler Slide Display

The size of the ruler changes with the type of object displayed on the PowerPoint slide.

Guides

Like the Ruler display, Guides help you position objects precisely on a PowerPoint slide. When you turn on the Guide display, a dotted-line cross is inserted on top of the current slide. When the guide lines are first displayed, they cross in the middle of the screen. This is designated as point 0,0. As you move one of the lines by grabbing it with the mouse pointer, PowerPoint shows the relative position from the center 0,0 position. You can display the Guides in conjunction with the Rulers to make it easier to tell where an object is located, or you can use the Guides alone.

The guides help you automatically position objects by causing them to snap to the guide, either as you move the center point of the guide near an object, or as you move an object near the center point of the guides. Either the center of the object or the edge of the object—whichever is nearest the guide intersection—will snap to the guide.

 The snap to guide action takes place while you are dragging the object, not when you release it. Move an object back and forth across a guide line and you can see it snap to the guide.

Zoom...

Use the **Zoom** command to display the Zoom dialog shown in Figure B.35.

Figure B.35 Zoom Dialog

If you click on 100%, the current slide fills up the slide space on the screen. Anything less than that reduces the display. You can enlarge a slide up to 400 percent if you want to study details or position objects precisely.

The Insert Menu

The Insert menu gives you a number of options for inserting information or objects onto a PowerPoint slide. The main Insert menu is shown in Figure B.36.

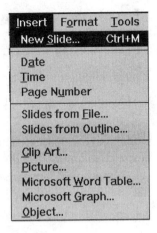

Figure B.36 Insert Menu

You can access many of the Insert menu options from the Standard toolbar.

New Slide...   Ctrl+M

Choosing the **New Slide...** command from the Insert menu is the same as clicking on **the New Slide** button at the bottom of the slide display. The New Slide dialog is displayed so that you can choose the layout you want for the new slide. PowerPoint inserts a new slide after the current slide in the presentation.

Date

The Date option is designed to format an entire presentation by inserting the current date on the Master pages. If you try to use Insert **Date** from any display other than a Master display, you will see the error dialog shown in Figure B.37.

Figure B.37 Date, Time, Page Number Error Dialog

If you are looking at a Master view, then the Insert Date command sequence results in a // object on the Master view. You can select this object like any other object and place it where you want PowerPoint to display the current date on all slides.

Time

The Insert Time command works like the Date command. You can only insert it on a Master view. When you use the command from a Master view, an :: object is inserted. You can move this place holder anywhere on the Master to display the current time on every slide.

Page Number

Like Date and Time, the Page Number code is inserted on a Master view. It can be moved into position, and will appear on all slides. The Page Number object is ##.

Slides from File...

When you use the **Slides from File...** command, PowerPoint displays the Insert File dialog, shown in Figure B.38.

Figure B.38 Insert File Dialog

You can choose a file from the list. PowerPoint inserts the slides from the selected file after the current slide in the current presentation. This is one way to use modules to build PowerPoint presentations. You can create short presentation files with slides that can be used in many presentations. Then, as you build new presentations, you can use Insert **Slides from File...** to place the modules you want.

Slides from Outline...

Like Slides from File, Slides from Outline lets you merge an existing presentation or presentation module with the current file. The Insert Outline dialog shown in Figure B.39 is displayed.

Figure B.39 Insert Outline Dialog

Choose a file name, and PowerPoint will insert the outline after the current slide.

Clip Art...

When you use **Insert Clip Art...**, PowerPoint displays the ClipArt Gallery, shown in Figure B.40.

Figure B.40 ClipArt Gallery

You can select from among the many clip art categories and images to insert a picture into the current slide. For more information about using clip art, refer to Chapter 4.

Picture...

Use Insert **Picture...** to place a graphics image (.TIFF, .PCX, or other file) onto a PowerPoint slide. The Insert Picture dialog, shown in Figure B.41, is displayed.

Figure B.41 Insert Picture Dialog

I've included more information about using graphics images in Chapter 5.

Microsoft Word Table...

The Word Table facility lets you insert a Microsoft Word table into a PowerPoint slide. When you choose this option, PowerPoint displays the Insert Word Table dialog, shown in Figure B.42.

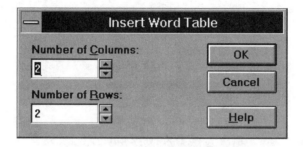

Figure B.42 Insert Word Table Dialog

The default table has two rows and two columns. You can change the table configuration by entering new values in these fields. You can also edit the table configuration after it is inserted onto your PowerPoint slide. Click on **OK** to insert the table form you have defined onto the current slide.

Microsoft Graph...

The Graph facility is like an Excel spreadsheet except that it is confined to row and column data that will be charted. When you choose this command, PowerPoint displays the Graph dialog shown in Figure B.43.

You can enter row and column information on the spreadsheet grid to construct a custom graph.

Object...

Use Insert **Object...** when you want to insert something not covered by one of the other Insert menu choices. When you choose this command, the Insert Object dialog shown in Figure B.44 is displayed.

Figure B.43 Microsoft Graph Dialog

Figure B.44 Insert Object Dialog

For more information about inserting objects into PowerPoint Presentations, refer to Chapter 8.

The Format Menu

The Format menu lets you choose fonts and apply attributes to text and other objects. The Format menu is shown in Figure B.45. Notice that many of the choices on the Format Menu apply to text. If you don't have text selected, many of the Format choices will be grayed out.

Figure B.45 Format Menu

Font...

The Font command applies to text inserted on a PowerPoint slide. When you use this menu choice, PowerPoint displays the Font dialog shown in Figure B.46.

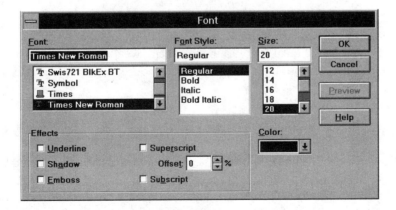

Figure B.46 Font Dialog

From this dialog you can choose the font, the font style (bold, italic, and so on), and the font size. In addition, you can specify other text attributes such as underline and color.

Bullet...

The Bullet menu choice displays the Bullet dialog shown in Figure B.47.

Figure B.47 Bullet Dialog

The default bullet list is from the Normal Text set of fonts, but you can select from a number of additional font groups to specify what characters will be used for bullet lists. First choose the font group, then choose a specific character from the Bullet dialog.

Alignment

The Alignment menu choice specifies how selected text will be aligned: Left, Center, Right, or Justify. Left alignment is the PowerPoint default. Choose **Center** to center the text on each line. Right justification makes the right side of text lines flush, but the left side ragged. Justified text is aligned so that both the left and right edges are smooth.

Line Spacing...

The Line Spacing menu choice displays the Line Spacing dialog shown in Figure B.48.

Figure B.48 Line Spacing Dialog

This is typical Windows text formatting, in which you set the line spacing and the amount of additional spacing before and after a paragraph. Once you change the PowerPoint defaults, the Preview button is active so that you can look at the results of your changes.

Change Case...

This command displays the Change Case dialog shown in Figure B.49.

Figure B.49 Change Case Dialog

This dialog provides five choices for setting the case of selected text. Sentence case is the default and it capitalizes the first character in a sentence. The lowercase option makes all of the selected text lowercase, while the UPPERCASE option makes all of the selected case uppercase. Title Case capitalizes each important word in a sentence. The tOGLE cASE option reverses the case of selected text: capital letters are changed to lowercase, and lowercase characters are changed to uppercase. Click on **OK** when you have selected the option you want.

Periods...

The Periods... menu choice displays the Periods dialog shown in Figure B.50.

Figure B.50 Periods Dialog

The Add Periods selection on this dialog adds periods to the ends of selected paragraphs, while Remove Periods removes periods.

Text Anchor...

The Text Anchor dialog, shown in Figure B.51, lets you specify how selected text will be anchored to the current slide.

Use this dialog to adjust the shape of a text object to the shape of the graphics object that contains it. The Anchor Point can be any one of six choices: Top, Middle, Bottom, Top Centered, Middle Centered, or Bottom Centered. The anchor point is the point on the text rectangle (text box) from which the text grows or to which it shrinks when edited. If you anchor the text in the middle center, for example, the text remains centered in the object's text area as the amount of text shrinks or grows.

Figure B.51 Text Anchor Dialog

As you adjust the Box Margins, you change the amount of space between the text and the graphics object that contains it. You can also force the object to adjust to the size of the text by clicking on the **Adjust Object Size to Fit Text** button. By default, PowerPoint wraps text in the object. You can disable this function by clicking on the **Word-wrap Text in Object** button to remove the **X** in this box.

Colors and Lines...

The Colors and Lines menu choice displays the Colors and Lines dialog shown in Figure B.52.

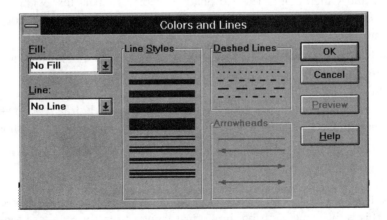

Figure B.52 Colors and Lines Dialog

The Line Styles area of this dialog lets you select from several line styles (various levels of thickness and types of compound lines). If you choose Dashed Lines, you can specify a dashed line format from among several formats available. The Arrowheads selection lets you specify left-facing arrowheads, right-facing arrowheads, or arrowheads that face in both directions. In addition, you can pull down Fill and Line menus to specify fill and line colors.

Shadow...

The Shadow menu choice displays the Shadow dialog shown in Figure B.53.

Figure B.53 Shadow Dialog

As with other PowerPoint and Windows-compliant dialogs, you can change the format of text with the pull-down menus available on this dialog. If you pull down the Color menu, you get three choices: No Shadow (the default), Embossed, and Other Color. The No Shadow choice formats text without any shadow. You can produce an Embossed effect by choosing Embossed from the Color menu.

Once you have chosen the color scheme, you can specify an offset for the shadow effect in points up and down, left and right. The best advice is to experiment with various settings to find the combination you want for the selected text. Click on **Preview** to see how the text will appear before you make a change. Click on **OK** to make the change and return to your PowerPoint slide.

Pick Up Text Style

The Pick Up Text Style command lets you copy the style of one object to another. This is the same as using the Format Painter from the Standard toolbar. The precise menu wording changes with the type of available objects you have.

Use **Pick Up Text Style** to copy attributes such as color, shadow, pattern, and so on. As with the Format Painter, you must first select the text or object whose text style you want to pick up. Then choose the **Pick up Text Style** command. This copies the text format to a temporary memory area.

Apply Style

This menu command is only available after you have copied a text style using Pickup Text Style. With a text style picked up, or copied, you can then apply this copied style by selecting new text and issuing the Apply Style command. As with the Pick Up Text Style command, you don't see a dialog when the command is used. Rather, you see the results of the command on the screen.

Apply To Defaults

If you haven't previously copied a text style with the Pick Up Text Style command, then the Apply Style menu choice is Apply to Defaults instead. As with the previous commands, this command does not present another dialog. Rather, it automatically resets the selected text to PowerPoint defaults. If you don't approve of the defaults, select the text again and use other text formatting commands to give the text the attributes you want.

Presentation Template...

The Presentation Template command displays the Presentation Template dialog shown in Figure B.54.

Figure B.54 Presentation Template Dialog

As I described in Chapter 4, you can choose from among a number of PowerPoint templates to set the mood and color scheme of your presentations. Template files are stored with the .ppt extension, like regular PowerPoint files. Select the template you want for the current presentation from the Presentation Template dialog.

Pick a Look Wizard...

PowerPoint Wizards are a way to use Interactive Macros to help you create PowerPoint presentations. When you choose **Pick a Look Wizard...** from the Format menu, you display the Pick a Look Wizard dialog shown in Figure B.55.

Figure B.55 Pick a Look Wizard—Step 1 of 9

To use any PowerPoint Wizard, just enter the information the Wizard asks for on each dialog, then choose **Next>** to move on to the next dialog. For more information on using PowerPoint Wizards, refer to Chapter 4.

Slide Layout...

The Slide Layout... dialog, shown in Figure B.56, is the same dialog you see when you start a new presentation in PowerPoint.

Figure B.56 PowerPoint Slide Layout Dialog

You can add one of these slide layout formats to a PowerPoint slide at any time.

Slide Background...

The default PowerPoint slide background is white. However, you can choose a new background at any time by displaying the Slide Background dialog, shown in Figure B.57.

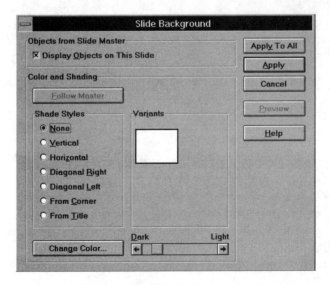

Figure B.57 Slide Background Dialog

The first field on this dialog determines whether or not objects from the Master view will be displayed on the slides. If you disable this feature, then date and time data, for example, won't be displayed on your slide.

You can also specify shading from this dialog. Click on different shade styles to view the variants on this dialog. Figure B.58 shows how PowerPoint displays the shading as you choose shade styles.

Figure B.58 Shade Style Variants on Slide Background Dialog

You can adjust the relative intensity of the shading by clicking on the **Dark** or **Light** buttons. You can display a dialog of available colors by clicking on the **Change Color...** button on this dialog. The Background Color dialog is shown in Figure B.59.

Finally, click on **Preview** on the Slide Background dialog to look at the changes you have made. Choose **Apply** to place the chosen background and other formatting onto the current slide. Choose **Apply To All** to apply the changes you make on this dialog to all slides in the presentation.

Figure B.59 Background Color Dialog

Slide Color Scheme...

When you choose the **Slide Color Scheme...** command, PowerPoint displays the Slide Color Scheme dialog shown in Figure B.60.

Figure B.60 Slide Color Scheme Dialog

Notice from Figure B.60 that you can specify individual color schemes for shadows, background, fills, and more. When you double-click on one of these color boxes, you can change the defaults by selecting a new color from the color dialog. Figure B.61 shows the color choices for background colors. Other color choices display similar dialogs.

Figure B.61 Background Color Dialog

If you choose **Apply** from the Slide Color Scheme dialog, the new color scheme is applied to the current slide. If you select **Apply to All**, then the new color scheme is applied to all slides in the presentation.

The Tools Menu

The Tools menu presents a number of utility features that help you fine-tune, format, or spell check your PowerPoint presentations. The basic Tools choices are shown in Figure B.62.

Spelling... F7

The Spelling... selection displays the PowerPoint Spelling dialog, shown in Figure B.63.

When you launch the Spelling routine, PowerPoint starts scanning your presentation with the current slide, looking for any misspelled words. When a word that isn't in the PowerPoint dictionary is found, the speller notes this and suggests other words or asks for input from you.

Figure B.62 Tools Menu

Figure B.63 Spelling Dialog

If you click on **Ignore**, the selected word is ignored once. If you click on **Ignore All**, then that spelling is ignored throughout the document. You can accept PowerPoint's suggested spelling by clicking on **Change**, or you can add the selected word to your own custom dictionary by clicking on **Add**.

Replace Fonts...

The Replace Fonts dialog lets you search the current presentation for a specified font and replace it with another one. In this way you can change the overall look of a presentation.

Transition...

I discussed transitions in Chapter 5. The Transition command displays the Transition dialog, shown in Figure B.64. This dialog lets you decide how PowerPoint will change from one slide to the next.

Figure B.64 Transition Dialog

If you specify Random Transition, then each slide will change with a different pattern. If you pull down the Effect list, you can specify how each slide will change. Note that you must specify the transition for each slide in your presentation. By default, PowerPoint changes slides with a straight cut.

Build...

Build slides, or Progressive Disclosure slides, display text one line at a time. You have some control over the build process through the Build dialog, shown in Figure B.65.

Click on **Build Body Text** to tell PowerPoint to display each body text element one at a time. If you click on **Dim Previous Points**, you can specify which color PowerPoint should use to dim the elements that have appeared prior to the current one. Finally, you can click on **Effect** to tell PowerPoint how to make each progressive element appear.

Figure B.65 Build Dialog

Hide Slide

Use **Hide Slide** to suppress the display of the current slide during a slide show presentation. If you click on this choice, a check mark appears beside the menu choice, but you won't see any change on the Slide display. When you start a slide show (View **Slide Show**), any slide for which Hide Slide is specified won't be displayed. You can reverse this setting at any time by clicking on **Hide Slide** again.

Play Settings...

Use the **Play Settings...** command to tell PowerPoint when to play any media clips and other embedded objects. This command presents the Play Settings dialog, shown in Figure B.66.

Figure B.66 Play Settings Dialog

PowerPoint selects the Category based on what is on the current slide. There are also defaults in the Start Play area of this dialog. You can change any of these defaults by simply clicking on the appropriate buttons.

Recolor...

Use the **Recolor...** command to change colors for existing PowerPoint objects. This command displays the Recolor dialog shown in Figure B.67.

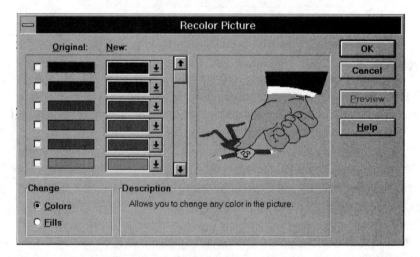

Figure B.67 Recolor Dialog

The colors that make up the selected object are shown in the Original area of the dialog. You can specify different colors for each of the original colors by pulling down a color list for each New color. If the range of colors you get with the pull-down list isn't enough, click on **Other Color** to display the Other Color dialog, which offers a number of new colors for each shade in the selected object.

Crop Picture

To use this command, select a picture on a PowerPoint slide, then issue the **Crop Picture** command. The PowerPoint mouse pointer changes to a small square. Move the square onto one of the sizing handles on the selected picture. Hold down the left mouse button and drag the picture border to the new size you want.

Customize...

The Customize Toolbars dialog, shown in Figure B.68, lets you add new icons to any displayed toolbar, remove existing icons, or move any icons to new locations.

Figure B.68 Customize Toolbars Dialog

Use this dialog by first selecting the category of commands or macros you want to add, then choose an icon from the Buttons area of the dialog. You can drag a button to a toolbar. While the Customize Toolbars dialog is displayed, you can drag any icon already on a toolbar to a new location, or you can drag an icon completely off of a toolbar.

Options...

The Options dialog, shown in Figure B.69, lets you specify a number of operational options for PowerPoint.

Each of the choices on this dialog is a toggle. If an **X** appears in the box beside an entry, then that entry is enabled. Remove the **X** by clicking on it. Click on a disabled option to place an **X** in the box and enable that option.

The Draw Menu

Use the Draw menu to manipulate various aspects of drawing objects within your PowerPoint presentation. As you can see from the menu in Figure B.70, some Draw menu items will not be available at times, depending on what types of objects are on your presentation slides, and whether or not you have selected one of these objects.

Figure B.69 Options Dialog

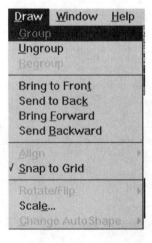

Figure B.70 Draw Menu

Group

You can group separate PowerPoint objects into a single graphic that you can move or edit as one. Hold down the **Shift** key as you click on individual components to select objects in a series. Then use Draw **Group** to put them together.

Ungroup

Many PowerPoint graphics objects are made up of collections of smaller objects that are grouped together into one. After you select a graphic on a PowerPoint slide, you can ungroup the object to separate it into individual components. This lets you edit these components separately.

Regroup

Use **Regroup** to reverse an Ungroup command. Simply select one of the objects that formed part of the original group and use the **Regroup** command to put the individual components back together.

Bring to Front

Many PowerPoint objects consist of several objects, some layered on top of others. You can use the **Bring to Front** command to control which object is most prominent. The Bring to Front command moves a selected object to the top of a stack of objects.

Send to Back

This is the reverse of the Bring to Front command. When you choose Send to Back, the selected object is sent to the bottom of the stack of objects.

Bring Forward

This command, along with the Send Backward command, moves objects in a stack one layer or level at a time. This is different from the Bring to Front command in that the selected object is moved only one level at a time instead of being moved to the front or top of the stack.

Send Backward

The Send Backward command is the opposite of the Bring Forward command. It sends the selected object back in the stack one level.

Align

The Align command helps you line up a group of objects along certain borders, such as the left, right, or top borders. To align objects, first select the objects you want to align, then choose the Draw **Align** command. This displays the Align pop-up menu shown in Figure B.71.

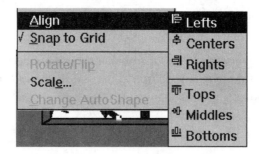

Figure B.71 Draw Align Pop-up Menu

Choose the type of alignment you want from the pop-up menu.

Snap to Grid

Each PowerPoint slide is crisscrossed by an invisible grid of lines that can help you keep individual objects aligned. By default, PowerPoint is set up to snap objects to the invisible grid. You can't see the grid, but you can see the effects of it as you move graphics objects around the screen. When you drop an object you are moving, it will snap to the nearest grid line.

If you want to have more precise control over the placement of PowerPoint objects, use the Draw **Snap to Grid** command to turn off the automatic Snap to Grid feature. You can tell whether this feature is enabled by a check mark beside the menu entry. A check mark means it is enabled; no check mark means it has been disabled.

Rotate/Flip

Select a PowerPoint object, then use Draw **Rotate/Flip** to display the additional menu shown in Figure B.72.

Figure B.72 Rotate/Flip Pull-down Menu

In addition to left, right, horizontal, and vertical rotation, you can choose **Free Rotate** to display the selected object with rotation handles. Grab a handle to move the object around a center axis, and rotate the object to the angle you want. Let go of the mouse button when the object is at the desired angle.

Scale...

After you select an object, you can choose **Scale** to display the Scale dialog shown in Figure B.73.

Figure B.73 Scale Dialog

The default scaling is 100 percent of the original object, as shown in the Scale To field of this dialog. Change the scaling by clicking on the up or down arrows to the right of this field, or by selecting the field contents and typing a new value.

You can click on **Preview** to see how the new scaling will look without actually making the change. You can specify that the size changes be made relative to the original picture size or that the best scale for the slide show be chosen. When the values on this dialog are set the way you want them, click on **OK** to close the dialog and return to the slide display.

Change AutoShape

PowerPoint includes a facility that makes it easy to draw a number of geometric shapes. The AutoShapes feature is accessible from the Draw toolbar. Once you have drawn one or more AutoShapes, you may decide that you want to change the basic shape. You can do this with the **Change AutoShape** selection from the Draw menu.

To use this feature, first select an AutoShape object. Then use Draw **Change AutoShape** to display the Change Autoshape dialog shown in Figure B.73.

Figure B.74 Change AutoShape Dialog

When you choose a shape, PowerPoint immediately changes the selected AutoShape to the new one.

The Window Menu

The PowerPoint Window menu is virtually the same as the Window menus of all Microsoft Windows applications (see Figure B.75).

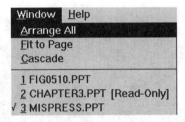

Figure B.75 PowerPoint Window Menu

This menu has four main components: Arrange All, Fit to Page, Cascade, and the open file list.

The Arrange All command displays all of the open files in memory like the sample display in Figure B.76.

Figure B.76 Sample Arrange All Display

Use the Fit to Page selection from the Window menu to properly size the current presentation to the specified page size (determined by File **Slide Setup...**).

The Cascade selection shrinks all of the open presentations and displays them like a stack of cards, as shown in Figure B.77.

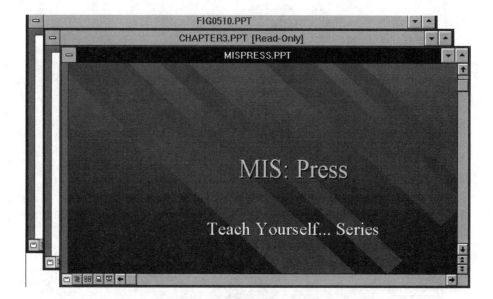

Figure B.77 Cascade Format

You can select and enlarge any of the presentations on the Cascade display by clicking on the title bar of the presentation you want to enlarge and make current.

The Help Menu

When you click on **Help**, PowerPoint displays the menu shown in Figure B.78.

For detailed information on using PowerPoint Help, refer to Chapter 9. Two choices on the Help menu are worth mentioning again here: Technical Support and About Microsoft PowerPoint.... The Technical Support choice displays the Help dialog shown in Figure B.79.

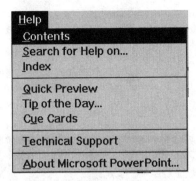

Figure B.78 Main Help Menu

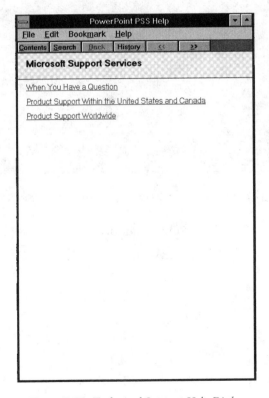

Figure B.79 Technical Support Help Dialog

As you can see, this dialog shows you how to get additional technical help with PowerPoint. Click on **Product Support within the United States and Canada** to display additional menus that will step you through getting online and telephone support for PowerPoint.

The About Microsoft PowerPoint window shows you what version of PowerPoint you are using and displays your product number (see Figure B.80).

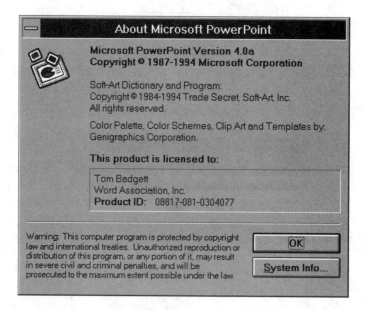

Figure B.80 About Microsoft PowerPoint Window

Click on **System Info** to have PowerPoint display a summary of your computer configuration.

Glossary

1-2-3   A popular spreadsheet software application from Lotus Development Corporation.

Applets   Utility programs that are shipped with main software packages such as PowerPoint and other Microsoft products. Many applets, such as WordArt, are common to several Microsoft products and are installed only once when the first package that includes the applet is installed.

Application window   In Microsoft Windows, a separate window object that contains a running program. Also, a window object that contains icons that represent other software applications. These applications can be launched into their own application windows by choosing the icon.

Aspect ratio   The relationship between an object's width and height. Different aspect ratios are common for different applications. A 35mm slide has a different ratio for pleasing appearance and fit than does an overhead projector foil, for example. You can restore a PowerPoint object's aspect ratio with the Draw **Scale...** command.

AutoContent Wizard   A PowerPoint Wizard that helps you build a presentation by inserting default slides for title, introduction, and other topics. Launch this Wizard with the File **New** command, then choose **AutoContent Wizard** from the New Presentation dialog.

AutoLayout   A feature of Microsoft PowerPoint and other Office products that lets you choose table and slide layout automatically from predefined screens. To use AutoLayouts, click on the **New Slide** button, or use **Format Slide Layout...**.

AutoShape

A PowerPoint utility that lets you insert a number of predefined shapes such as arrow points, squares, and rectangles onto a slide. AutoShape tools are accessed through the AutoShape toolbar. Point to an existing toolbar and click the right mouse button to display the toolbar menu, and then select **AutoShapes**.

Backtab

Backtab or reverse tab moves the insertion point to the left a standard tab width. This is the reverse of the standard tab key. Insert a backtab code by pressing **Shift+Tab**.

Bookmark

An electronic place holder that allows you to return to a specific screen or record of information. In PowerPoint Help, you can insert a bookmark with the Bookmark command from the main Help menu.

Brainstorming

A creative process that can be used for planning and designing PowerPoint presentations. Brainstorming consists of stream-of-consciousness planning through repetitive lists, in which a broad topic is narrowed to topics of smaller scope.

Branching

In computer programming or PowerPoint presentations, the ability of a program to go directly from one program module or slide to another based on some decision process. Presenters frequently design PowerPoint presentations with built-in branching to allow for different audience skill levels or reactions to the standard material.

Bullet list

A succinct list of information set off by relatively large dots or other symbols called bullets. A bullet list is useful in summarizing data for an audience.

Cascade

A computer screen design that stacks several programs or program components one on top of the other with slight offsets, like a deck of cards fanned out. A cascade arrangement usually lets you see a title line or other distinguishing feature of each screen object so you can access any object you wish.

Click

In using a computer mouse, the process of pointing to or selecting a specific screen object. A click is a single,

	rapid depression of one of the mouse buttons (usually the left one unless specified otherwise).
Clip art	Relatively simple drawings that can be inserted into a PowerPoint presentation. PowerPoint is supplied with hundreds of clip art images. Third-party companies also sell clip art collections in a variety of file formats that you can use with PowerPoint and other applications.
ClipArt Gallery	A PowerPoint utility that makes finding and choosing clip art images fast and easy.
Clipboard	A section of temporary memory in Windows-compliant applications where objects can be stored during copy and paste operations.
Context sensitive help	An electronic help system that provides information about specific software operations. Context sensitive help displays specific help messages that relate to the current software operation rather than displaying a general help message or requiring you to step through menus or search for specific information.
Control Menu	In Microsoft Windows, a menu common to all window objects that lets you close the current window, move the window, size it, or switch to another running application. The control menu is represented by a short horizontal bar at the upper left corner of all window objects.
Control Panel	In Microsoft Windows, a system utility that lets you set up the operation of various Windows components, including the printer, screen colors, and networking. The Control Panel icon is located in the Main application window.
Copy	The process of making a duplicate of an object within PowerPoint or another application. In Windows-compliant applications, the copy process usually involves placing a duplicate image on the Clipboard, then copying it from the Clipboard to the new location.
Cross hair	A graphics tool designed to help with object design or placement. In PowerPoint, cross hairs are used for pre-

cise placement or alignment of objects. The View **Guides** command displays a large cross hair, for example.

Cue Card Pop-up help dialogs in PowerPoint and other Microsoft Office applications that help you conduct specific tasks. These help screens include step-by-step instructions for completing common tasks within an application.

Cut The process of removing a selected object from a document or display. A cut is frequently used in Windows-compliant applications to move the object to a new location. The selected object is removed from its present location and placed on the Clipboard. Then it is copied from the Clipboard into a new location.

Desktop In Windows applications, the basic user interface in which most operations are conducted. The desktop generally consists of an editing area, a set of menus, tool bars, and so on. Individual documents or objects can be loaded onto the desktop for manipulation.

Dialog box In Windows, a pop-up object that either presents information to the user or asks the user for information.

Directory A logical disk structure used to associate or group information on a computer. Sometimes called subdirectory when it is subordinate to another directory.

Dissolve The process of changing from one display to another by fading out the first display and fading in the second. Dissolves can be used as transitions between PowerPoint slides during a presentation.

DOS Disk Operating System. Each computer design has its own disk operating system. Most operating systems have a name, such as UNIX, VMS, and so on. For PCs, the disk operating system is called simply DOS.

DOS prompt The disk operating system prompt, a character or characters that tells the user that the operating system is waiting for input.

Double-click The process of choosing a Windows object by pointing to the object and then pressing the left mouse button twice in quick succession. A single click usually selects an object, and a double-click chooses it or causes it to carry out its intended operation.

Drag
The process of moving an on-screen object by grabbing it with the mouse pointer and dragging it from one location to another.

Driver
A software device that enables a specific piece of hardware or sometimes another software application to function properly. The most common types of drivers are printer drivers, which help an application send the proper codes and formatting instructions to a specific printer.

Drop shadow
A graphics device for offsetting a portion of an object and making it appear that it is casting a shadow. Useful with lettering, borders, and other objects to provide the illusion of depth.

Equation editor
An applet within other applications that lets you enter mathematical equations and, in some cases, calculate them. An equation editor usually serves as an adjunct to other mainstream applications such as a word processor or presentation products such as PowerPoint.

Excel
Microsoft Excel is a spreadsheet application that is popular for conducting "what if", bookkeeping, and financial projection operations.

Fade
A process for removing an on-screen object by causing it to get progressively darker until it disappears. Fades can be used as a transition between PowerPoint slides during a presentation.

Flow chart
A series of boxes connected by lines that show the progression of an activity or show relationships among various people or projects within a company.

Font
A collection of typefaces in a certain style.

Format Bar
A specialized toolbar in PowerPoint and other Microsoft applications that displays current font information as well as details about other text formatting.

	The Format Bar also can be used to set font attributes through pull-down menus and buttons.
FORTAN	A high level computer programming language, rarely used with microcomputers but once very popular in the development of engineering or other technical applications on minicomputers and mainframes.
Graphical user interface	A computer interface, such as Microsoft Windows, that shows the user graphically how to conduct applications and system level operations.
Handles	Protrusions around the perimeter of graphics objects that can be used to move or size the object. Handles make it easier to grab an object's border for sizing or moving.
Handouts	In PowerPoint, printed sheets based on a presentation that are designed to be handed out to the audience during or after a presentation. Handout sheets contain one or more of the presentation's slides and perhaps some descriptive text.
Hot key	A key or keystroke combination designed to invoke a software application, applet, or utility. A hot key bypasses the usual menu or mouse access methods to make utility or feature access faster and easier for experienced users.
I Beam	The insertion point in Windows-based applications. Usually used to indicate where text will be typed.
Icon	A simple picture used to represent an application, applet, or utility in a Windows environment.
Interactive presentation	A presentation that can take input from a user and change the direction of the presentation based on user input.
Landscape	Page or screen orientation where the longest part of an image or text is oriented left to right instead of top to bottom like a standard business letter.
Layout	The process of designing a screen, slide, or printed page. Layout includes margin descriptions, object placement, attributes, and other display or print characteristics.

Live links A process for creating a continuous relationship between a PowerPoint object and the application that created it. When an object that is part of a live link is modified within its host application, the copy of it on a PowerPoint slide changes automatically to reflect that modification.

LPT1 Shorthand for the main printer port on an MS-DOS computer.

Menu bar A colored, (usually) horizontal bar that holds the main menu items for a computer program. In PowerPoint, the main menu bar is located beneath the title bar and above the Standard toolbar.

Microsoft Graph A Microsoft applet that is used in PowerPoint and other applications to create graphs from rows and columns of numbers.

Microsoft Office A collection of Microsoft software applications that includes PowerPoint, Word, Excel, Mail, and Access.

Microsoft Windows Microsoft's graphical user interface for MS-DOS computers.

Mouse A data input and pointing device used to select screen objects within a graphical user interface such as Microsoft Windows.

Mouse pointer The small graphics character—usually an arrow—that represents the current position on the graphics screen of the mouse input device. The pointer is used to select objects in conjunction with the left mouse button.

MSAPPS The subdirectory where Microsoft stores its common applets such as WordArt, Chart, and so on. This subdirectory usually is located within the Windows directory.

Object Anything displayed on a graphical user interface screen. Objects can consist of text, graphics, pictures, clip art, or a combination of items.

Object Linking and Embedding Microsoft's term for the ability to embed or link objects from one application into the files of another application.

OLE	See **Object Linking and Embedding**.
OLE 2.0	Microsoft's second version of Object Linking and Embedding. OLE 2.0 includes the ability to do in-place editing, in which the source application is launched in the background, but you edit its objects from within the target application.
OrgChart	A Microsoft applet that helps you create organizational chart objects for inclusion in PowerPoint or other applications.
Outline toolbar	A special toolbar with buttons and icons is that displayed when you enter an outline view.
Paste	The process of copying information stored on the Clipboard into a new file or document or to a new location in the same file or document.
Pick a Look Wizard	In PowerPoint, an interactive macro that helps you establish a slide design.
Point	The process of moving the mouse pointer over or near an on-screen object prior to selecting or choosing it.
Port	A physical or logical doorway to attach a computer system to another computer, a printer, an input device, or a software application.
Portrait	A page or screen orientation that places the longest portion of the page or screen in an up-and-down orientation like a standard business letter. See also **Landscape**.
PostScript	A printer control language frequently used for printing complex graphics or text. To use PostScript output, your printer must be designed with a PostScript language interpreter.
Print Manager	In Microsoft Windows, a software utility that manages the printer output from one or more software applications. The Print Manager cues information designated for the printer, manages conflicts, and spools output to disk to free up printing applications more quickly. See also **Print spooler**.

Print spooler   A software or hardware device that accepts software output intended for a printer and stores it temporarily on disk or in RAM memory. A print spooler frees up the printing application more quickly than printing directly to a printer, because memory and the hard disk work more quickly than the printer. Most print spoolers also manage output from more than one printing application at a time. See also **Print Manager**.

Program Manager   In Microsoft Windows, the main user interface software that contains application windows and icons. The Program Manager launches programs, displays program icons, and otherwise provides the user a graphical interface into the computer system.

Resizing   The process of reshaping or changing the size of on-screen objects. Resizing usually is done by grabbing a sizing handle and dragging an object border to a new size.

Report It   In PowerPoint, a facility for automatically launching Microsoft Word and inserting the current presentation outline. The outline can be edited or enhanced before sending it back to PowerPoint.

Restore button   In Microsoft Windows, a triangular icon at the upper right corner of most window objects that enlarges the window after it has been reduced.

Rich Text Format   A document format frequently used to transfer text files among different word processing or text editing programs. The RTF format can transfer many text attributes such as bold and italics, even among incompatible programs.

Routing slip   In Microsoft Mail, a software attachment that tells the mail program where to send the current document and in what order. The File **Add Routing Slip...** command lets you add a routing slip attachment to a PowerPoint document.

RTF   See **Rich Text Format**.

Sans serif Type without serifs (the accenting protrusions on some characters). Sans serif type is plain and clean, and is good for titles and headings. However, serif type is better for body text. See also **Serif**.

Scroll bars In Windows, horizontal and vertical objects with arrows that let you move the contents of a display screen up and down or left and right.

Serif The small accenting protrusions on some typefaces, designed to add emphasis and make text easier to read. See also **Sans serif**.

Shadowed text Text that is formatted with a background or side shadow.

Slide shows In PowerPoint, a method of displaying a presentation as sequential on-screen slides or as graphics slides converted to 35mm film.

Slide Sorter In PowerPoint, a view that displays several slides from the current presentation on the same screen. Use View **Slide Sorter** to access this view.

Slides Graphics in PowerPoint used as individual elements of a presentation.

Speaker's Note view In PowerPoint, a view that includes a slide and room beneath it to type notes about the slide or the topics it covers. These notes can be used to help you remember major topics you want to mention in conjunction with each slide.

Spreadsheet A software application designed to make projections, mathematical analysis, and "what if" computations easy. See also **Excel**.

Storyboard In PowerPoint or other graphics-oriented applications, small sequential drawings of a presentation that show how the presentation will be designed. Storyboards usually are temporary devices used during the design of a slide show or other visual presentation, including motion pictures.

Straight cuts	In PowerPoint, a straight transition between two slides that does not include any special effects such as fades or dissolves.
Subdirectory	See **Directory**.
Submenu	A menu subordinate to a main menu entry. A submenu is displayed when you choose a main menu item that has additional choices under it.
Template	A computer file that is used as a guide or form for designing additional files. In PowerPoint, template files are provided to give your slides creative and colorful backgrounds and graphics characters. You can start with a template and design your own presentation to produce professional results.
Text tool	In a graphics program such as PowerPoint, an icon that represents a character or text application. To use a text tool you usually select it from a toolbar or icon. Then you place it within a graphics object where you want to apply text, and type text from the keyboard.
Tip of the Day	In PowerPoint and other Microsoft Office applications, a random pop-up Help dialog that presents tips on how to conduct various software applications.
Title bar	In Microsoft Windows, the topmost horizontal bar of a window object that carries the name of the object or application.
Toolbar buttons	Small icons that reside together on a toolbar that represent software utilities or applets. You launch the feature represented by the button by clicking on the button. Toolbar buttons frequently represent commands or features that also are available from a standard menu.
Toolbars	Collections of icons that represent software utilities or features.
ToolTips	In Microsoft Office applications, a feature that displays the function of an on-screen object when the mouse pointer is moved over the object. This feature helps users understand the function of software buttons and icons.

Transition	A technique for switching between two PowerPoint slides by placing a special effect on the screen between the slides. See also **Fade**, **Dissolve**, **Wipe**.
TrueType	A Microsoft Windows scalable font technology that maximizes the probability that on-screen text will appear precisely as printed text. TrueType is an outline font technology used by Apple and Microsoft. It does not necessarily produce WYSIWYG (What You See Is What You Get) displays, but that is the goal and it is close to WYSIWYG.
User interface	A method of communication between a computer and computer user that enables the user to respond to an application's request for data. Microsoft Windows is a graphical user interface. Other interfaces use straight menus or command prompts (like MS DOS, for example).
Windows for Workgroups	An implementation of Microsoft Windows that includes networking and mail components. A system of computers, each running Windows for Workgroups and connected by standard Ethernet cable, that can function as a local area network.
Wipe	A transition technique for advancing from one PowerPoint slide to another.
Wizard	A series of interactive screens in Microsoft applications that helps the user conduct a specific task.
WordArt	A Microsoft applet that helps you format text as a graphics image. WordArt is used to build creative text titles for PowerPoint slides, word processing letterhead, and so on.

Index